# NORTHWEST
## HOME LANDSCAPING

Fourth Edition

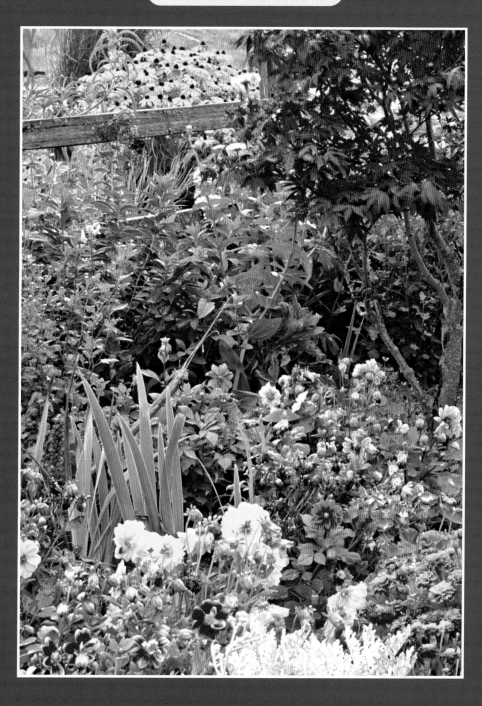

Other titles available in the *Home Landscaping* series:

# CALIFORNIA

# MID-ATLANTIC

# MIDWEST
*including South-Central Canada*

# NORTHEAST
*including Southeast Canada*

# SOUTHEAST

# SOUTHERN COASTAL

# TEXAS

# WESTERN

## Publisher's Note

I am pleased to present the newest edition of this classic book on Northwestern home landscaping. In this edition, you will find new content, including information on the impact of climate change on Northwestern landscaping and detailed descriptions of plants to avoid so you may cultivate the healthiest garden possible. Perhaps the biggest change to this book, however, is what you **won't** find: invasive plants that we removed from designs and plant profiles and replaced with Northwestern natives or non-invasive plants. As you read and begin your landscaping journey with us, you can feel confident that no matter the home, it will be surrounded by lush, vibrant plants that invite pollinators, guests, and yourself into your yard every day of the year with a warm welcome. Also, I would like to give a special thank you to Felicia Brower, the technical editor for this edition, for lending her expertise in home landscaping.

Alan Giagnocavo, CEO and Publisher
Fox Chapel Publishing

# NORTHWEST
## HOME LANDSCAPING

**48 Landscape Designs**
**200+ Plants & Flowers Best Suited to the Northwest**

Fourth Edition

**Roger Holmes and Don Marshall**

**Technical Editor for Current Edition: Felicia Brower**

CREATIVE HOMEOWNER®, Upper Saddle River, New Jersey

NORTHWEST HOME LANDSCAPING, FOURTH EDITION

| | |
|---|---|
| Managing Editor | Gretchen Bacon |
| Editor | Madeline DeLuca |
| Technical Editor | Felicia Brower |
| Designer | Freire, SL |

Manufactured in China

First Printing

*Northwest Home Landscaping, Fourth Edition*
ISBN-13: 978-1-58011-598-8

CREATIVE HOMEOWNER® *www.CreativeHomeowner.com*, is an imprint of New Design Originals Corporation and distributed exclusively by Fox Chapel Publishing, 800-457-9112, 903 Square Street, Mount Joy, PA 17552.

## About the Authors

**Roger Holmes** is the founding editor of *Fine Gardening* magazine. He co-edited the monumental Taylor's *Master Guide to Gardening* and other highly regarded gardening books, and produced the landscaping series of which this book is part. He also co-wrote Creative Homeowner's *Creating Good Gardens*.

**Don Marshall** heads up the Environmental Horticultural Program at Lake Washington Technical College, in Kirkland, Washington, where he has been Horticulture Instructor for over 20 years. He is also the sole proprietor of Plant Designs, a landscaping company that designs, installs, and maintains commercial and residential landscapes.

## About the Technical Editor

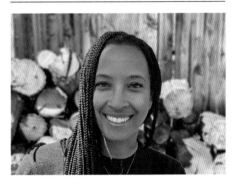

**Felicia Brower** is a Colorado-based freelance writer, editor, and master gardener. As a member of the *Colorado Native Plant Society* and *Wild Ones: Native Plants, Natural Landscapes*, Felicia has a deep interest in incorporating low-water plants native to the arid west into the home garden and landscape. She regularly attends courses and workshops to stay up-to-date on new trends in home landscaping, especially those catered towards growing in the Rocky Mountain region.

# Safety First

Though all concepts and methods in this book have been reviewed for safety, it is not possible to overstate the importance of using the safest working methods possible. What follows are reminders—dos and don'ts for yard work and landscaping. They are not substitutes for your own common sense.

- *Always* use caution, care, and good judgment when following the procedures described in this book.

- *Always* determine locations of underground utility lines before you dig, and then avoid them by a safe distance. Buried lines may be for gas, electricity, communications, or water. Start research by contacting your local building officials. Also contact local utility companies; they will often send a representative free of charge to help you map their lines. In addition, there are private utility locator firms listed online. Note: previous owners may have installed underground drainage, sprinkler, and lighting lines without mapping them.

- *Always* read and heed the manufacturer's instructions for using a tool, especially the warnings.

- *Always* ensure that the electrical setup is safe; be sure that no circuit is overloaded and that all power tools and electrical outlets are properly grounded and protected by a ground-fault circuit interrupter (GFCI). Do not use power tools in wet locations.

- *Always* wear eye protection when using chemicals, sawing wood, pruning trees and shrubs, using power tools, and striking metal onto metal or concrete.

- *Always* read labels on chemicals, solvents, and other products; provide ventilation; heed warnings.

- *Always* wear heavy rubber gloves rated for chemicals, not mere household rubber gloves, when handling toxins.

- *Always* wear appropriate gloves in situations in which your hands could be injured by rough surfaces, sharp edges, thorns, or poisonous plants.

- *Always* wear a disposable face mask or a special filtering respirator when creating sawdust or working with toxic gardening substances.

- *Always* keep your hands and other body parts away from the business ends of blades, cutters, and bits.

- *Always* obtain approval from local building officials before undertaking construction of permanent structures.

- *Never* work with power tools when you are tired or under the influence of alcohol or drugs.

- *Never* carry sharp or pointed tools, such as knives or saws, in your pockets. If you carry such tools, use special-purpose tool scabbards.

---

# The Landscape Designers

**John Ahrens,** with Barry Landry and Nena Scott, King's Creek Landscape Management, Austin, Texas. Their design appears on pp. 58-59.

**Lee Buffington and Gordon Iwata,** Arcadia Design, Mercer Island, Washington. Their designs appear on pp. 54-57, 94-97, and 106-109.

**Laura Crockett,** Sylvan Designs, Hillsboro, Oregon. Her designs appear on pp. 16-19, 46-49, and 82-85.

**Kate Day** is a landscape architect and certified arborist in the Seattle area. Her designs appear on pp. 28-31, 70-73, and 88-91.

**Rosa Finsley, with Cheryl Bryant,** King's Creek Gardens, Cedar Hill, Texas. Their design appears on pp. 86-87.

**Lucy Hardiman** is the principal of Perennial Partners, a garden-design collective in Portland. Her designs appear on pp. 74-77 and 66-69.

**Daniel Lowery,** Queen Anne Gardens, Seattle. His designs appear on pp. 22-25, 36-39, and 108-111.

**Glenn Morris** has designed southern landscapes for many years. His design appears on pp. 64-65.

**Ruth Olde,** Blasig Landscape Design and Construction Ltd., Vancouver, British Columbia. Her designs appear on pp. 60-63, 78-81, and 98-101.

**Jana Ruzicka** operates her own landscape design business in Laguna Beach, California. Her design appears on pp. 106-107.

**Dan Sears,** Sears Design Group of Raleigh, North Carolina. His design appears on pp. 40-41.

**Carolyn Singer** owns Foothill Cottage Gardens, Grass Valley, California. Her design appears on pp. 20-21.

**Jimmy and Becky Stewart** are professional gardeners in Atlanta, Georgia. Their design appears on pp. 92-93.

**Mary Wilhite and Sharon Lee Smith,** Blue Moon Gardens, Tyler, Texas. Their design appears on pp. 26-27.

**Phil Wood** owns Phil Wood Garden Design in Seattle. His designs appear on pp. 32-35, 42-45, and 50-53.

# Contents

# About This Book

**Of all the home improvement projects** homeowners tackle, few offer greater rewards than landscaping. Paths, patios, fences, arbors, and, most of all, plantings can enhance home life in countless ways, large and small, functional and pleasurable, every day of the year. At the main entrance, an attractive brick walkway flanked by eye-catching shrubs and perennials provides a cheerful send-off in the morning and welcomes you home from work in the evening. A carefully placed grouping of small trees, shrubs, and fence panels creates privacy on the patio or screens a nearby eyesore from view. An island bed showcases your favorite plants, while dividing the backyard into areas for several different activities.

Unlike with some home improvements, the rewards of landscaping can be as much in the activity as in the result. Planting and caring for lovely shrubs, perennials, and other plants can afford years of enjoyment. And for those who like to build things, outdoor construction projects can be especially satisfying.

While the installation and maintenance of plants and outdoor structures are within the means and abilities of most people, few of us are as comfortable determining exactly which plants or structures to use and how best to combine them. It's one thing to decide to dress up the front entrance or patio, another to come up with a design for doing so.

That's where this book comes in. Here, in the Portfolio of Designs, you'll find designs for more than twenty-eight common home-landscaping situations, created by landscape professionals who live and work in the Northwest. Drawing on years of experience, these designers balance functional requirements and aesthetic possibilities, choosing the right plant or structure for the task, confident of its proven performance in similar situations.

Complementing the Portfolio of Designs is the second section, Plant Profiles, which gives information on all the plants used in the book. The book's third section, the Guide to Installation, will help you install and maintain the plants and structures called for in the designs. The discussions that follow take a closer look at each section; we've also printed representative pages of the sections on pp. 9-10 and pointed out their features.

## Portfolio of Designs

This section is the heart of the book, providing examples of landscaping situations and solutions that are at once inspiring and accessible. Some are simple, others more complex, but each one can be installed in a few weekends by homeowners with no special training or experience.

For each situation, we present two designs, the second a variation of the first. As the sample pages on the facing page show, the first design is displayed on a two-page spread. A perspective illustration (called a "rendering") depicts what the design will look like several years after installation, when the perennials and many of the shrubs have reached mature size. (For more on how plantings change as they age, see "As Your Landscape Grows," pp. 12–13.) The rendering also shows the planting as it will appear at a particular time of year. A site plan indicates the positions of the plants and structures on a scaled grid. Text introduces the situation and the design and describes the plants and projects used.

The second design, presented on the second two-page spread, addresses the same situation as the first but differs in one or more important aspects. It might show a planting suited for a shady rather than a sunny site, or it might incorporate different structures or kinds of plants to create a different look. As for the first design, we present a rendering, site plan, and written information, but in briefer form. The second spread also includes photographs of a selection of the plants featured in the two designs. The photos showcase noteworthy qualities—lovely flowers, handsome foliage, or striking forms—that these plants contribute to the designs.

Installed exactly as shown here, the designs will provide years of enjoyment. But individual needs and properties will differ, and we encourage you to alter the designs to suit your site and desires. Many types of alterations are easy to make. You can add or remove plants and adjust the sizes of paths, patios, and arbors to accommodate larger or smaller sites. You can rearrange groupings and substitute favorite plants to suit your taste. Or you can integrate the design with your existing landscaping. If you are uncertain about how to solve specific problems or about the effects of changes you'd like to make, consult with staff at a local nursery or with a landscape designer in your area.

# PORTFOLIO OF DESIGNS

## FIRST DESIGN OPTION

**Summary**
*An overview of the situation
and the design*

**Site Plan**
*Positions all plants and
structures on a scaled grid*

**Plants & Projects**
*Noteworthy qualities of
the plants and structures
and their contributions
to the design*

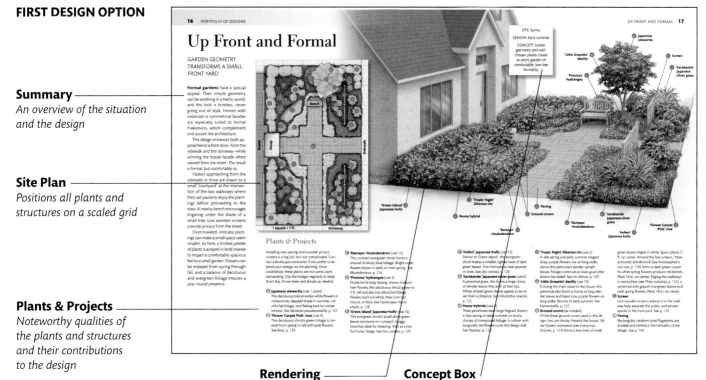

**Rendering**
*Shows how the design
will look when plants
are well established*

**Concept Box**
*Summarizes an important aspect of the design;
tells whether the site is sunny or shady and
what season is depicted in the rendering*

## SECOND DESIGN OPTION

**Rendering**
*Depicts the design
when plants are well
established*

**Concept Box**
*Site, season, and design
summary*

**Summary**
*Addressing the same situation
as the first design, an overview
of differences in design concept,
site conditions, or plant
selection*

**Site Plan**
*Plants and structures
on a scaled grid*

**Variations on a Theme**
*Photos of inspiring designs
in similar situations*

# PLANT PROFILES

**Plant Portraits**
*Photos of selected plants*

**Detailed Plant Information**
*Descriptions of each plant's noteworthy qualities and requirements for planting and care*

**Choices**
*Selections here help you choose from the many varieties of certain popular plants.*

# GUIDE TO INSTALLATION

**Sidebars**
*Detailed information on special topics, set within ruled boxes*

**Step-by-Step**
*Process illustrations; steps keyed by number to discuss in the main text*

## Plant Profiles

The second section of the book includes a description of each of the plants featured in the Portfolio. These profiles outline the plants' basic preferences for environmental conditions—such as soil, moisture, and sun or shade—and provide advice about planting and ongoing care.

Working with plant experts in the Northwest, we selected plants carefully, following a few simple guidelines. Every plant should be a proven performer in the region; once established, it should thrive without pampering. All plants should be available from a major local nursery or garden center. If they're not in stock, they could be ordered, or you could ask the nursery staff to recommend suitable substitutes.

In the Portfolio section, you'll note that plants are referred to by their common name but are cross-referenced to the Plant Profiles section by their latinized scientific name. While common names are familiar to many people, they can be confusing. Distinctly different plants can share the same common name, or one plant can have several different common names. Scientific names, therefore, ensure greatest accuracy and are more appropriate for a reference section such as this. Although you can confidently purchase most of the plants in this book from local nurseries using the common name, knowing the scientific name allows you to ensure that the plant you're ordering is the same one shown in our design.

## Guide to Installation

In this section you'll find detailed instructions and illustrations covering all the techniques you'll need to install any design from start to finish. Here we explain how to think your way through a landscaping project and anticipate the various steps. Then you'll learn how to do each part of the job: readying the site; laying out the design; choosing materials; addressing basic irrigation needs; building paths, trellises, or other structures; preparing the soil for planting; buying the recommended plants and putting them in place; and car-

ing for the plants to keep them healthy and attractive year after year.

We've taken care to make installation of built elements simple and straightforward. The paths, trellises, and arbors all use basic, readily available materials, and they can be assembled by people who have no special skills or tools beyond those commonly used for home maintenance. The designs can easily be adapted to meet specific needs or to fit in with the style of your house or other landscaping features.

Installing different designs requires different techniques. You can find the techniques that you need by following the cross references in the Portfolio to pages in the Guide to Installation, or by skimming the Guide. You'll find that many basic techniques are reused from one project to the next. You might want to start with one of the smaller, simpler designs. Gradually you'll develop the skills and confidence to do any project you choose.

Most of the designs in this book can be installed in several weekends; some will take a little longer. Digging planting beds and erecting fences and arbors can be strenuous work. If you lack the energy for such tasks, consider hiring a neighborhood teenager to help out; local landscaping services can provide more comprehensive help.

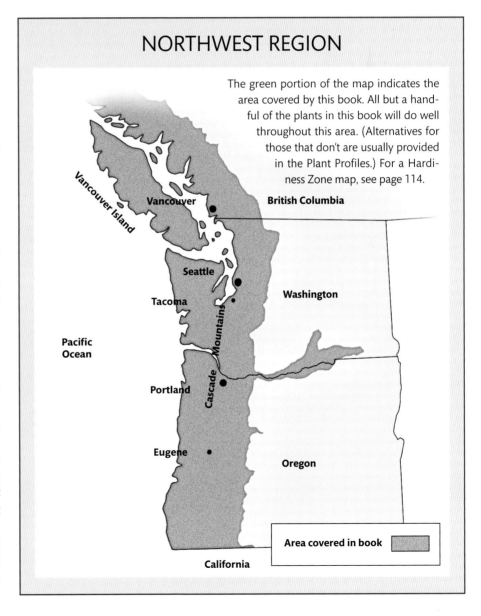

**NORTHWEST REGION**

The green portion of the map indicates the area covered by this book. All but a handful of the plants in this book will do well throughout this area. (Alternatives for those that don't are usually provided in the Plant Profiles.) For a Hardiness Zone map, see page 114.

Vancouver Island

Vancouver — British Columbia

Seattle

Tacoma — Washington

Pacific Ocean

Cascade Mountains

Portland

Eugene — Oregon

Area covered in book

California

# As Your Landscape Grows

## AT PLANTING

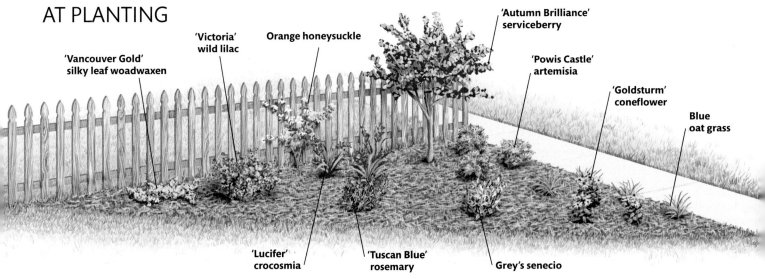

'Vancouver Gold'
silky leaf woadwaxen

'Victoria'
wild lilac

Orange honeysuckle

'Autumn Brilliance'
serviceberry

'Powis Castle'
artemisia

'Goldsturm'
coneflower

Blue
oat grass

'Lucifer'
crocosmia

'Tuscan Blue'
rosemary

Grey's senecio

**Landscapes change** over the years. As plants grow, the overall look evolves from sparse to lush. Trees cast cool shade where the sun used to shine. Shrubs and hedges grow tall and dense enough to provide privacy. Perennials and ground covers spread to form colorful patches of foliage and flowers. Meanwhile, paths, arbors, fences, and other structures gain the comfortable patina of age.

Continuing change over the years—

sometimes rapid and dramatic, sometimes slow and subtle—is one of the joys of landscaping. It is also one of the challenges. Anticipating how fast plants will grow and how big they will eventually become is difficult, even for professional designers, and was a major concern in formulating the designs for this book.

To illustrate the kinds of changes to expect in a planting, these pages show one

of the designs at three different "ages." Even though a new planting may look sparse at first, it will soon fill in. And because of careful spacing, the planting will look as good in 10 to 15 years as it does after 3 to 5. It will, of course, look different, but that's part of the fun.

## THREE TO FIVE YEARS

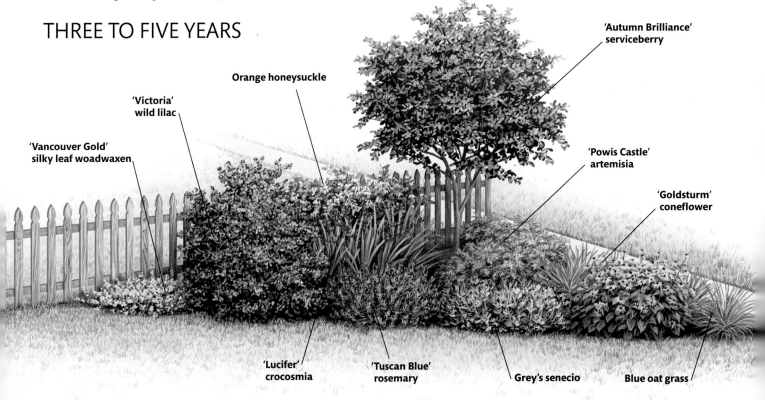

'Autumn Brilliance'
serviceberry

Orange honeysuckle

'Victoria'
wild lilac

'Vancouver Gold'
silky leaf woadwaxen

'Powis Castle'
artemisia

'Goldsturm'
coneflower

'Lucifer'
crocosmia

'Tuscan Blue'
rosemary

Grey's senecio

Blue oat grass

**At Planting**—Here's how the corner planting (pp. 32–35) might appear in spring immediately after planting. The branches of the orange honeysuckle, 2 to 3 ft. long, have been tied to the fence, where they can begin to twine. The serviceberry is 4 to 5 ft. tall, and the shrubby wild lilac is about 18 in. tall. Bought in 1-gal. containers, the rosemary, Grey's senecio, coneflower, artemisia, and blue oat grass are about a foot in height; the crocosmia a little taller. Silky leaf woadwaxen hugs the ground near the fence. In addition to mulch, you can fill the spaces between the small plants with short annuals.

**Three to Five Years**—As shown here in early summer, the planting has filled out nicely. The serviceberry rises to a height of about 8 ft. Below, the honeysuckle twines along much of the fence. The wild lilac has filled in significantly. Its blue flowers pair attractively with the carpet of yellow woadwaxen flowers. The rosemary, senecio, coneflower, and artemisia have become bushy plants with handsome foliage and flowers. The blue oat grass has grown into bristly clumps 12 to 18 in. tall; the taller crocosmia now forms a small patch.

**Ten to Fifteen Years**—Shown again in early summer, the serviceberry, now 10 to 12 ft. tall, has a graceful habit and casts dappled shade over the planting. Its lower limbs have been removed as the tree has grown, making room for the wild lilac, which has overgrown the woadwaxen. Annual pruning has kept the honeysuckle vigorous but confined to the fence. The crocosmia has been divided over the years to keep it in scale (and provide starts for other clumps around the yard). The rosemary, senecio, coneflower, artemisia, and blue oat grass commingle, with just enough pruning each year to keep the planting tidy and the clumps defined.

## TEN TO FIFTEEN YEARS

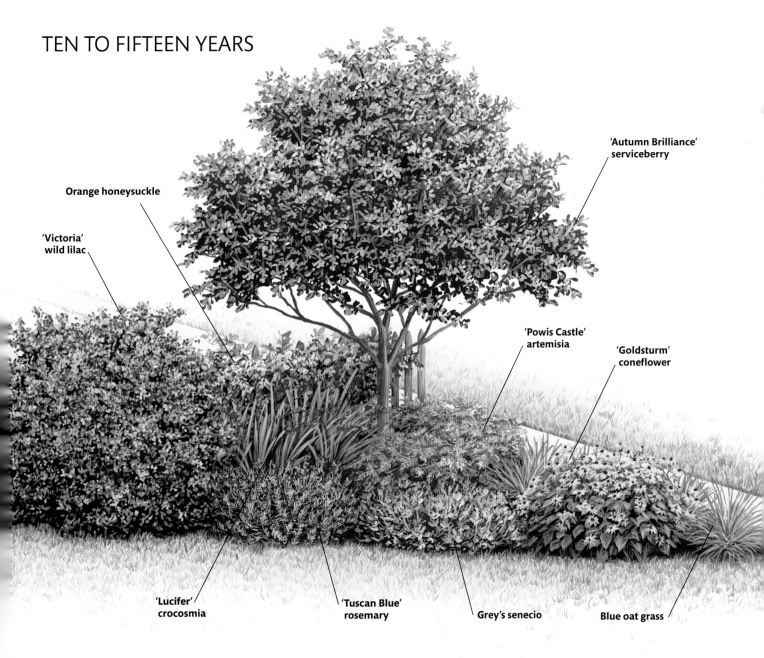

'Autumn Brilliance' serviceberry

Orange honeysuckle

'Victoria' wild lilac

'Powis Castle' artemisia

'Goldsturm' coneflower

'Lucifer' crocosmia

'Tuscan Blue' rosemary

Grey's senecio

Blue oat grass

# Portfolio *of* Designs

**You can use** any of the forty-eight professional landscape designs presented in this section outright or adapt them to suit your property or personal preferences. Each design solves a common landscape problem and provides a plan to create a stunning landscape with plants that thrive in the Pacific Northwest. There are gardens of colorful perennials and shrubs, as well as structures and plantings that create shady hideaways, dress up nondescript walls, and even make a centerpiece of a lowly recycling area. Large color illustrations show what the designs will look like, and site plans delineate the layout and planting scheme. The text explains the designs and describes the plants and projects appearing in them. These designs can make your property more attractive, more useful, and—most importantly—more enjoyable for you, your family, and your friends.

# Up Front and Formal

### GARDEN GEOMETRY TRANSFORMS A SMALL FRONT YARD

**Formal gardens** have a special appeal. Their simple geometry can be soothing in a hectic world, and the look is timeless. Homes with balanced or symmetrical facades are especially suited to formal makeovers, which complement and accent the architecture.

This design enhances both approaches to a front door—from the sidewalk and the driveway—while echoing the house facade when viewed from the street. The result is formal, but comfortably so.

Visitors approaching from the sidewalk or drive are drawn to a small "courtyard" at the intersection of the two walkways where they can pause to enjoy the plantings before proceeding to the door. A nearby bench encourages lingering under the shade of a small tree. Low wooden screens provide privacy from the street.

Overcrowded, intricate plantings can make a small space seem smaller. So here, a limited palette of plants is arrayed in bold masses to impart a comfortably spacious feel to a small garden. Flowers can be enjoyed from spring through fall, and a balance of deciduous and evergreen foliage ensures a year-round presence.

1 square = 1 ft.

Driveway

'Green Island' Japanese holly

## Plants & Projects

Installing new paving and wooden privacy screens is a big job, but not complicated. Contact a landscape contractor if you prefer to expend your energy on the planting. Once established, these plants are not particularly demanding. Clip the hedges regularly to keep them tidy. Prune trees and shrubs as needed.

**Ⓐ Japanese stewartia** (use 1 plant)
This deciduous tree provides white flowers in midsummer, dappled shade in summer, colorful fall foliage, and flaking bark for winter interest. See *Stewartia pseudocamellia*, p. 144.

**Ⓑ 'Flower Carpet Pink' rose** (use 8)
This deciduous shrub's green foliage is covered from spring to fall with pink flowers. See *Rosa*, p. 139.

**Ⓒ 'Ramapo' rhododendron** (use 12)
This compact evergreen shrub forms a mound of silvery blue foliage. Bright-violet flowers bloom in early or mid-spring. See *Rhododendron*, p. 139.

**Ⓓ 'Preziosa' hydrangea** (use 3)
Prized for its long-lasting, showy midsummer flowers, this deciduous shrub grows to 5 ft. tall and also has attractive foliage. Flowers start out white, then turn red, mauve, or blue. See *Hydrangea macrophylla*, p. 132.

**Ⓔ 'Green Island' Japanese holly** (use 16)
This evergreen shrub's small shiny green leaves are borne on compact, twiggy branches ideal for shearing. Trim as a tidy, but loose, hedge. See *Ilex crenata*, p. 133.

SITE: Sunny

SEASON: Early summer

CONCEPT: Subtle geometry and well-chosen plants create an entry garden of comfortable, low-key formality.

**A** Japanese stewartia

**J** 'Little Grapette' daylily

**L** Screen

**G** 'Sarabande' Chinese silver grass

**D** 'Preziosa' hydrangea

**I** 'Tropic Night' Siberian iris

**M** Paving

**K** Ground covers

**H** Peony hybrid

**C** 'Ramapo' rhododendron

**C** 'Ramapo' rhododendron

**G** 'Sarabande' Chinese silver grass

**F** 'Helleri' Japanese holly

**B** 'Flower Carpet Pink' rose

**F** **'Helleri' Japanese holly** (use 10)
Similar to 'Green Island', this evergreen shrub makes a smaller, tighter mass of dark-green leaves. Trim formally to neat geometric lines. See *Ilex crenata*, p. 133.

**G** **'Sarabande' Chinese silver grass** (use 6)
A perennial grass, this forms a large clump of slender leaves that arch at their tips. White-striped green leaves appear to be silver from a distance. See *Miscanthus sinensis*, p. 135.

**H** **Peony hybrids** (use 6)
These perennials bear large fragrant flowers in late spring or early summer on bushy clumps of compound foliage. A cultivar with burgundy-red flowers suits this design well. See *Paeonia*, p. 136.

**I** **'Tropic Night' Siberian iris** (use 6)
In late spring and early summer, elegant deep-purple flowers rise on long stalks above this perennial's slender upright leaves. Foliage continues to look good after bloom has faded. See *Iris sibirica*, p. 133.

**J** **'Little Grapette' daylily** (use 10)
Echoing the irises closer to the house, this perennial also forms a clump of long slender leaves and bears rosy purple flowers on long stalks. Blooms in early summer. See *Hemerocallis*, p. 131.

**K** **Ground covers** (as needed)
Of the three ground covers used in this design, two are shrubs. Nearest the house, 'Silver Queen' euonymus (see *Euonymus fortunei*, p. 127) forms a low mass of small green leaves edged in white. Space plants 2 ft. on center. Around the low screens, 'Massachusetts' kinnikinnick (see *Arctostaphylos uva-ursi*, p. 120) forms a dark-green carpet. Its white spring flowers produce red berries. Plant 18 in. on center. Edging the walkways is moss phlox (see *Phlox subulata*, p. 136) a perennial with grayish evergreen leaves and pink spring flowers. Plant 18 in. on center.

**L** **Screen**
Low wooden screens adjacent to the walkway help separate the public and private spaces in the front yard. See p. 178.

**M** **Paving**
Rectangular, random-sized flagstones are durable and reinforce the formality of the design. See p. 157.

**K** 'Lucifer' crocosmia

**A** Chaste tree

**P** 'Sarabande' Chinese silver grass

**O** Path and seating

**H** Penstemon

**C** 'Victoria' wild lilac

**F** Grey's senecio

**B** Indian grass

'Magnus' purple coneflower **J**

**N** Pot

**M** Ground cover

**L** 'Autumn Joy' sedum

**G** 'Hidcote' English lavender

Ground **M** cover

**I** 'May Night' salvia

**D** Rockspray cotoneaster

**E** Dwarf eastern white pine

**G** 'Hidcote' English lavender

SITE: Sunny

SEASON: Late summer

CONCEPT: An imaginative informal planting transforms a front yard into a pleasant stroll garden.

# Free-spirited front yard

If formality isn't your style and you prefer gardens to lawns, consider this design. Here, sweeping masses of shrubs and perennials create a colorful undulating landscape. The foliage is varied in form, color, and texture, and there are flowers and striking seed heads from spring through fall.

Though informal, the composition is subtly purposeful. Eye-catching plants define the planting at the corners. Distinctive pines frame the doorway, while walkways from drive and sidewalk invite entry.

But for the visitor or resident inclined to dally, a meandering flagstone path leads not to the front door but to a comfortable bench where the plants can be enjoyed at leisure. You might consider removing any concrete walkway from the drive to emphasize the garden stroll.

You need undertake no major construction for this design, and you can install the planting in stages, retaining lawn in areas yet to be planted.

## Plants & Projects

**A** **Chaste tree** (use 1 plant)
Long clusters of fragrant lavender-colored flowers bloom on this deciduous shrub summer through early fall. See *Vitex agnus-castus*, p. 146.

**B** **Indian grass** (use 1)
A perennial grass with upright blue-green foliage that turns orange and yellow in fall and hints of those colors through winter. See *Sorghastrum nutans*, p. 143.

**C** **'Victoria' wild lilac** (use 1)
This upright shrub offers attractive evergreen foliage and clusters of deep-blue flowers in spring. See *Ceanothus*, p. 123.

**D** **Rockspray cotoneaster** (use 1)
A low deciduous shrub with pinkish-white spring flowers and long-lasting red berries. Leaves turn red in fall. See *Cotoneaster horizontalis*, p. 126.

**E** **Dwarf eastern white pine** (use 3)
This evergreen tree or shrub grows slowly and has soft blue-green needles. See *Pinus strobus* 'Nana', p. 137.

**F** **Grey's senecio** (use 3)
An evergreen shrub with small gray leaves and yellow daisylike flowers in summer. See *Senecio greyi*, p. 142.

**G** **'Hidcote' English lavender** (use 23)
The gray foliage of this compact evergreen shrub bristles with spikes of dark-purple flowers in early summer. See *Lavandula angustifolia*, p. 134.

**H** **Penstemon** (use 9)
This late-spring and summer flowering perennial has showy dark and blue-and-purple tubular flowers on a spike. See *Penstemon serrulatus*, p. 136.

1 square = 1 ft.

House · Stoop · Walkway · Ornamental stones · Sidewalk · Driveway · Bench

# PLANT PORTRAITS

These plants add character to front yards that are geometric or free-ranging, formal or informal.

● = First design, pp. 16–17

▲ = Second design, pp. 18–19

Moss phlox (*Phlox subulata*, p. 136) ●

'Ramapo' rhododendron (*Rhododendron*, p. 139) ●

---

**ⓘ 'May Night' salvia** (use 7)
For months in summer this perennial bears numerous spikes of deep-purple flowers above dark-green leaves. See *Salvia* x *superba*, p. 141.

**ⓙ 'Magnus' purple coneflower** (use 13)
Large daisylike purple flowers with orange centers rise on stiff stems above this perennial's dark-green leaves. See *Echinacea purpurea*, p. 126.

**ⓚ 'Lucifer' crocosmia** (use 3)
This perennial makes a clump of long narrow leaves. In summer, arching stalks bear sprays of red-orange flowers. See *Crocosmia*, p. 126.

**ⓛ 'Autumn Joy' sedum** (use 18)
A perennial with fleshy gray-green foliage and flat clusters of tiny flowers that turn from pink to russet from summer through fall. See *Sedum*, p. 142.

**ⓜ Ground covers** (as needed)
Woolly thyme (see *Thymus pseudolanuginosus*, p. 145) runs through the center of the planting. Plant 1 ft. apart. Bearberry cotoneaster (see *Cotoneaster dammeri*, p. 125) carpets areas at the front of the planting and to the left of the stoop. Plant 2 ft. on center.

**ⓝ Pots**
Large, colorfully planted pots accent the planting. Try combinations of boxwood, amaranth, zinnias, verbena, coleus, scaevola, and helichrysum.

**ⓞ Path and seating**
A path of irregular flagstones leads to a seating area of crushed rock (for both, see p. 156) and a comfortable bench.

**See p. 17 for the following:**

**ⓟ 'Sarabande' Chinese silver grass** (use 2)

Chaste tree (*Vitex agnus-castus*, p. 146) ▲

'Preziosa' hydrangea (*Hydrangea macrophylla*, p. 132) ●

# Front-Door Makeover

## ENHANCE YOUR MAIN ENTRY IN A WEEKEND

**Sometimes the simplest landscaping projects** pack a surprisingly big punch. This design uses only a few plants and can be easily installed in a single weekend. Yet this small investment of time and money can transform one of the most important parts of your property, welcoming visitors to your home as well as presenting a pleasing face to passersby.

Small plantings often suffer from busyness—too many different kinds of plants in too little space. This design makes a bold display with just five different plants. Potted shrubs and upright viburnums with a skirt of candytuft frame the doorway, while low masses of pinks and daylilies border the walkway. There are pretty flowers and a variety of foliage textures to catch the eye, as well as a subtle mix of scents. The planting is enticing to visitors but not overpowering. And it offers a pleasant spot to chat as guests enter or leave the house.

'Little Gem' **B**
evergreen candytuft

**D** 'Stella de Oro'
daylily

Cottage pink **C**

**A** 'Spring Bouquet'
viburnum

House

Stoop

**B**

**E**

**A**

**C**

Walkway

**D**

**B**

**E**

**A**

**C**

**D**

Lawn

1 square = 1 ft.

SITE: Sunny

SEASON: Late winter

CONCEPT: A few well-chosen plants and a few hours work can invigorate a nondescript entry.

Black chokeberry **E**

Cottage pink **C**

'Little Gem' evergreen candytuft **B**

**A** 'Spring Bouquet' viburnum

**D** 'Stella de Oro' daylily

## Plants & Projects

This simple planting is easy to maintain. Clip the candytuft after its spring bloom to encourage rebloom in the fall. Deadhead the daylilies and pinks to keep them tidy. As the years pass, you may need to prune the viburnum in spring or fall to keep them an attractive size.

**A** **'Spring Bouquet' viburnum** (use 2 plants)
This compact evergreen shrub blooms from late fall to spring, bearing white flowers with a rosy pink tinge and light fragrance. Dense, dark-green foliage looks good year-round. See *Viburnum tinus*, p. 146.

**B** **'Little Gem' evergreen candytuft** (use 6)
Forming a solid mass at the feet of the viburnums, the dark leaves of this evergreen perennial are covered with white flowers for several weeks in spring; in some areas, they bloom all year. See *Iberis sempervirens*, p. 133.

**C** **Cottage pink** (use 6)
This perennial is prized for its delicious scent. Single or double flowers in shades of white, pink, and red float on wiry stems above a mat of gray-green foliage from late spring into summer. See *Dianthus plumarius*, p. 126.

**D** **'Stella de Oro' daylily** (use 6)
A remarkably long-blooming daylily, it bears cheerful yellow flowers on sturdy stalks from late spring through fall on mounds of grassy foliage. See *Hemerocallis*, p. 131.

**E** **Black chokeberry** (use 2)
Planted in containers, this evergreen shrub greets visitors with showy white flowers in mid-spring, long-lasting dark-purple berries in summer, and colorful eye-catching red foliage in fall. See *Aronia melanocarpa*, p. 120.

# A Foundation with Flair

## CREATE A FRONT GARDEN OF STRIKING FOLIAGE

**Rare is the home** without foundation plantings. These simple skirtings of greenery hide unattractive underpinnings and help integrate a house with its surroundings. Useful as these plantings are, they are too frequently no more than monochromatic expanses of clipped evergreens, dull as dishwater. But, as this design shows, a low-maintenance foundation planting can be varied, colorful, and fun.

The planting enhances the house as seen from the street, frames the walkway to the front door for visitors, and can be enjoyed when viewed from inside the house as well. Extending the planting beyond the ends of the house helps "settle" an upright, boxy house more comfortably on its site.

The design combines trees and shrubs in a deep, gently curving bed. Small maples and a plume cedar lend height and presence, while providing some screening and privacy from the street. Lower evergreen shrubs and ferns add a variety of leaf textures and colors that make an eye-catching display for much of the year, peaking in fall, the season shown here. In addition to woody plants, carefully chosen perennials accent the entry and, in spring, swaths of tulips brighten the scene.

SITE: Sunny

SEASON: Early fall

CONCEPT: A mixture of distinctive foliage textures and colors makes a foundation planting with four-season interest.

## Plants & Projects

This is a low-care planting. Once established, the plants will thrive without much more attention than seasonal cleanup and renewing the mulch in the summer to conserve water. Shear the candytuft after bloom and divide and refurbish the tulips every fall.

A Spicebush

C Dwarf Hinoki cypress

F Barnes' narrow male fern

E Red chokeberry

D David viburnum

C Dwarf Hinoki cypress

Barnes' narrow male fern F

H 'Little Gem' candytuft

G 'Lucifer' crocosmia

**A Spicebush** (use 3 plants)
This multi-stemmed decid-uous shrub offers months of interest. In spring, tiny fragrant green-yellow flowers are fol-lowed by red berries. Leaves turn yellow in fall and have a spicy fragrance when crushed. Male and female plants re-quired to cross-pollinate. See *Lindera benzoin*, p. 134.

**B Plume cedar** (use 1)
Making a neat cone, this ev-ergreen tree contrasts nicely with the nearby maples. Needlelike blue-green foliage turns bronze in winter. Peeling, cinnamon-colored bark is also attractive. See *Cryptomeria ja-ponica* 'Elegans', p. 126.

**C Dwarf Hinoki cypress** (use 2)
Flanking the steps, a pair of these small evergreen trees form mounds of layered em-erald-green scalelike foliage. Plant has a sculpted look. See *Chamaecyparis obtusa* 'Nana Gracilis', p. 123.

**D David viburnum** (use 11)
A compact evergreen shrub with handsome, leathery, dark-green leaves. In spring, pink buds produce flat clusters of small white flowers. It bears metallic-blue fruits in fall. See *Viburnum davidii*, p. 146.

**E Red chokeberry** (use 8)
This multi-stemmed bushy shrub explodes with small white flowers in late spring be-fore being covered in bright-red berries in summer. Glossy green foliage turns bright-or-ange and red in the fall. See *Aronia arbutifolia*, p. 120.

**F Barnes' narrow male fern** (use 9)
This semievergreen fern forms a narrow clump of upright fronds with slightly ruffled leaflets. See Ferns: *Dryopteris filix-mas* 'Bar-nesii', p. 128.

**G 'Lucifer' crocosmia** (use 6)
Clusters of bright-red-orange flowers hover on graceful arch-ing stems among this perennial's swordlike leaves from summer into fall. See *Crocosmia*, p. 126.

**H 'Little Gem' candytuft** (as needed)
This perennial ground cover forms mounds of glossy ever-green leaves. Flat clusters of white flowers cover the foliage in spring. See *Iberis semper-virens*, p. 133.

**I Tulips** (as needed)
Plant a generous number (100 or more) of these colorful bulbs in the candytuft for a striking spring display. See Bulbs: *Tulipa*, p. 122.

## PLANT PORTRAITS

These plants will dress up the most nondescript foundation or front porch while requiring little care.

● = First design, pp. 22–23

▲ = Second design, pp. 24–25

**Weeping hemlock**
(*Tsuga canadensis* 'Pendula', p. 146) ▲

**Tulips** (*Tulipa*, p. 122) ●

**'Setsugekka' sasanqua camellia**
(*Camellia sasanqua*, p. 123) ▲

**Spicebush** (*Lindera benzoin*, p. 134) ●

**Bird's-nest Norway spruce**
(*Picea abies* 'Nidiformis', p. 137) ▲

# Setting for a shady porch

This foundation planting graces a front porch on a site shaded from the afternoon sun. Like the previous design, this one mixes the year-round attractions of evergreens with deciduous trees and perennials. From spring through fall, many-stemmed vine maples screen porch sitters from activity on the street. In late winter, fragrant flowers entice visitors to linger on the porch.

Here again, foliage is the key. Conifers, broad-leaved evergreens, ferns, and leafy hostas combine a pleasing variety of forms, leaf textures, and colors. Unlike many plantings, this one reaches its flowering peak in late winter (shown here). Seasonally planted hanging baskets and containers accent the foliage during the rest of the year.

## Plants & Projects

**Ⓐ Vine maple** (use 6 plants)
This deciduous Northwest-native tree forms an open thicket of stems that is interesting year-round. Green leaves turn red, yellow, and orange in fall. See *Acer circinatum*, p. 118.

**Ⓑ Weeping hemlock** (use 1)
A slow-growing evergreen tree, its arching branches form a wide mound of soft blue-green foliage. A striking contrast to the vine maples. See *Tsuga canadensis* 'Pendula', p. 146.

**Ⓒ Bird's-nest Norway spruce** (use 3)
This slow-growing evergreen tree makes a hassocklike mound of dark-green needles. Commonly has a slight depression on top, which gives rise to its name. See *Picea abies* 'Nidiformis', p. 137.

Hanging basket **J**

Vine maple **A**

Weeping hemlock **B**

Fragrant sarcococca **E**

Soft shield fern **G**

Lenten rose **H**

Lenten rose **H**

Bird's-nest Norway spruce **C**

**J** Container

Variegated winter daphne **F**

**D** 'Setsugekka' sasanqua camellia

**C** Bird's-nest Norway spruce

**G** Soft shield fern

See site plan for **I** .

SITE: Shady

SEASON: Late winter

CONCEPT: An eye-catching selection of plants enhance gatherings on a shady porch.

Column

Porch

Steps

Lawn

Sidewalk

1 square = 1 ft.

**D** 'Setsugekka' sasanqua camellia (use 3)
An evergreen shrub prized for its winter offering of white, semidouble flowers displayed against a backdrop of glossy green foliage. See *Camellia sasanqua*, p. 123.

**E** Fragrant sarcococca (use 6)
This evergreen shrub forms a mass of glossy green foliage beneath the porch. In late winter, small, but very fragrant, white flowers cluster among the leaves. See *Sarcococca ruscifolia*, p. 142.

**F** Variegated winter daphne (use 3)
The glossy green leaves of this evergreen shrub are edged in gold. Fragrant, rose-tinged white flowers bloom from late winter into spring. See

*Daphne odora* 'Aureomarginata', p. 126.

**G** Soft shield fern (use 18)
Clumps of lacy bright-green fronds accent the planting in several spots. The foliage is evergreen and soft to the touch. See Ferns: *Polystichum setiferum*, p. 128.

**H** Lenten rose (use 12)
A popular late-winter-blooming perennial has distinctive fleshy

flowers and shiny evergreen leaves. See *Helleborus orientalis*, p. 130.

**I** Hosta (use 20)
This popular perennial is prized for its foliage. To complement this planting, choose a medium-size cultivar with variegated white-and-green leaves. See *Hosta*, p. 132.

**J** Containers and hanging baskets (as needed)

For winter, we've shown trailing glacier ivy and primroses in the baskets hanging on the porch columns. For the large pots on the porch and by the steps, use a tall plant (such as a dwarf conifer, evergreen fern, or spike plant) underplanted with seasonal annuals. Here we've shown winter pansies and kale.

# Another Fancy Foundation

## FLOWERS AND FOLIAGE CREATE A LUSH GARDEN

**By adding smaller plants** in front of the taller shrubs near the house and including a small flowering tree, a mix of shrubs and perennials, and a flowering vine along the railing, the design transforms a foundation planting into a small garden. Here, there's something for everyone to enjoy, from porch sitters to passersby.

Starting in early spring with fragrant jessamine and rosemary and the eye-stopping flowers of the esperanza and verbena, the garden reaches full exuberance in summer, with bright flowers in yellows, purples, blues, and oranges. Foliage in a mixture of greens and grays and a variety of textures showcases the flowers, several of which attract beautiful butterflies and hummingbirds. And the evergreen leaves of many of the plants extend this foundation planting's appeal through the winter.

SITE: Sunny

SEASON: Midsummer

CONCEPT: Mixing small trees, vines, shrubs, and perennials makes a colorful foundation planting.

Carolina jessamine **J**

Firebush **C**

Chinese maiden grass **F**

'Blue Princess' verbena **H**

Chokeberry **B**

'Gold Star' esperanza **D**

'Catawba' crapemyrtle **A**

'Goldsturm' black-eyed Susan **I**

'Autumn Joy' sedum **G**

Firebush **C**

'Blue Princess' verbena **H**

**Porch**

Porch columns

J

J

J

B

F

H

C

C

B

E

I

G

C

A

D

D

**Steps**

**Lawn**

C

**Walk**

H

1 square = 1 ft.

H

B   Red
     chokeberry

E   Rosemary

F   Chinese
     maiden
     grass

C   Firebush

D   'Gold Star'
     esperanza

H   'Blue Princess'
     verbena

## Plants & Projects

This is a low-care planting that offers a dazzling display of color in summer and fall. In addition to routine seasonal pruning, cut the firebush back in midsummer to keep it in check. If the verbena quits blooming, shear it back to about one-third to encourage new bloom. Train the jessamine up porch columns by attaching the vines to wires with twist ties. Add trellising if you want additional shade on the porch. For winter color in the beds, consider planting pansies or snapdragons when perennials fade.

**A** **'Catawba' crapemyrtle** (use 1 plant)
Next to the steps, this small shrublike tree greets guests with showy purple flowers in summer and brilliant orange leaves in fall. See *Lagerstroemia indica* 'Catawba', p. 134.

**B** **Red chokeberry** (use 5)
This multi-stemmed bushy shrub is covered with small white flowers in late spring before being bright-red berries in summer. Glossy green foliage turns vibrant orange and red in the fall. See *Aronia arbutifolia*, p. 120.

**C** **Firebush** (use 6)
Small red-orange flowers light up this bushy tropical shrub in summer, attracting butterflies and hummingbirds. See *Hamelia patens*, p. 130.

**D** **'Gold Star' esperanza** (use 6)
Known also as Texas yellow bells, this shrub bears big bright clusters of yellow flowers from spring to fall, creating a colorful contrast with the crapemyrtle and firebush beside it. See *Tecoma stans* 'Gold Star', p. 144.

**E** **Rosemary** (use 2)
This shrubby perennial herb forms a tight bouquet of branches clad in small needlelike leaves and topped with small blue flowers in early spring. It makes a fragrant edging next to the steps, in easy reach to snip a few leaves for cooking. See *Rosmarinus officinalis*, p. 140.

**F** **Chinese maiden grass** (use 3)
This beautiful fine-textured grass looks like a fountain. Flower plumes appear in late summer, and both leaves and flowers stay attractive through winter. See *Miscanthus sinensis*, p. 135.

**G** **'Autumn Joy' sedum** (use 3)
This bold-textured perennial grows in neat mounds of grayish-green succulent leaves. Dense clusters of tiny burnt-orange flowers appear in fall, turn pink, and gradually fade to tan. See *Sedum* 'Autumn Joy', p. 142.

**H** **'Blue Princess' verbena** (use 8)
Butterflies can't resist this perennial's lavender-blue flowers, which bloom continuously from spring to fall in clusters the size of silver dollars. See *Verbena* x *hybrida* 'Blue Princess', p. 146.

**I** **'Goldsturm' black-eyed Susan** (use 4)
In early summer golden dark-eyed daisylike flowers rise above this perennial's deep-green heart-shaped foliage. See *Rudbeckia fulgida* var. sullivantii 'Goldsturm', p. 140.

**J** **Carolina jessamine** (use 3)
Shiny neat evergreen leaves and a show of fragrant yellow flowers in spring make this vigorous vine ideal for training up porch columns or along a railing. See *Gelsemium sempervirens*, p. 129.

# First Impressions

## MAKE A PLEASANT PASSAGE TO YOUR FRONT DOOR

SITE: Sunny

SEASON: Midsummer

CONCEPT: Easy-care plantings and a distinctive walkway enhance a home's main entrance.

**Why wait** until a visitor reaches the front door to extend a cordial greeting? An entry-way landscape of well-chosen plants and a revamped walkway make the short journey a pleasant one. They also enrich your home's most public face and help settle it comfortably in its surroundings.

The flagstone paving here creates a walkway with the feel of a cozy courtyard, an atmosphere enhanced by the small trees, shrubs, and a bench. Extending along the driveway, the paving makes it easier for passengers to get in and out of a car. Attractive plants lead the way to the door and make the stroll inviting, while providing interest to viewers inside the house and on the street.

Flowering trees and shrubs bloom from spring through fall in whites and pinks. Perennial flowers add blues, reds, and purples. A mix of evergreen leaves and eye-catching fruit and bark make winter visitors welcome, too.

## Plants & Projects

Preparing the planting beds and laying the flagstone walkway are the main tasks in this design. Once plants are established, they require only seasonal cleanup and pruning to keep them looking their best.

**A Sourwood** (use 7 plants)
This small deciduous tree provides light shade and helps create a casual privacy for the entryway. Leaves change from bronze to green to orangey red from spring to summer to fall. Clusters of bell-shaped white flowers dangle from the ends of branches in mid- to late summer. See *Oxydendrum arboreum*, p. 136.

**B Peegee hydrangea** (use 1)
Pruned as a standard (a mass of foliage above a single bare trunk), this deciduous shrub greets visitors by the drive. Elongated clusters of creamy white flowers stand out against the dull-green foliage from midsummer into fall. See *Hydrangea paniculata* 'Grandiflora', p. 132.

**C Bigleaf hydrangea** (use 3)
Large hemispherical clusters of white, pink, red, or blue flowers grace this vase-shaped shrub from midsummer into fall. Deciduous leaves are shiny green. See *Hydrangea macrophylla*, p. 132.

**D Compact strawberry tree** (use 3)
Framing the window and door, this upright shrub offers glossy evergreen leaves with red margins and stems and colorful peeling bark. Bears clusters of white flowers and red fruit simultaneously in fall. See *Arbutus unedo* 'Compacta', p. 120.

**E Black chokeberry** (use 21)
This versatile evergreen shrub can tolerate any lighting. It boasts showy white flowers in mid-spring, dark-purple berries in summer, and eye-catching red foliage in fall. See *Aronia melanocarpa*, p. 120.

**F 'Goldflame' spirea** (use 10)
This deciduous shrub has striking leaves—red in spring and fall and golden-yellow in summer. In addition, flattened clusters of carmine-pink flowers bloom in summer and again in early fall. See *Spiraea japonica*, p. 143.

**G 'Harmony' reticulata iris** (use 9)
Sky blue flowers with yellow throats bloom in spring before the grassy foliage of this perennial appears. See *Iris reticulata*, p. 133.

**H Perennial salvia** (use 7)
This popular plant bears numerous upright spikes of violet-blue flowers on a mass of dull-green foliage. Blooms off and on from spring through fall. See *Salvia* x *superba*, p. 141.

**I 'Autumn Joy' sedum** (use 9)
The fleshy gray-green leaves of this perennial are topped by flat clusters of tiny flowers in late summer. Clusters turn from pale-greenish-pink to russet over a long period. See *Sedum*, p. 142.

**J Columbine** (use 3)
From spring into summer, exquisite flowers of blue, pink, or purple float on wiry stems over this perennial's airy blue-green foliage. See *Aquilegia*, p. 119.

**K Wintergreen** (use 16)
This low, creeping evergreen shrub displays small, glossy green leaves at the ends of short stems. In summer, bell-shaped, white-to-pink flowers dangle among the foliage. Red berries follow. Leaves and berries have wintergreen scent when crushed. See *Gaultheria procumbens*, p. 129.

**L Paving**
Laid on a sand-and-gravel base, rectangular flagstones in a variety of sizes provide an attractive, level surface. See p. 156.

Sourwood **A**

Black chokeberry **E**

House

Stoop

Bench

Lawn

1 square = 1 ft.

**Compact D strawberry tree**

**B Peegee hydrangea**

**C Bigleaf hydrangea**

**I 'Autumn Joy' sedum**

**E Black chokeberry**

**J Columbine**

**H Perennial salvia**

**I 'Autumn Joy' sedum**

**L Paving**

**See site plan for G.**

**F 'Goldflame' spirea**

**K Wintergreen**

House

Stoop

Lawn

1 square = 1 ft.

SITE: Shady

SEASON: Spring

CONCEPT: A selection of plants native and adapted to the region creates an enticing entryway on a shaded site.

# Native plants offer a shady welcome

If your entry is shady, perhaps with morning sun and afternoon shade, you can try this planting scheme. The configuration remains the same as that of the previous design, but here we've used Northwest-native plants and others well adapted to shadier conditions in the region. Overall, the emphasis is still on year-round good looks.

Following nature's woodland models, the planting is layered. The vine maple's leafy canopy casts dappled summer shade on flowering evergreen shrubs and richly textured ground covers below. Spring (shown here) bursts with bloom, and a profusion of evergreen foliage guarantees interest throughout the rest of the year.

## Plants & Projects

**ⒶVine maple** (use 7 plants)
Choose multitrunked specimens of this deciduous tree to make the most of its striking form. Broad, lobed leaves are colorful in the spring and fall. See *Acer circinatum*, p. 118.

**ⒷSilk-tassel bush** (use 1)
This evergreen is pruned here as a shrub with room for underplantings. Elliptical, wavy-edged leaves are dark-green above and gray below. Male plants produce long pendulous catkins in winter. See *Garrya elliptica*, p. 129.

**ⒸEvergreen huckleberry** (use 11)
This low-branching evergreen shrub features small, glossy green leaves tinged with red; new stems are burgundy. Bears pinkish-white flowers in spring. Berries are edible. See *Vaccinium ovatum*, p. 146.

**ⒹLeucothoe** (use 16)
A low-growing evergreen shrub has arching branches. Small

Vine maple Ⓐ

'Dora Amateis' rhododendron Ⓔ

Silk-tassel bush Ⓑ

Leucothoe Ⓓ

Evergreen huckleberry Ⓒ

Leucothoe Ⓓ

Creeping mahonia Ⓕ

Sword fern Ⓖ

Paving Ⓛ

White bleeding heart Ⓙ

Creeping mahonia Ⓕ

Compact strawberry tree Ⓚ

Japanese painted fern Ⓗ

Bunchberry Ⓘ

clusters of white flowers nestle on stems at the base of the lance-shaped leaves in spring. Foliage turns bronze with cold weather in fall. See *Leucothoe axillaris*, p. 134.

**E** **'Dora Amateis' rhododendron** (use 8)
This is a compact form of the popular evergreen shrub. In spring, it lights up the space beneath the window with a blizzard of green-throated white flowers. Glossy green foliage is attractive year-round. See *Rhododendron*, p. 139.

**F** **Creeping mahonia** (use 7)
An evergreen shrub with hollylike blue-green leaflets, it spreads by underground stems to form a patch. Bears clusters of dusty yellow flowers in spring. Leaves turn bronze-green in winter. See *Mahonia repens*, p. 135.

**G** **Sword fern** (use 9)
The shiny evergreen fronds of this Northwest-native fern contrast handsomely with nearby foliage. See Ferns: *Polystichum munitum*, p. 128.

**H** **Japanese painted fern** (use 15)
A smaller, lacier fern with delicately colored fronds showing shades of purple, green, and silver. See Ferns: *Athyrium niponicum* 'Pictum', p. 128.

**I** **Bunchberry** (use 12)
The small oval leaves of this semievergreen ground cover appear near the ends of short stems. A perennial, bunchberry bears small flowers with showy white bracts in spring, followed by eye-catching shiny red fruit in autumn. See *Cornus canadensis*, p. 125.

**J** **White bleeding heart** (use 3)
A perennial with lacy, fernlike, blue-green foliage. In late spring, rows of small white heart-shaped flowers dangle from arching stems. See *Lamprocamprios spectabilis* 'Alba', p. 134.

See p. 28 for the following:

**K** **Compact strawberry tree** (use 3)

**L** **Paving**

# PLANT PORTRAITS

In sun or shade, these plants will provide a warm welcome at the front entry of your home.
● = First design, pp. 28–29
▲ = Second design, pp. 30–31

**Wintergreen**
(*Gaultheria procumbens*, p. 129) ●

**Black chokeberry**
(*Aronia melanocarpa*, p. 120) ●

**'Dora Amateis' rhododendron**
(*Rhododendron*, p. 139) ▲

**Evergreen huckleberry**
(*Vaccinium ovatum*, p. 146) ▲

**White bleeding heart**
(*Lamprocamprios spectabilis* 'Alba', p. 134) ▲

**Columbine** (*Aquilegia*, p. 119) ●

**Creeping mahonia** (*Mahonia repens*, p. 135) ▲

# An Eye-Catching Corner

## BEAUTIFY A BOUNDARY WITH EASY-CARE PLANTS

**The corner** where two properties and the sidewalk meet is often a kind of grassy no-man's-land. Neighbors hesitate to garden there for fear of offending one another. This design defines that boundary with a planting that can be enjoyed by both property owners, as well as by passersby. Good gardens make good neighbors, so we've used well-behaved, low-maintenance plants that won't make extra work for the person next door—or for you.

Because of its exposed location, remote from the house and close to the street, a corner planting is often less personal than those in more private and frequently used parts of a property. This design is meant to be appreciated from a distance. Anchored by a small tree, the planting combines shrubs and perennials in an attractive scheme of colorful foliage and flowers. An existing fence provides scaffolding for a vigorous vine. While not intended as a barrier, the planting also provides a modest psychological, if not physical, screen from activity on the sidewalk and street.

Here, something is in bloom from spring through fall, with flowers in shades of yellow, blue, orange-red, and white. The foliage is also colorful, mixing gray, silver, and blue with green. The small tree provides a blaze of color in fall, while evergreen plants ensure a year-round presence.

Fence

Lawn

1 square = 1 ft.

Sidewalk

SITE: Sunny

SEASON: Summer

CONCEPT: A colorful planting that looks good year-round marks the property line in a neighborly fashion.

'Victoria' **B**
wild lilac

'Vancouver Gold' **D**
silky leaf woadwaxen

# Plants & Projects

As befits a planting some distance from the house, these durable, reliable plants require little care beyond some seasonal pruning and cleanup. As they reach maturity, the shrubs and vine may need occasional pruning to control their size.

**A** **'Autumn Brilliance' serviceberry** (use 1 plant)
This small deciduous tree is a three-season performer, with white flowers in spring, blue berries in summer, and colorful foliage in fall. See *Amelanchier* x *grandiflora*, p. 119.

**B** **'Victoria' wild lilac** (use 1)
In spring, this evergreen shrub displays small deep-blue flowers at the ends of its branches.

Small, glossy dark-green leaves make an effective background. See *Ceanothus*, p. 123.

**C** **Grey's senecio** (use 1)
Grown primarily for its soft gray foliage, this evergreen shrub bears pretty yellow flowers in summer. Bloom is unreliable. Flowers are sometimes sheared off, as shown here, to emphasize the foliage. See *Senecio greyi*, p. 142.

**D** **'Vancouver Gold' silky leaf woadwaxen** (use 1)
A low deciduous ground cover whose twiggy matlike stems are

covered with tiny green leaves. In late spring and early summer it bears a mass of bright-yellow pealike flowers. See *Genista pilosa*, p. 129.

**E** **'Tuscan Blue' rosemary** (use 3)
This evergreen shrub has fragrant gray-green leaves. Periwinkle-blue flowers bloom in late winter and sporadically the rest of the year. See *Rosmarinus officinalis*, p. 140.

**F** **Orange honeysuckle** (use 1)
A deciduous twining vine with dark-green leaves and clusters

of bright-orange tubular flowers spring through mid-summer, followed by orange-red berries. See *Lonicera ciliosa*, p. 134.

**G** **Blue oat grass** (use 5)
This evergreen grass forms a clump bristling with thin pale-blue leaves. Trim off the sparse flower spikes, as shown here, if you wish. See *Helictotrichon sempervirens*, p. 130.

**H** **'Powis Castle' artemisia** (use 3)
A perennial, this forms a spreading mound of deeply cut silvery leaves that adds a striking accent to the planting. See *Artemisia*, p. 120.

**I** **'Goldsturm' coneflower** (use 3)
From summer into fall this perennial's daisylike flowers rise on sturdy stems above clumps of green leaves. Flowers are yellow with dark centers. See *Rudbeckia*, p. 140.

**J** **'Lucifer' crocosmia** (use 3)
This perennial forms attractive clumps of sword-shaped leaves. In summer, bright-red-orange flowers line the ends of tall branched stems. See *Crocosmia*, p. 126.

**A** 'Autumn Brilliance' serviceberry

**F** Orange honeysuckle

**H** 'Powis Castle' artemisia

**G** Blue oat grass

**I** 'Goldsturm' coneflower

**J** 'Lucifer' crocosmia

**E** 'Tuscan Blue' rosemary

**C** Grey's senecio

# A winter full of flowers

Like the previous design, this one provides a handsome mix of foliage and flowers, but for a shady site. Again, low maintenance and year-round interest are priorities. To relieve the dreary days of the rainy season, this planting offers a lovely, often-fragrant, array of flowers from fall to spring.

A large deciduous viburnum anchors the design, while evergreen or nearly evergreen plants fill out the space. Foliage colors and textures take center stage from late spring through fall. Mounding and spreading shrubs are accented by lacy fern fronds and sword-leaved irises. The dominant flower colors are pink and white. Adding highlights are splashes of yellow barrenwort and magenta geranium blossoms, along with the bright-orange-red seedpods of the Gladwin irises.

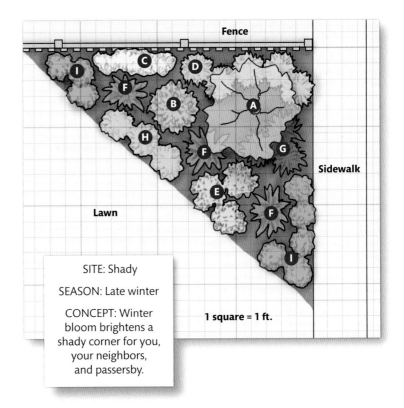

SITE: Shady

SEASON: Late winter

CONCEPT: Winter bloom brightens a shady corner for you, your neighbors, and passersby.

1 square = 1 ft.

'Apple Blossom' sasanqua camellia **C**

Low sarcococca **D**

**A** 'Dawn' viburnum

**G** Gladwin iris

**F** 'Robust' male fern

**I** Bigroot geranium

**H** 'Colchicum' barrenwort

**B** David viburnum

**F** 'Robust' male fern

**E** 'Silver Queen' euonymus

Bigroot geranium **I**

## Plants & Projects

**Ⓐ 'Dawn' viburnum** (use 1 plant)
This large deciduous shrub has very fragrant pink flowers from fall into spring, peaking in late winter. Its dark-green leaves turn scarlet in fall. See *Viburnum* x *bodnantense*, p. 146.

**Ⓑ David viburnum** (use 1)
This compact evergreen shrub has leathery dark-green leaves. In spring, pink buds open into flat-topped clusters of white flowers. See *Viburnum davidii*, p. 146.

**Ⓒ 'Apple Blossom' sasanqua camellia** (use 1)
Trained along the fence, this shrub displays pink-and-white flowers against a backdrop of glossy evergreen leaves from late fall into winter. See *Camellia sasanqua*, p. 123.

**Ⓓ Low sarcococca** (use 5)
This low, spreading evergreen shrub bears tiny white flowers that nestle at the base of its green lancelike leaves. Blooms in late winter. See *Sarcococca humilis*, p. 142.

**Ⓔ 'Silver Queen' euonymus** (use 3)
Another low-growing evergreen, this shrub has small, white-edged green leaves that take on a pink tinge in winter. See *Euonymus fortunei*, p. 127.

**Ⓕ 'Robust' male fern** (use 3)
A graceful bright-green fern. Its lacy evergreen fronds do well in winter conditions. See Ferns: *Dryopteris* x *complexa*, p. 128.

**Ⓖ Gladwin iris** (use 3)
This perennial forms a clump of glossy upright leaves and bears clusters of purple flowers in summer. Long-lasting pods follow, splitting to reveal bright-orange-red seeds. See *Iris foetidissima*, p. 133.

**Ⓗ 'Colchicum' barrenwort** (use 3)
This perennial ground cover is prized for its heart-shaped evergreen foliage, which changes color with the seasons. Bears yellow flowers in spring. See *Epimedium pinnatum*, p. 127.

**Ⓘ Bigroot geranium** (use 8)
Bushy clumps of colorful and fragrant semievergreen foliage distinguish this perennial. Late-spring flowers are magenta or purple. See *Geranium macrorrhizum*, p. 130.

## PLANT PORTRAITS

Viewed from the house, sidewalk, or street, these easy-care plants provide good-looking foliage and flowers year-round.
● = First design, pp. 32–33
▲ = Second design, pp. 34–35

**'Apple Blossom' sasanqua camellia** (*Camellia sasanqua*, p. 123) ▲

**'Dawn' viburnum** (*Viburnum* x *bodnantense*, p. 146) ▲

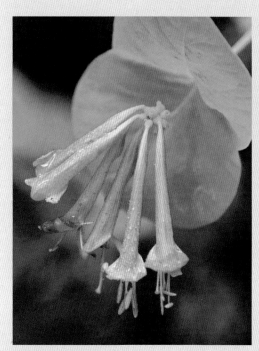

**Orange honeysuckle** (*Lonicera ciliosa*, p. 134) ●

**Blue oat grass** (*Helictotrichon sempervirens*, p. 130) ●

**Gladwin iris** (*Iris foetidissima*, p. 133) ▲

**'Powis Castle' artemisia** (*Artemisia*, p. 120) ●

# Streetwise and Stylish

## GIVE YOUR CURBSIDE STRIP A NEW LOOK

**Homeowners seldom give a thought** to the part of their property adjacent to the street. Often bounded by a sidewalk, this area is at best a tidy patch of lawn and at worst a weed-choked eyesore. Yet this is one of the most public parts of many properties. Filling this strip with attractive plants and paths from street to walkway can give pleasure to passersby and visitors who park at the curb, as well as enhancing the streetscape you view from the house. (Plant-ings on curbside strips are often regulated by local ordinances, so check with officials about restrictions before you start a remake.)

This can be a difficult site, subject to summer drought, pedestrian and car traffic, and errant dogs. Plants need to be tough to perform well here. Those in this design fill the bill and look good, too. The two Persian parrotias that anchor the planting may reach 8 ft. or more (if you let them), partially screening the yard from the street in the summer. While the parrotias are deciduous, the other plants are evergreen, providing an all-season display. Bloom peaks in spring (shown here). Small red flowers sprout from the bare branches of the parrotias, while the ornamental strawberry, rosemary, and spring bulbs bloom beneath them.

Easily laid pavers afford access from the street to the sidewalk and front-entry walk. To unify the look of your front yard, incorporate the same plants in plantings on the other side of the sidewalk. If your curbside property doesn't include a sidewalk, you can extend the planting farther into the yard.

A Persian parrotia
C Black chokeberry
E Spring bulbs
E Spring bulbs
D 'Pink Panda' ornamental strawberry
B 'Majorca Pink' rosemary
F Paving

## Plants & Projects

The flagstone paving is easy to lay on a sand-and-gravel base. Once established, the plants require very little care. You can let the parrotias grow into small trees, or prune them in spring to keep them whatever size you wish. Heavily planted bulbs will require dividing after several years.

**A** **Persian parrotia** (use 2 plants) An all-season performer, this large deciduous shrub bears small clusters of red flowers before the leaves appear in spring. Dark-green leaves turn yellow, red, and then purple in fall. Peeling bark looks good in winter. Use single-trunked, low-branching specimens here. See *Parrotia persica*, p. 136.

**B** **'Majorca Pink' rosemary** (use 6) This evergreen shrub bears narrow, fragrant blue-green leaves on upright branches. Small lavender-pink flowers bloom from late winter into spring. See *Rosmarinus officinalis*, p. 140.

**C** **Black chokeberry** (use 5) This versatile evergreen shrub offers year round interest. It boasts showy white flowers in mid-spring, dark-purple berries in summer, and green foliage that turns into an eye-catching red in the fall. See *Aronia melanocarpa*, p. 120.

**D** **'Pink Panda' ornamental strawberry** (as needed) This fast-growing evergreen ground cover resembles the vegetable-garden favorite but is grown

SITE: Sunny

SEASON: Spring

CONCEPT: Tall plants help separate your property from the street, while welcoming visitors parked curbside.

**A** Persian parrotia

**E** Spring bulbs

**B** 'Majorca Pink' rosemary

**B** 'Majorca Pink' rosemary

**D** 'Pink Panda' ornamental strawberry

**E** Spring bulbs

**C** Black chokeberry

**E** Spring bulbs

1 square = 1 ft.

Lawn

Sidewalk

Driveway

more for its ornamental qualities than its fruit (which is edible). Bears pink flowers in spring. See *Fragaria*, p. 129.

**E** **Spring bulbs** (as needed) Underplant the strawberry ground cover with crocuses and daffodils for a long spring blooming season. Swaths of white-and-blue crocuses edge the pavers, while groups of white, yellow, and orange daffodils appear in several spots. Large numbers of bulbs make a bigger splash. See Bulbs: *Crocus* and *Narcissus,* p. 122.

**F** **Paving** Rectangular flagstones in random sizes provide easy access. See p. 156.

# A low-profile planting

As in the previous design, this planting dresses up the often-neglected curbside, while easily accommodating visitors who park on the street. Lacking tall shrubs, it offers less privacy but makes a smoother transition to the street than the other design.

Though there are flowers from spring into fall, foliage is the main event here. Planted in bold masses that echo the angled lines of the paving, the foliage makes a simple but effective composition of varied colors and textures. There are also seasonal accents, from cheerful daffodils in the spring to flat-topped russet seed heads of sedum in the fall. Most of the planting is evergreen and is attractive in winter as well.

## Plants & Projects

**Ⓐ 'Newport Dwarf' escallonia** (use 6 plants)
This low, bushy evergreen shrub carpets the planting with glossy green leaves. It is sprinkled with small clusters of red flowers in summer. See *Escallonia rubra*, p. 127.

**Ⓑ Mugo pine** (use 2)
This popular evergreen conifer forms a low shrubby mound of dark-green needles. Its solid mass contrasts nicely with the airy Russian sage nearby. See *Pinus mugo*, p. 137.

**Ⓒ 'Silver Queen' euonymus** (use 20)
The white-and-green variegated foliage of this low, spreading shrub makes a distinctive edging for the pavers, sidewalk, and driveway.

Evergreen leaves take on a pink tinge in winter. See *Euonymus fortunei*, p. 127.

**Ⓓ 'Longin' Russian sage** (use 2)
A multistemmed perennial with fine gray-green leaves. Delicate spikes of lavender-blue flowers hover among foliage and woody light-gray stems from summer into fall. See *Perovskia atriplicifolia*, p. 136.

**Ⓔ 'Autumn Joy' sedum** (use 8)
This perennial forms a mound of fleshy light-green leaves. Flat-topped clusters of tiny

greenish-pink flowers appear in late summer, turning deeper red with age, finally becoming long-lasting russet-colored seed heads. See *Sedum*, p. 142.

**Ⓕ Daffodils** (as needed)
Plant your favorite daffodils among the euonymus for a spring spectacular. Use 100 or more of the same color for a strong showing. See Bulbs: *Narcissus*, p. 122.

**Ⓖ Paving**
Use materials that go with your house. Here, roughly square flagstones are laid with fairly large gaps on a sand-and-gravel base. The stair-stepped outline is echoed in the adjacent plantings. See p. 156.

> SITE: Sunny
>
> SEASON: Summer
>
> CONCEPT: Simple massings of handsome foliage transform an often-neglected area and treat visitors and passersby to an eye-catching display.

1 square = 1 ft.

Lawn

Sidewalk

Driveway

'Autumn Joy' Ⓔ sedum

'Longin' Ⓓ Russian sage

Ⓑ Mugo pine

Ⓒ 'Silver Queen' euonymus

Ⓓ 'Longin' Russian sage

Ⓐ 'Newport Dwarf' escallonia

See site plan for Ⓕ.

'Newport Dwarf' Ⓐ escallonia

'Silver Queen' Ⓒ euonymus

Paving Ⓖ

'Newport Dwarf' Ⓐ escallonia

Mugo pine Ⓑ

'Silver Queen' Ⓒ euonymus

# PLANT PORTRAITS

These low-maintenance plants will improve any curb-side area, while withstanding the rigors of life by the street.
● = First design, pp. 36–37
▲ = Second design, pp. 38–39

**Crocus** (Bulbs: *Crocus*, p. 122) ●

**Black chokeberry** (*Aronia melanocarpa*, p. 120) ●

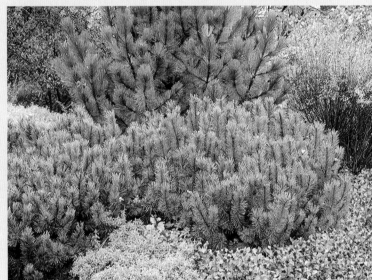

**Mugo pine** (*Pinus mugo*, p. 137) ▲

**'Pink Panda' ornamental strawberry** (*Fragaria*, p. 129) ●

**'Majorca Pink' rosemary** (*Rosmarinus officinalis*, p. 140) ●

**Persian parrotia** (*Parrotia persica*, p. 136) ●

# Front-Yard Border

## ARBOR AND PLANTINGS MAKE A WELCOMING ENTRY

**The waist-high hedge** of evergreen hollies in this design creates a friendly attractive barrier, just enough to signal the confines of the front yard. The simple wisteria-covered arbor provides welcoming access, particularly when it is enveloped in the pleasing aroma of the vine's striking flowers.

Curved planting beds face the house, defined by a lower, more informal hedge of evergreen azaleas. At one end, a pictur-esque multitrunked holly forms a canopy for shade-loving astilbes, with their feathery foliage and long summer display of white flower plumes. Flanking the arch, Russian sage adds months of purple flowers in summer and fall. Spring, however, offers the most bloom, with pink flowers covering the azaleas, low patches of moss phlox, and lavender flower clusters dangling from the wisteria-like bunches of aromatic grapes.

Arbor **H**

**A** American wisteria

'Compacta' **C** Japanese holly

'Compacta' **C** Japanese holly

Moss phlox **G**

**D** 'Gumpo Pink' azalea

See site plan for **E** **F**.

Sidewalk

Existing walkway

Lawn

1 square = 1 ft.

**B** Yaupon holly

**D** 'Gumpo Pink' azalea

SITE: Sunny

SEASON: Spring

CONCEPT: An arbor, hedge, and simple plantings define boundaries and provide an inviting entry.

## Plants & Projects

On the planting plan shown here, the small bed could be tucked between the arbor and a driveway or the wall of a house or garage. You can easily expand the design in either direction by extending the hedges and adding more perennials. The structures and plantings are easy to build, install, and care for. After the tree, hedges, and wisteria are trained and shaped to your taste, seasonal pruning will keep them tidy.

**A** **American wisteria** (use 1 plant)
This is a vigorous deciduous vine with spectacular clusters of fragrant pealike purple or blue flowers in summer. Prune in spring to control its size and to stimulate abundant bloom. See *Wisteria frutescens*, p. 147.

**B** **Yaupon holly** (use 1)
A small, tough, easy-to-grow evergreen tree features glossy dark-green leaves and masses of red berries. Buy a multitrunked specimen and prune it to best display the interesting crooked trunks and branches. See *Ilex vomitoria*, p. 133.

**C** **'Compacta' Japanese holly** (use 8)
The dense twiggy habit and small evergreen leaves make this an excellent shrub for a sheared hedge, as we've shown here, or you can prune it more lightly for an informal effect. Either way, prune it in summer. See *Ilex crenata*, p. 133.

**D** **'Gumpo Pink' azalea** (use 16)
This low-growing evergreen shrub is well suited to the informal hedge that defines the curved edge of the bed. Clusters of large pink flowers are a splendid sight in late spring. Prune in early summer. See *Rhododendron*, p. 139.

**E** **White astilbe** (use 5)
The white plumelike flowers of this hardy perennial shine out from the shade of the holly tree in summer. When not blooming, mounds of dark-green, deeply divided leaves are an effective ground cover. See *Astilbe*, p. 121.

**F** **Russian sage** (use 14)
This perennial's clusters of lavender-blue flowers float in the air above clumps of silver-gray foliage, attracting pollinators as a bonus. See *Perovskia*, p. 136.

**G** **Moss phlox** (use 10)
Edging the walkway, this tough evergreen ground cover will creep under the azaleas to form a mat of prickly leaves covered with flowers in spring. Choose a pale-pink cultivar that complements the azaleas. See *Phlox subulata*, p. 136.

**H** **Arbor**
You can build this simple arbor in a weekend. Its 6x6 posts are sturdy enough to support the vigorous growth of the wisteria. Let the wood weather to gray-brown, or stain it to complement your house. See p. 172.

# A Pleasant Passage

## RECLAIM A NARROW SIDE YARD FOR A STROLL GARDEN

**Many residential lots** include a slim strip of land between the house and a property line. Usually overlooked by everyone except children and dogs racing between the front yard and the back, this often-shady corridor can become a valued addition to the landscape. In this design, a lovely little stroll garden invites adults, and even children, to linger as they move from one part of the property to another.

The wall of the house and a fence on the property line give the space an enclosed feeling, like a narrow room. A gently curving gravel path widens the passage visually and lengthens the stroll through it. A wooden bench set on flagstones offers a comfortable place for a pause.

On both sides of the path, evergreen and deciduous shrubs and trees provide color all year. Pink rhododendron blossoms line the path in spring. Flowering clematis on the fence is a focal point from the bench in summer. The red-and-purple foliage of the hydrangea and maple catches the eye in fall. Fragrant yellow witch hazel flowers brighten the passage in winter.

1 square = 1 ft.

SITE: Sunny

SEASON: Summer

CONCEPT: Plants with colorful foliage and pretty flowers make an enticing stroll garden in a frequently neglected area.

## Plants & Projects

Lay out and install the path and edging. Then prepare and plant the beds. As the maple grows, you'll need to prune it to provide headroom for strollers. To encourage the witch hazel to grow as a small tree rather than a shrub, prune the suckers after it flowers. Once established, the plants require seasonal care as well as pruning to maintain size and shape.

**Ⓐ Japanese maple**
(use 1 plant)
This deciduous tree has a delicate open habit that offers dappled shade along the path. We've shown a seed-grown plant with green summer foliage and red fall color, but you can choose a favorite cultivar. See *Acer palmatum*, p. 118.

**Ⓑ Chinese witch hazel** (use 1)
A small deciduous tree or shrub has large bold gray-green leaves that turn yellow in fall. It's striking in winter when fragrant yellow flowers bloom on bare wood. See *Hamamelis mollis*, p. 130.

**Ⓒ 'Nana Gracilis' dwarf Hinoki cypress** (use 1)
A narrow, naturally sculpted conifer, its glossy emerald foliage is a bright spot at one end of the path. See *Chamaecyparis obtusa*, p. 123.

**Ⓓ Silk-tassel bush** (use 1)
Showy gray-green flower tassels dangle from this evergreen shrub in the winter months. Leaves are gray-green and have wavy mains. See *Garrya elliptica*, p. 129.

**Ⓔ 'Shirobana' spirea** (use 1)
Another little gem at path's end, this deciduous shrub has dark-green leaves and flat clusters of white, pink, and rose flowers all summer. See *Spiraea japonica*, p. 143.

**Ⓕ Oakleaf hydrangea** (use 1)
This deciduous shrub has large lobed leaves, lacy flowers from spring through fall, and good fall color. The peeling reddish bark looks good in winter. See *Hydrangea quercifolia*, p. 132.

**Ⓖ Oregon grape** (use 1)
A spreading evergreen shrub with handsome deeply divided leaves. The showy yellow flower clusters in spring produce blackish-blue berries later in the year. See *Mahonia aquifolium*, p. 135.

**Ⓗ 'Cilpinense' evergreen rhododendron** (use 5)
Small leaves and a compact habit make this evergreen shrub ideal for narrow spaces. It bears light-pink flowers very early in spring. See *Rhododendron*, p. 139.

**Ⓘ Small-flowered clematis** (use 1)
A vigorous climber, this deciduous vine becomes a focal point from the bench in summer and fall when its dark-green leaves are covered with flowers. Many cultivars are available. See *Clematis* hybrids, p. 124.

**Ⓙ Frikart's aster** (use 3)
Tough and carefree, this perennial bears clusters of purple flowers that last for many weeks starting in late summer. See *Aster x frikartii*, p. 121.

**Ⓚ Geranium** (use 6)
An evergreen perennial that forms a leafy mound with clusters of pale-purple flowers in summer. See *Geranium x cantabrigiense*, p. 130.

**Ⓛ Mother-of-thyme** (use 6)
In summer, this shrubby perennial bears small purple flowers on a mat of tiny aromatic evergreen leaves. See *Thymus serpyllum*, p. 145.

**Ⓜ Path**
Curving gently through the planting is a gravel path edged by cobblestones. See p. 156.

**Ⓝ Seating area**
Random-sized flagstones laid on a sand-and-gravel base support a comfortable bench of your choice. See p. 156.

See site plan for **E**.

**A** Japanese maple

**B** Chinese witch hazel

**F** Oakleaf hydrangea

**G** Oregon grape

**C** 'Nana Gracilis' dwarf Hinoki cypress

**N** Seating area

**D** Silk-tassel bush

**L** Mother-of-thyme

Frikart's aster **J**

Path **M**

**H** 'Cilpinense' evergreen rhododendron

Geranium **K**

**I** Small-flowered clematis

# A shady corridor

If a side of your house has a shady exposure, try this design. Here, shade-loving trees, shrubs, perennials, and ground covers create a pleasing mix of textures and colors.

A curved path of flagstones opens at one end into a terrace that allows room for seating and a potted camellia. Along the path, the large bold leaves of aucuba, penstemon, and hostas mingle with the glossy chokeberry leaves, astilbes, and ferns.

Spring is the season of peak bloom. For many months, the seating area will be filled with pleasant scents. Sweet-smelling sarcococca blooms in early spring. Summer brings the fragrance of leucothoe flowers. And almost any time of year you can reach down from your chair and rub a bigroot geranium leaf to savor its scent.

## Plants & Projects

**Ⓐ Stripebark maple** (use 1 plant)
This narrow deciduous tree features a wide repertoire: yellow clusters of flowers in spring; a dark-green leaf canopy in summer; yellows, reds, and oranges in fall; and bark that shows off green-and-white stripes in winter. See *Acer davidii*, p. 118.

**Ⓑ Red chokeberry** (use 2)
This multi-stemmed bushy shrub is covered with tiny white flowers in late spring before bright-red berries appear in summer. Glossy green foliage turns vibrant orange and red in the fall. Popular with na-

tive pollinators. See *Aronia arbutifolia*, p. 120.

**Ⓒ 'Rainbow' drooping leucothoe** (use 1)
Evergreen shrub features shiny cream, pink, and green leaves. Fragrant white flower clusters appear under the drooping leaves in spring. See *Leucothoe fontanesiana*, p. 134.

**Ⓓ Fragrant sarcococca** (use 1)
This small evergreen shrub with glossy leaves and very fragrant white flowers will scent the seating area in early spring. See *Sarcococca ruscifolia*, p. 142.

See site plan for Ⓓ, Ⓘ, and Ⓙ.

Stripebark maple Ⓐ

Red chokeberry Ⓑ

Soft shield fern Ⓖ

Hosta Ⓗ

'Rainbow' drooping leucothoe Ⓒ

Japanese camellia Ⓛ

SITE: Shady

SEASON: Early summer

CONCEPT: Fragrant plants with colorful foliage create a passage garden of sweet-scented informality.

Lawn

House

Fence

1 square = 1 ft.

Gold dust aucuba Ⓔ

Bigroot geranium Ⓚ

Path and seating area Ⓜ

Cascade penstemon Ⓕ

**E** **Gold dust aucuba** (use 1)
The large, yellow-speckled glossy leaves of this evergreen shrub make an attractive background for the small maroon flowers in spring. See *Aucuba japonica* 'Variegata', p. 121.

**F** **Cascade penstemon** (use 3)
This shade-tolerant native perennial has showy tubular dark-purple-and-blue flowers on 1- to 2-ft. stalks summer through early fall. See *Penstemon serrulatus*, p. 136.

**G** **Soft shield fern** (use 3)
This dense evergreen fern has lovely soft fronds and upright growth. See Ferns: *Polystichum setiferum*, p. 128.

**H** **Hosta** (use 6)
Carefree, shade-tolerant perennial features distinctive leaves. There are many colors and shapes to choose from. A blue-leaved cultivar works well here. See *Hosta*, p. 132.

**I** **Astilbe** (use 3)
Plumes of tiny flowers rise on stalks above the lacy leaves of this shade-loving perennial in early summer. Choose one of the many pink cultivars. See *Astilbe*, p. 121.

**J** **Bishop's hat** (use 3)
An outstanding ground cover, this evergreen perennial forms a low mass of heart-shaped leaves that are tinged red-and-purple in summer. In early spring, it bears sprays of small white to pinkish flowers. See *Epimedium grandiflorum*, p. 127.

**K** **Bigroot geranium** (use 4)
A perennial with attractive semievergreen leaves that are aromatic when crushed. Its pink to magenta flowers bloom in late spring. See *Geranium macrorrhizum*, p. 130.

**L** **Japanese camellia** (use 1)
Planted in a pot, this glossy evergreen shrub bears large white, pink, or red flowers in spring. You can choose from many cultivars. See *Camellia japonica*, p. 123.

**M** **Path and seating area**
A curved path widens into a cozy terrace. Both are made of flagstones laid on a sand-and-gravel base. See p. 156.

# PLANT PORTRAITS

Eye-catching plants for an overlooked spot: here are flowers, foliage, and fragrances to make your side-yard stroll garden a favorite.
● = First design, pp. 42–43
▲ = Second design, pp. 44–45

**Gold dust aucuba**
(*Aucuba japonica* 'Variegata', p. 121) ▲

**Stripebark maple**
(*Acer davidii*, p. 118) ▲

**Japanese camellia**
(*Camellia japonica*, p. 123) ▲

**Red chokeberry**
(*Aronia arbutifolia*, p. 120) ▲

**Mother-of-thyme** (*Thymus serpyllum*, p. 145) ●

**Astilbe** (*Astilbe*, p. 121) ▲

# Landscaping a Low Wall

## A COLORFUL TWO-TIER GARDEN REPLACES A BLAND SLOPE

**Some things** may not love a wall, but plants and gardeners do. For plants, walls offer warmth for an early start in spring. Gardeners appreciate the rich visual potential of composing a garden on two levels, as well as the practical advantage of working on two relatively flat surfaces instead of a single sloping one.

This design places two complementary perennial borders above and below a wall bounded at one end by a set of stairs. While each bed is relatively narrow, when viewed from the lower level they combine to form a border almost 10 ft. deep, with plants rising to eye level or more. The planting can be extended farther along the wall with the same or similar plants.

Anchored by its wall, steps, and path, this design can separate two areas on your property, serving as an entrance and boundary for both. Its mix of foliage textures and colors, including a number of evergreens, gives it a year-round presence. And flowers displayed from spring to fall make the planting a destination on its own.

Building the wall that makes this design possible doesn't require the time or skill it once did. Nor is it necessary to scour the countryside for tons of fieldstone or to hire an expensive contractor. Thanks to precast retaining-wall systems, anyone with a healthy back (or access to energetic teenagers) can install a knee-high do-it-yourself wall in as little as a weekend.

> SITE: Sunny
>
> SEASON: Early summer
>
> CONCEPT: A low retaining wall creates easy-to-maintain beds for a distinctive two-level planting of shrubs and perennials.

Wall and walkway **L**

## Plants & Projects

Installing the wall and steps is the major task in this design. Once the plants are established, they'll thrive with just some seasonal pruning, mulching, and cleanup. You'll need to renew the spade-cut edge between beds and lawn several times a year to keep it tidy.

**A** **'Victoria' wild lilac** (use 1 plant)
Anchoring the top bed, this evergreen shrub is a mass of small, glossy, crinkled leaves. In spring it bears blue to purple lilac-like flowers. See *Ceanothus*, p. 123.

**B** **Grey's senecio** (use 1)
Soft woolly gray foliage covers this evergreen shrub. Yellow daisylike flowers appear in summer; some gardeners remove them to emphasize the foliage. See *Senecio greyi*, p. 142.

**C** **New Zealand flax** (use 1)
Focal point of the lower bed, this perennial forms a clump of long, upright, swordlike leaves. Cultivars offer a range of eye-catching leaf colors. See *Phormium tenax*, p. 137.

**D** **'Blue Star' juniper** (use 5)
This evergreen shrub makes a low sculpted mass of silvery blue foliage. Plants will eventually grow together and form a single clump. See *Juniperus squamata*, p. 134.

**E** **'Hidcote' English lavender** (use 3)
Spikes of small purple flowers rise above this perennial's mounding blue-green foliage in early summer. Leaves are fragrant and evergreen. See *Lavandula angustifolia*, p. 134.

**F** **Penstemon** (use 3)
Choose a variety of this perennial with eye-catching tubular dark-purple-and-blue flowers on 1- to 2-ft. stalks summer through early fall. See *Penstemon serrulatus*, p. 136.

**G** **Russian sage** (use 3)
This woody perennial makes an airy upright clump of stiff gray stems and small silver-gray, lance-shaped leaves. Tiny lavender-blue flowers appear to float above the leaves in summer. See *Perovskia*, p. 136.

**H** **Cushion spurge** (use 3)
A many-stemmed perennial, this forms a compact mound of neat green leaves. Long-lasting bright-yellow flowers form at the ends of the stems in spring. Foliage turns red in fall. See *Euphorbia polychroma*, p. 128.

**I** **Corsican hellebore** (use 1)
This perennial produces distinctive pale-green flowers in late winter. Leathery leaves are dark-green and edged with small spines. See *Helleborus argutifolius*, p. 130.

**J** **Ground covers** (as needed)
The planting uses three ground covers. On the right side of the top bed, Carpathian bellflower (see *Campanula carpatica*, p. 123) makes heart-shaped leaves and violet-blue flowers. At left in the top bed and covering much of the bottom bed is a carpet of creeping thyme (see *Thymus praecox* ssp. *articus*, p. 145), which bears tiny green leaves and violet flowers. On the left side of the bottom bed, 'Dragon's Blood' sedum (see *Sedum spurium*, p. 142) forms a mat of small fleshy evergreen leaves and rosy red flowers.

**K** **Planters**
Available at many garden centers, troughs formed of lightweight cement make excellent planters. You can plant them with fibrous begonias in a mix of colors, as we've shown here. They're also ideal for small sedums or alpine plants.

**L** **Wall and walkway**
The low, precast retaining wall shown here is typical of those available at home-and-garden centers and local landscaping suppliers. (See p. 168). The walkway is made of durable crushed stone. (See p. 156.)

**A** 'Victoria' wild lilac

**B** Grey's senecio

**F** Penstemon

**E** 'Hidcote' English lavender

**H** Cushion spurge

**K** Planter

**K** Planter

**G** Russian sage

**J** Ground cover

**K** Planter

**F** Penstemon

**I** Corsican hellebore

**J** Ground cover

**D** 'Blue Star' juniper

**F** Penstemon

**C** New Zealand flax

1 square = 1 ft.

Lawn

# Two tiers in the shade

A retaining wall and plantings can be equally alluring in a shady backyard. This design echoes the one on the preceding pages but with plants that thrive in morning sun and afternoon shade. The planting provides an enjoyable setting for relaxing or reading on the bench.

The top level has a striking and rather exotic look, combining the rustling feather reed grass, the dramatic leaves and flowers of penstemon, and the upright ruffled fronds of narrow ferns. The lower level is less flamboyant but offers a pleasant range of flowers and foliage.

SITE: Shady

SEASON: Early summer

CONCEPT: Bold plants create a shade-tolerant planting of interest from a distance or up close.

1 square = 1 ft.          Lawn

## Plants & Projects

**A Feather reed grass** (use 7 plants)
A showy, ornamental grass that has tall stalks with red-bronze feathery heads that turn tan in fall. See *Calamagrostis × acutiflora* 'Karl Foerster', p. 122.

**B Cascade penstemon** (use 1)
A native perennial with showy tubular dark-purple-and-blue flowers on stalks that rise 1 to 2 ft. above its foliage summer through early fall. See *Penstemon serrulatus*, p. 136.

**C 'Nana Gracilis' dwarf Hinoki cypress** (use 1)
This small evergreen tree forms a narrow cone of glossy green, scalelike foliage. See *Chamaecyparis obtusa*, p. 123.

**D Sasanqua camellia** (use 1)
From late fall into winter, this evergreen shrub displays lovely

A **Feather reed grass**

B **Cascade penstemon**

G **'Tropic Night' Siberian iris**

C **'Nana Gracilis' dwarf Hinoki cypress**

M **Wall and walkway**

E **Barnes' narrow male fern**

K **River rock**

J **Ground cover**

D **Sasanqua camellia**

I **'Velvet Night' heuchera**

H **'Cattleya' astilbe**

L **Seating area**

F **Large-leaved hosta**

J **Ground cover**

flowers against a background of glossy foliage. Train on wires attached to the wall and prune to maintain size. See *Camellia sasanqua*, p. 123.

**E Barnes' narrow male fern** (use 5)
Small ruffled leaflets add character to the fronds of this narrow upright fern. It is evergreen in mild winters. See Ferns: *Dryopteris filix-mas* 'Barnesii', p. 128.

**F Large-leaved hosta** (use 1)
A large-leaved form of this popular perennial nestles next to the bench. A cultivar with large chartreuse leaves would look good in this planting. See *Hosta*, p. 132.

**G 'Tropic Night' Siberian iris** (use 1)
A perennial with striking slender, upright leaves produces deep-purple flowers in late spring. See *Iris sibirica*, p. 133.

**H 'Cattleya' astilbe** (use 5)
This perennial's lacy green-bronze foliage is attractive for many months. In early summer, clusters of tiny crimson-pink flowers are borne on tall stalks above the foliage. See *Astilbe* x *arendsii*, p. 121.

**I 'Velvet Night' heuchera** (use 7)
This perennial is prized for its deep-purple foliage. From spring into summer, it bears airy plumes of small greenish-white flowers. See *Heuchera americana*, p. 131.

**J Ground covers** (as needed)
Two perennial ground covers are used here. Blue star creeper (see *Pratia pedunculata*, p. 137) edges the lower bed with tiny bright-green leaves and sky-blue flowers. In the top bed, Irish moss (see *Sagina subulata*, p. 140) forms a mat of kelly green mosslike foliage.

**K River rock**
Round rocks in a range of sizes add interest to the beds.

**L Seating area**
Set a comfortable bench on a graveled surface (see p. 162) for enjoying the planting.

**See p. 46 for the following:**

**M Wall and walkway**

**Irish moss**
(*Sagina subulata*, p. 140) ▲

# PLANT PORTRAITS

These plants make the most of a two-tiered garden created by a low retaining wall.
● = First design, pp. 46–47
▲ = Second design, pp. 48–49

'Dragon's Blood' sedum (*Sedum spurium*, p. 142) ●

Large-leaved hosta (*Hosta*, p. 132) ▲

**Feather reed grass**
(*Calamagrostis* × *acutiflora* 'Karl Foerster', p. 122) ▲

**Corsican hellebore**
(*Helleborus argutifolius*, p. 130) ●

**New Zealand flax**
(*Phormium tenax*, p. 137) ●

# Angle of Repose

## MAKE A BACK-DOOR GARDEN IN A SHELTERED NICHE

**Many homes** offer the opportunity to tuck a garden into a protected corner. In the front yard, such spots are ideal for an entry garden or a landscaping display that enhances the view of your house from the sidewalk or the street. If the niche is in the backyard, like the site shown here, the planting can be more intimate, part of a comfortable outdoor "room" you can stroll through at leisure or enjoy from a nearby patio or window.

This design gives pleasure year-round. From spring into summer the garden is awash with flowers in white, pink, purple, and blue. Some attract hummingbirds and butterflies. Holly osmanthus entices family and friends to the small patio with its lovely springtime aroma. Yellow coreopsis and bold deep-blue asters maintain a flowering presence from summer into fall. The showy copper-colored sepals of the abelia flowers also last into late fall.

Although flowers are lovely, they are fleeting. For lasting appeal, this planting relies on its foliage. Featuring many evergreen plants, the design combines interesting, sometimes arresting, foliage textures and colors. The leaves sport a range of green and purple hues. The shrubs are either loose and bushy or dense and mounded. Bristling near the center of the planting, New Zealand flax adds an exotic touch. At the bed edges, perennials make the transition to the lawn by picking up the green-and-purple color scheme.

'Java Red' **B** weigela

**B** 'Java Red' weigela

**F** Variegated boxleaf Japanese euonymus

**H** 'Monch' Frikart's aster

Moss phlox **L**

David **C** viburnum

Lawn

1 square = 1 ft.

SITE: Sunny

SEASON: Summer

CONCEPT: This private garden can be enjoyed from inside the house, on a small patio, or by strolling around and through it.

'Edward Goucher' abelia — D

A 'Snowdrift' crabapple

G 'Rubrum' New Zealand flax

I 'Moonbeam' coreopsis

F Variegated boxleaf Japanese euonymus

J 'Palace Purple' heuchera

E Holly osmanthus

M Stepping-stones

K Bigroot geranium

K Bigroot geranium

## Plants & Projects

Once established, the crabapple and shrubs will require seasonal pruning to keep them healthy and the right size. Divide the perennials when they become crowded.

**A** **'Snowdrift' crabapple** (use 1 plant)
In spring this small deciduous tree bears red buds and showy white flowers. Small orange-red fruits ripen in fall and last all winter, if the birds don't get them. See *Malus*, p. 135.

**B** **'Java Red' weigela** (use 2)
This deciduous shrub makes a fountain of dark-green leaves with a purple tint. In early summer, hummingbirds are attracted to nectar in the tubular deep-pink flowers. See *Weigela*, p. 147.

**C** **David viburnum** (use 3)
An evergreen shrub, this has bold, leathery dark-green leaves. Clusters of white flowers blushed with pink bloom in late spring and produce metallic-blue fruit in autumn. See *Viburnum davidii*, p. 146.

**D** **'Edward Goucher' abelia** (use 1)
This shrub's evergreen leaves turn from bronzy green, to dark-green, to pur-

ple-bronze from spring through winter. It bears masses of small rosy pink-purple flowers in summer. See *Abelia* x *grandiflora*, p. 118.

**E** **Holly osmanthus** (use 1)
This slow-growing evergreen shrub with toothed, dark-green leaves. Small fragrant white flowers in spring. See *Osmanthus burkwoodii*, p. 136.

**F** **Variegated boxleaf Japanese euonymus** (use 12)
This evergreen shrub has tiny white-and-green leaves. Massed in three places, it helps tie the planting together. See *Euonymus japonicus* 'Microphyllus Variegatus', p. 128.

**G** **'Rubrum' New Zealand flax** (use 1)
This perennial makes a striking display of saberlike purple-red leaves. Its reddish-purple summer flowers are undependable in the region. See *Phormium tenax*, p. 137.

**H** **'Monch' Frikart's aster** (use 3)
From late summer through fall, this perennial bears striking lavender-blue flowers with bright golden centers. Foliage looks good the rest of the season. See *Aster* x *frikartii*, p. 121.

**I** **'Moonbeam' coreopsis** (use 6)
Abundant sunny yellow flowers cover this perennial's mound of lacy green foliage in summer. See *Coreopsis verticillata*, p. 124.

**J** **'Palace Purple' heuchera** (use 3)
This perennial is grown primarily for its deep-purple, maplelike leaves. It bears feathery spikes of tiny white flowers from spring into summer. See *Heuchera*, p. 131.

**K** **Bigroot geranium** (use 7)
This perennial forms a mass of fragrant semievergreen foliage. Magenta or pink flowers bloom in late spring. See *Geranium macrorrhizum*, p. 130.

**L** **Moss phlox** (use 7)
A spreading, mat-growing perennial with semi-evergreen dark leaves and masses of blue, pink, purple, scarlet, or white flowers. See *Phlox subulata*, p. 136.

**M** **Stepping-stones**
Irregular flagstone stepping-stones allow up-close viewing and access for maintenance. See p. 157.

# A touch of the Orient

Chosen for a shady site, these plants provide a subtle flavor of the Far East. The Japanese stewartia, andromeda, camellia, enkianthus, and Japanese painted fern all suggest an Asian woodland.

Attractive throughout the year, the planting is particularly effective in early spring and late winter, the season shown here. As winter moves to spring, buds and flowers, colorful foliage, and interesting patterns of bare branches entice viewers inside the house to get back outdoors. Interplant spring-flowering bulbs with the hosta for even more color. As in the previous design, handsome foliage, accented by the flowers of the stewartia, hydrangeas, and geraniums, provides enjoyment in the summer and fall.

Lawn

1 square = 1 ft.

SITE: Shady

SEASON: Late winter

CONCEPT: Fill a private niche on a shady site with plants that give pleasure year-round.

**F** Bigleaf hydrangea

**G** Fragrant sarcococca

**A** Japanese stewartia

**C** Sasanqua camellia

Red chokeberry **D**

Lenten rose **I**

Stepping-stones **M**

See site plan for **J**.

**B** Redvein enkianthus

**K** 'Colchicum' barrenwort

**H** Japanese painted fern

Geranium **L**

**F** Bigleaf hydrangea

**E** 'Mountain Fire' Japanese andromeda

**L** Geranium

## Plants & Projects

**Ⓐ Japanese stewartia**
(use 1 plant)
This deciduous tree offers attractive bark and silky buds in winter and spring, white flowers in summer, and colorful fall foliage. See *Stewartia pseudocamellia*, p. 144.

**Ⓑ Redvein enkianthus** (use 1)
This upright deciduous shrub has small blue-green leaves that turn orange-red in fall. Bears pinkish flowers in late spring. See *Enkianthus campanulatus*, p. 126.

**Ⓒ Sasanqua camellia** (use 1)
Large flowers bloom on this shrub from late fall into winter. Evergreen foliage looks good year-round. There are many cultivars to choose from. See *Camellia sasanqua*, p. 123.

**Ⓓ Red chokeberry** (use 1)
This shrub is covered with white flowers in spring and red berries in summer. Foliage turns orange and red in the fall. See *Aronia arbutifolia*, p. 120.

**Ⓜ Stepping-stones**

**Ⓔ 'Mountain Fire' Japanese andromeda** (use 1)
This evergreen shrub forms a dense mound of glossy foliage. New leaves are bright-red and appear after clusters of pink flowers bloom in late winter. See *Pieris japonica*, p. 137.

**Ⓕ Bigleaf hydrangea** (use 2)
Large clusters of papery blue, pink, or white flowers bloom on this deciduous shrub for months in the summer. See *Hydrangea macrophylla*, p. 132.

**Ⓖ Fragrant sarcococca** (use 3)
The glossy green leaves of this evergreen shrub are a good backdrop for the fragrant white flowers borne in late winter. See *Sarcococca ruscifolia*, p. 142.

**Ⓗ Japanese painted fern** (use 3)
Evergreen in mild winters, the lacy fronds of this fern are an iridescent mix of green, silver, and maroon. See Ferns: *Athyrium niponicum* 'Pictum', p. 128.

**Ⓘ Lenten rose** (use 3)
This evergreen perennial has shiny green, toothed leaves and distinctive flowers in pink, purple, white, or green. Blooms late winter into spring. See *Helleborus orientalis*, p. 130.

**Ⓙ Hosta** (use 7)
A perennial grown for its attractive foliage. Choose a midsize cultivar with green leaves for this design. See *Hosta*, p. 132.

**Ⓚ 'Colchicum' barrenwort** (use 5)
This evergreen perennial has heart-shaped leaves that turn from copper to green to maroon during the year. It bears small yellow flowers in spring. See *Epimedium pinnatum*, p. 127.

**Ⓛ Geranium** (use 12)
This perennial bears light-purple flowers on light-green foliage in summer. See *Geranium* x *cantabrigiense*, p. 130.

**See p. 51 for the following:**

**Ⓜ Stepping-stones**

# PLANT PORTRAITS

Evergreen and deciduous plants provide interest all year in a colorful planting.
● = First design, pp. 50–51
▲ = Second design, pp. 52–53

'Snowdrift' crabapple (*Malus*, p. 135) ●

'Mountain Fire' Japanese andromeda (*Pieris japonica*, p. 137) ▲

Variegated boxleaf Japanese euonymus (*Euonymus japonicus* 'Microphyllus Variegatus', p. 128) ●

'Java Red' weigela (*Weigela*, p. 147) ●

# Beautify a Blank Wall

## A VERTICAL GARDEN MAKES THE MOST OF A NARROW SITE

**Just as you can enhance a wall** in your home with a painting, you can decorate a blank wall outdoors with plants. The design shown here transforms a nondescript front entrance by showcasing perennials, shrubs, and vines against an adjacent garage wall. Such entrances are common in suburban homes, but a vertical garden like this is also ideal for other spots where yard space is limited.

Selected for a sunny site, these plants offer something in every season. There are flowers spring through fall, and evergreen shrubs provide fresh-looking foliage year-round. The garden is at its flowering peak in early and midsummer, with blooms in yellow, blue, purple, and red. The flowers and foliage of the two lavenders offer fragrance as well. Two trellises laden with clematis flowers draw the eye upward, making a canvas of an otherwise blank wall. When flowers fade, the planting's varied foliage colors, shapes, and textures provide interest on the walk to the front door.

## Plants & Projects

Once established, these plants require little more than seasonal maintenance. As they mature, the shrubs will need to be pruned to limit their size. In late fall, cut down the perennials along the walk to keep the bed tidy. Or, instead, let the escallonia expand to displace the perennials and fill their space during the winter.

**Ⓐ Clematis hybrid** (use 2 plants)
Trained up matching trellises, the generous foliage of these deciduous vines is covered with eye-catching flowers for months. Choose from numerous cultivars. For winter presence, try an evergreen type. See *Clematis*, p. 124.

**Ⓑ 'Sunshine' Grey's senecio** (use 1)
An evergreen shrub, this makes a loose mound of soft paddle-shaped green leaves. Bears yellow flowers in summer. See *Senecio greyi*, p. 142.

**Ⓒ 'Newport Dwarf' escallonia** (use 4)
Shading the roots of the clematis, this evergreen shrub has a tight, compact form. Shiny green leaves and red flowers cluster at the ends of stems in summer. See *Escallonia rubra*, p. 127.

**Ⓓ 'Tuscan Blue' rosemary** (use 1)
The upright stems of this evergreen shrub are lined with fragrant blue-green leaves. Bears deep-blue flowers sporadically throughout the year. See *Rosmarinus officinalis*, p. 140.

**Ⓔ 'Flower Carpet White' rose** (use 3)
This shrub forms a low, spreading ground cover of reddish-green leaves. From spring through autumn it bears clusters of single white flowers. See *Rosa*, p. 139.

**Ⓕ 'Provence' lavender** (use 1)
This evergreen shrub's spikes of fragrant deep-purple flowers and fragrant gray-green foliage combine well with the nearby roses. It blooms in early summer. See *Lavandula x intermedia*, p. 134.

**Ⓖ 'Hidcote' English lavender** (use 6)
An evergreen shrub, it forms a compact clump of upright stems bearing small gray-green leaves. Spikes of deep-purple flowers rise above the foliage in summer. See *Lavandula angustifolia*, p. 134.

**Ⓗ 'Moonbeam' coreopsis** (use 3)
A perennial, this forms a neat patch of lacy green foliage covered from summer to fall with sunny yellow flowers. See *Coreopsis verticillata*, p. 124.

**Ⓘ 'Vera Jameson' sedum** (use 3)
The floppy stems of this perennial bear succulent blue-gray and purple leaves. From summer to fall, flat clusters of tiny flowers turn from pinkish green to rose-pink to rust. See *Sedum*, p. 142.

**Ⓙ 'Johnson's Blue' geranium** (use 3)
This perennial makes a sprawling mass of pretty lobed green leaves. Bears periwinkle-blue flowers in early summer. See *Geranium*, p. 130.

'Flower Carpet **Ⓔ**
White' rose

'Provence' **Ⓕ**
lavender

SITE: Sunny

SEASON: Summer

CONCEPT: Handsome plants arrayed against a blank wall make a picture that pleases year-round.

**Ⓚ Trellis**
This pair of simple trellises provides support for the clematis and look good in winter, too. See p. 179.

Trellis **K**

**A** Clematis
hybrid

'Vera Jameson' **I**
sedum

'Sunshine' **B**
Grey's senecio

'Newport **C**
Dwarf'
escallonia

**D** 'Tuscan Blue'
rosemary

'Newport Dwarf' **C**
escallonia

**J** 'Johnson's Blue'
geranium

**G** 'Hidcote'
English lavender

'Moonbeam' **H**
coreopsis

'Hidcote' **G**
English
lavender

Driveway    Garage

**F**    **A**    **K**    **K**    **A**

**B**

**C**    **C**    **D**

**E**    **G**    **H**    **I**    **J**    **G**

Front entry

Walkway

Lawn

1 square = 1 ft.

# PLANT PORTRAITS

These perennials and shrubs enhance a blank wall and narrow entry walk with handsome foliage and pretty flowers all year.

- ● = First design, pp. 54–55
- ▲ = Second design, pp. 56–57

**'Moonbeam' coreopsis**
(*Coreopsis verticillata*, p. 124) ●

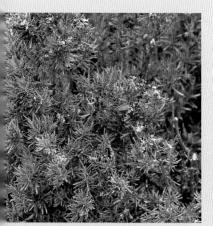

**'Tuscan Blue' rosemary**
(*Rosmarinus officinalis*, p. 140) ●

**'Bressingham White' bergenia**
(*Bergenia cordifolia*, p. 121) ▲

**Barrenwort**
(*Epimedium*, p. 127) ▲

**'Provence' lavender**
(*Lavandula* x *intermedia*, p. 134) ●

# Dressing up a shady wall

A site with morning sun and afternoon shade calls for a different palette of plants. The basic idea of this design remains the same as before: incorporate wall space to make the best use of a narrow plot.

Arrayed on a wooden trellis, the star of this planting is a striking camellia. It graces the late-winter to early-spring floral display (shown here) with soft white flowers. At its feet, a supporting cast of plants adds flowers in pink, white, and blue. And the powerful scent of winter daphne welcomes visitors on the entry walk. After the spring show has faded, the foliage creates a pleasant scene through summer, fall, and winter.

## Plants & Projects

**Ⓐ Sasanqua camellia** (use 1 plant)
Trained to the trellis, this shrub displays lovely flowers against glossy evergreen foliage from late fall through early spring. Choose a white-flowered cultivar suitable for trellis training. See *Camellia sasanqua*, p. 123.

**Ⓑ 'Cilpinense' evergreen rhododendron** (use 1)
Branching low to the ground, this shrub forms a handsome mound of small evergreen leaves. In late winter and early spring, it bears pale-pink flowers that fade to white. See *Rhododendron*, p. 139.

**Ⓒ Variegated winter daphne** (use 1)
This evergreen shrub has shiny green leaves edged in yellow. In spring, purple buds open into clusters of rose-tinged white flowers near the ends of the branches and perfume the entire area. See *Daphne odora* 'Aureomarginata', p. 126.

**Ⓓ Low sarcococca** (use 3)
This spreading evergreen shrub with glossy green, leathery leaves bears clusters of very fragrant, tiny white flowers in late winter. See *Sarcococca humilis*, p. 142.

**Ⓔ Lenten rose** (use 3)
Grown for its distinctive flowers and shiny evergreen leaves, this perennial blooms in late winter and early spring. See *Helleborus orientalis*, p. 130.

Driveway | Garage

SITE: Shady

SEASON: Early spring

CONCEPT: Early-season flowers and evergreen foliage add interest to a short entry walk next to a wall.

1 square = 1 ft.

Walkway

**L** Trellis

**D** Low sarcococca

**A** Sasanqua camellia

Barrenwort **F**

**I** Christmas rose

**H** Lungwort

**G** Tassel fern

**J** 'Bressingham White' bergenia

**E** Lenten rose

**C** Variegated winter daphne

Annual **K**

**B** 'Cilpinense' evergreen rhododendron

**F** **Barrenwort** (use 5)
This perennial's evergreen leaves change from bronze to green to maroon from spring to winter. Bears flowers in yellow, pink, red, or white in spring. See *Epimedium,* p. 127.

**G** **Tassel fern** (use 1)
This evergreen fern forms an attractive clump of stiff, finely divided, and glossy fronds. See Ferns: *Polystichum polyblepharum,* p. 128.

**H** **Lungwort** (use 6)
The fuzzy gray-green leaves of this perennial are sprinkled with white spots. Spikes of tiny blue, red, or pink flowers appear in early spring. See *Pulmonaria saccharata,* p. 139.

**I** **Christmas rose** (use 5)
This perennial closely resembles Lenten rose but bears showy white flowers in winter and early spring. See *Helleborus niger,* p. 130.

**J** **'Bressingham White' bergenia** (use 3)
A perennial with large, shiny green leaves and white flowers that bloom on stalks in spring. See *Bergenia cordifolia,* p. 121.

**K** **Annuals** (as needed)
Use seasonal annuals, such as the pansies shown here.

**L** **Trellis**
You can make this trellis using the same construction as in the previous design. See p. 179.

# Decorate a Sunny Wall

## PERENNIALS, VINES, AND A FLOWERING SHRUB ENLIVEN A TIGHT SPACE

**Selected for a sunny site,** these plants offer something in every season. Many are evergreen, with foliage that looks fresh year-round. From March to December, flowers enhance the entrance with color and fragrance. In fall, the pomegranate will decorate the wall with large, cream-colored fruits.

The garden has two flowering peaks: spring and autumn. Fragrant white flowers of jessamine greet visitors to the front door early in spring. Chiming in later are the bold blossoms of the pomegranate,

iris, and daylily, and the more delicate blooms of dianthus and sage. Daylillies and sages continue to flower through the heat of summer, joined by santolina's bright-yellow buttonlike blooms. Expect another round of bloom that covers much of the color wheel when the weather turns cool in fall.

> SITE: Sunny
>
> SEASON: Spring
>
> CONCEPT: Handsome plants arrayed against a blank wall make a picture that pleases year-round.

Star jessamine **B**

Bearded iris **F**

Gray santolina **E**

'Bath's Pink' dianthus **H**

## Plants & Projects

Training the pomegranate and the jessamine is the most demanding aspect of this planting. As the pomegranate grows, select horizontal branches that grow parallel with the wall and fasten them to wires attached to the wall. Prune or restrict growth to the wires. Train the jessamine vines by securing the runners to the trellises. The perennials are generally carefree.

**A** **'Wonderful' pomegranate** (use 1 plant)
This upright deciduous shrub is easily trained against a wall. It bears bright-green glossy foliage and dazzling orange-red flowers in spring. A bounty of sweet, juicy pomegranates follows. Leaves are colorful in fall. See *Punica granatum* 'Wonderful', p. 139.

**B** **Star jessamine** (use 2)
This twining climber will cover the trellis year-round in small, shiny, dark-green leaves. It bears abundant and fragrant pinwheel-shaped white flowers in spring. See *Trachelospermum jasminoides*, p. 145.

**C** **Mealycup sage** (use 5)
From spring to fall this upright perennial produces showy blue flower spikes that rise in clusters from clumps of slender gray-green leaves. See *Salvia farinacea*, p. 141.

**D** **Autumn sage** (use 3)
This bushy perennial has tiny oval leaves that contrast with the strappy foliage of the daylilies nearby. Colorful flower spikes surround the plant all season. We've shown a purple variety, but pink, white, and red are also available. See *Salvia greggii*, p. 141.

**E** **Gray santolina** (use 4)
This evergreen perennial forms a tight mound of narrow silver-gray foliage, just right for borders and tucked into corners. Small yellow flowers top the foliage in summer. See *Santolina chamaecyparissus*, p. 141

**F** **Bearded iris** (use 3)
Prized for handsome swordlike foliage as well as large lavender blossoms, this perennial is a standout against the daintier dianthus. It often blooms again in autumn. See *Iris* x *germanica*, p. 133.

**G** **'Black Eyed Stella' daylily** (use 5)
This popular perennial thrives in hot sunny spots. Forms a clump of long, slender evergreen leaves crowned all summer with golden trumpet-shaped flowers tinged dark red in the centers. See *Hemerocallis* 'Black Eyed Stella', p. 131.

**H** **'Bath's Pink' dianthus** (use 15)
Sprinkled with small pink flowers in spring, this perennial trims the walk the rest of the year with a fringe of fine silvery foliage. See *Dianthus* 'Bath's Pink', p. 126.

**D** Autumn sage

**G** 'Black Eyed Stella' daylily

**A** 'Wonderful' pomegranate

**C** Mealycup sage

**H** 'Bath's Pink' dianthus

**G** 'Black Eyed Stella' daylily

**D** Autumn sage

**E** Gray santolina

Driveway

Garage

House

Door

1 square = 1 ft.

Walkway

# A No-Mow Slope

## A TERRACED PLANTING TRANSFORMS A STEEP SITE

**Steep slopes** can be a landscaping headache. Planted with lawn grass, they're a chore to mow, and they can present problems of erosion and maintenance if you try to establish other ground covers or plantings. One solution to this dilemma is shown here: tame the slope with low retaining walls and steps. Then plant the resulting flat (or flatter) beds with attractive trees, shrubs, and perennials.

Steep slopes near the house are common in many Northwest communities. Here, a narrow, steeply sloping front yard has been terraced with low retaining walls and wide steps. The result transforms the home's pub-

lic face and creates an enticing path to the front door.

Visitors approaching from the sidewalk or the driveway pass through colorful plantings. Shrubs and perennials bloom in whites, pinks, and purples in late winter and spring. Trees and shrubs offer fall color and handsome evergreen foliage in winter. Near the house, you can extend the foundation shrubs along the wall or tie them in to existing plantings.

Japanese **A** snowbell

'Goldflame' **D** spirea

Evergreen **K** candytuft

See site plan for **M**.

'Vancouver Gold' **F** silky leaf woadwaxen

## Plants & Projects

Reshaping the slope and building the retaining walls, steps, and walkways is a big job. Even if you plan to do much of the work yourself, it's best to consult a landscape contractor for advice and local building officials about regulations. Once established, the plants will give years of enjoyment and need only seasonal maintenance.

**Ⓐ Japanese snowbell**
(use 2 plants)
This deciduous tree is a three-season performer. Fragrant white flowers dangle from its branches in spring and green summer leaves turn yellow in fall. See *Styrax japonicum*, p. 144.

**Ⓑ 'Royal Purple' smoke tree**
(use 1)
This large deciduous shrub is red in spring and dark-purple in summer. In summer and fall it bears plumes of tiny pink flowers. Prune lower limbs to approximate a tree form. See *Cotinus coggygria*, p. 125.

SITE: Sunny

SEASON: Spring

CONCEPT: Retaining walls, steps, and attractive plants tame this slope and enhance the home's public face.

House

Lawn

Driveway

Sidewalk

1 square = 1 ft.

Red laceleaf **C**
Japanese maple

'Hidcote' **H**
English lavender

'Springwood **I**
Pink' heath

**D** 'Goldflame' spirea

Variegated **E**
winter daphne

**J** 'Massachusetts'
kinnikinnick

**B** 'Royal Purple'
smoke tree

**L** Retaining wall
and steps

**G** Dwarf
rhododendron

**K** Evergreen
candytuft

**C Red laceleaf Japanese maple** (use 1)
An eye-catching presence by the door, this shrubby tree offers delicate lacy foliage that is red in summer and redder in fall. See *Acer palmatum* 'Dissectum Atropurpureum', p. 118.

**D 'Goldflame' spirea** (use 8)
This deciduous shrub forms a mass of thin arching stems. Bright-gold leaves are tinged with orange in spring and turn red in fall. Bears flat clusters of pink flowers in summer. See *Spiraea japonica*, p. 143.

**E Variegated winter daphne** (use 1)
The rose-tinged flowers of this evergreen shrub bloom from late winter into spring. Shiny green-and-cream leaves look good year-round. See *Daphne odora* 'Aureomarginata', p. 126.

**F 'Vancouver Gold' silky leaf woadwaxen** (use 8)
This low, spreading shrub forms a mat of small, deciduous, dark-green leaves. In summer, it is covered with yellow flowers. See *Genista pilosa*, p. 129.

**G Dwarf rhododendron** (use 6)
This compact evergreen shrub tucks into the spaces by the steps and sidewalk. In spring, its dark-purple flowers look good against the gray-green leaves. See *Rhododendron impeditum*, p. 139.

**H 'Hidcote' English lavender** (use 12)
Masses of fragrant dark-purple flowers top the gray-green leaves of this small bushy shrub in early summer. Its aromatic evergreen foliage looks good the rest of the year. See *Lavandula angustifolia*, p. 134.

**I 'Springwood Pink' heath** (use 14)
This low, spreading evergreen shrub has fine needlelike leaves. A profusion of tiny pink bell-shaped flowers bloom in late winter and spring. See *Erica carnea*, p. 127.

**J 'Massachusetts' kinnikinnick** (use 19)
Ideal for dry slopes, this evergreen ground cover forms a low mass of dark glossy leaves on reddish stems. Small pinkish-white flowers bloom in spring and produce red berries in summer. See *Arctostaphylos uva-ursi*, p. 120.

**K Evergreen candytuft** (use 17)
This bushy evergreen perennial ground cover has bright clusters of white flowers that stand out against its dark glossy leaves for weeks in spring. See *Iberis sempervirens*, p. 133.

**L Retaining walls and steps**
The walls and steps are made with a precast-concrete retaining-wall system available at garden centers. See p. 168.

**M Paving**
Choose a surface that complements the house. See p. 156.

# PLANT PORTRAITS

These durable, low-care plants will help transform difficult hillside sites.
- ● = First design, pp. 60–61
- ▲ = Second design, pp. 62–63

**Evergreen candytuft** (*Iberis sempervirens*, p. 133) ●

**'Goldflame' spirea**
(*Spiraea japonica*, p. 143) ●

**'Sango Kaku' coralbark maple**
(*Acer palmatum*, p. 118) ▲

**Fuchsia**
(*Fuchsia magellanica*, p. 129) ▲

**Red laceleaf Japanese maple**
(*Acer palmatum* 'Dissectum Atropurpureum', p. 118) ●

**'Caesar's Brother' Siberian iris** (*Iris sibirica*, p. 133) ▲

# Working with a hillside

If terracing a steep slope with retaining walls and steps does not appeal to you, or is beyond your budget, consider this design. Here we've worked with the existing hillside, replacing turfgrass with tough, easy-care ground covers. Once the plants are established, their roots will hold the hillside soil in place, and they will require little supplemental watering during the summer.

The planting is as attractive as it is durable. Mounding deciduous and evergreen shrubs contrast with the swordlike foliage of Siberian iris and airy clumps of Russian sage. Above these lower-growing plants, the striking coralbark maple provides dappled shade and a sense of separation from street and sidewalk traffic. There are months of bloom in reds, pinks, purples, and lavender from the spikes of tiny Russian sage flowers to the exotic blossoms of fuchsia.

## Plants & Projects

Ⓐ **'Sango Kaku' coralbark maple**
(use 1 plant)
Colorful in all seasons, this small deciduous tree has lacy leaves that open reddish, turn light-green, and then yellow in fall. Bare winter bark is coral red. See *Acer palmatum*, p. 118.

Ⓑ **Fuchsia** (use 3)
Deep red-and-purple flowers cover this small shrub all summer long. They'll invite hummingbirds to your front yard. Evergreen in mild winters and needs watering in summer. See *Fuchsia magellanica*, p. 129.

Ⓒ **Spreading English yew** (use 9)
An evergreen shrub with flat needlelike leaves that stay dark-green all year. Left unpruned, the shrubs will blend together to form a soft mass. See *Taxus baccata* 'Repandens', p. 144.

Ⓓ **'Dwarf Pavement' rose** (use 34)
This tough deciduous shrub produces masses of glossy green leaves and wonderfully fragrant pink flowers from spring into fall. Its stems are very thorny, so if you have small children you might consider a less prickly rose. See *Rosa rugosa*, p. 139.

63

SITE: Sunny

SEASON: Summer

CONCEPT: Tough but attractive plants make a colorful, easy-care front yard on a sloping site.

Fuchsia **B**

'Dwarf Pavement' rose **D**

'Caesar's Brother' **G** Siberian iris

Spreading **C** English yew

'Vancouver Gold' **I** silky leaf woadwaxen

'Newport Dwarf' **E** escallonia

Spreading **C** English yew

'Sango Kaku' **A** coralbark maple

'Dwarf **D** Pavement' rose

Russian **F** sage

'Caesar's Brother' **G** Siberian iris

See site plan for **H**.

**E** **'Newport Dwarf' escallonia** (use 9)
Compact and glossy-leaved, this evergreen shrub grows thick enough to hide the foundation and stays low enough to frame the windows without pruning. It bears clusters of red flowers in summer. See *Escallonia rubra*, p. 127.

**F** **Russian sage** (use 5)
This perennial makes a wispy clump of small gray-green leaves on upright stems. For many weeks in summer, lavender flower spikes appear above and among the leaves. See *Perovskia*, p. 136.

**G** **'Caesar's Brother' Siberian iris** (use 8)
This perennial has narrow grassy leaves and deep blue-purple flowers that bloom on stiff stalks in late spring. It provides a nice splash of texture and color in front of the yews. See *Iris sibirica*, p. 133.

**H** **'Autumn Joy' sedum** (use 7)
This perennial forms a mass of thick stems and succulent gray-green leaves. Large flat flower heads turn from shades of pink to rusty red as summer progresses into autumn. See *Sedum*, p. 142.

**See p. 61 for the following:**

**I** **'Vancouver Gold' silky leaf woadwaxen** (use 22)

1 square = 1 ft.

# Easy-Care Hillside

## LANDSCAPING TAMES A SEVERE SLOPE

A River birch

Mexican orange E

'Savannah' holly B

C Wax myrtle

G Daylily

D Forsythia

F Creeping willowleaf cotoneaster

H Retaining wall

**In this steep-slope design,** the low retaining wall creates two terraces that mirror the curve of the driveway. On the lower level, shapely woody evergreens rise above a carpet of colorful daylilies. On the top level, massed ranks of deciduous and evergreen shrubs define the gentle curve of the remaining slope. Farther from the house an attractive tree punctuates the end of the wall. Low-growing shrubs spill down the retaining hill, uniting the upper and lower planting terraces and marking the transition to the front lawn.

The planting provides good-looking flowers in spring and summer and handsome foliage, pretty berries, and striking bark in fall and winter. It is attractive whether viewed from above or below. Seen from the sidewalk, it frames the house and directs attention to the front entrance. It also screens the semiprivate area of drive and garage from the more public entrance. As the large shrubs grow, they overlap, tying the planting together and creating horizontal layers that further reduce the visual impact of the once-dominant slope.

The planting can easily be altered to accommodate existing foundation plants along the facade of the house. Or you can extend it to create a new foundation planting by adding more Mexican oranges and cotoneasters, with perhaps a wax myrtle or two where you need some height.

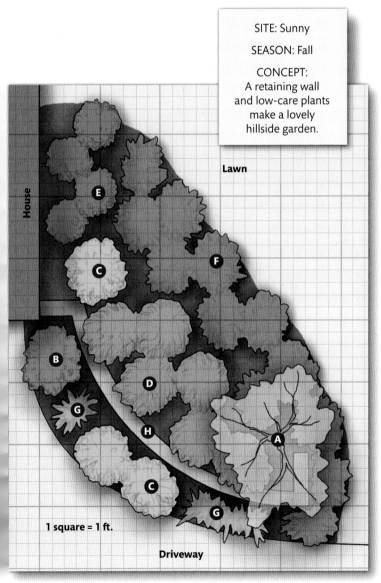

SITE: Sunny

SEASON: Fall

CONCEPT:
A retaining wall and low-care plants make a lovely hillside garden.

Lawn

House

1 square = 1 ft.

Driveway

## Plants & Projects

Building the retaining wall, re-shaping the slope, and preparing the planting beds is a big job—you might want to line up some energetic helpers or hire someone with a small earthmover. Once that job is done and the plants are established, this design will provide years of enjoyment with a minimum amount of maintenance. If you'd like extra flowers, plant small bulbs (crocus, squill, grape hyacinth, small daffodils) in clumps of six or more, scattered among the shrubs.

**A River birch** (use 1 plant)
The multiple trunks of this fast-growing tree transform winter days with their exquisite bark, which peels back to reveal orange, tan, and creamy white layers. Medium-green leaves cast a light summer shade. See *Betula nigra*, p. 121.

**B 'Savannah' holly** (use 1)
This pyramidal tree with shiny evergreen leaves and red berries makes a fine accent by the garage. See *Ilex* x *attenuata*, p. 133.

**C Wax myrtle** (use 3)
This evergreen shrub has aromatic leaves and a graceful form. Birds like the clusters of gray berries in fall and winter. See *Myrica cerifera*, p. 135.

**D Forsythia** (use 6)
With cheery yellow flowers in early spring, this deciduous shrub covers lots of ground with its arching branches. Foliage is green in summer, purple in fall. See *Forsythia* x *intermedia*, p. 128.

**E Mexican orange** (use 4)
An evergreen shrub with shiny compound leaves. Clusters of fragrant white flowers bloom in spring and sporadically through summer making this a great choice to dress up the foundation. See *Choisya ternata*, p. 123.

**F Creeping willowleaf cotoneaster** (use 12)
This tough, low-growing evergreen shrub is an excellent ground cover for a slope—its stems root where they touch ground, holding the soil in place. Bears white flowers in spring, red berries in fall, and its shiny leaves turn purple in cold weather. See *Cotoneaster salicifolius* 'Repens', p. 126.

**G Daylily** (use about 3 dozen)
For an extended show of lovely lilylike flowers, combine early- and late-blooming cultivars of this useful perennial in your favorite colors. Its grassy foliage and cheerful blooms make a bright informal edging for the drive. See *Hemerocallis*, p. 131.

**H Retaining wall**
Using a precast concrete wall system, you can build a curved wall like the one shown here in a weekend. See p. 168.

# A Beginning Border

## FLOWERS AND A FENCE OFFER A TRADITIONAL DESIGN

**A mixed border** can be one of the most delightful of all gardens. Indeed, that's usually its sole purpose. Unlike many other types of landscape plantings, a traditional border is seldom yoked to any function beyond that of providing as much beauty as possible. From the first neat mounds of foliage in the spring to the fullness of summer bloom and autumn color, the mix of flowers, foliage, textures, tones, and hues brings pleasure.

This border is designed for a beginning or busy gardener, using durable plants that are easy to establish and care for. Behind the planting, screening out distraction, is a simple fence. The border is meant to be viewed from the front, so tall plants need to go at the back. There are interesting plant combinations to enjoy from every vantage point, from a distance or close-up. It is easy to extend the planting along the fence to suit your site and energy.

The plants here provide months of bloom. To complement the spring flowers of the clematis, plant bulbs that will bloom among the emerging perennials. In summer and fall, the garden is a subtle tapestry of color, with flowers in shades of pink, violet, and blue woven among leaves in many shades of green. Attractive foliage of the grasses, red chokeberry, and other plants carries interest through the winter.

SITE: Sunny

SEASON: Fall

CONCEPT: Even a novice can make this flower border flourish. Attractive plants displayed against a simple fence will provide months of enjoyment.

Lawn

1 square = 1 ft.

'Sarabande' Chinese silver grass C

'Elsa Spath' clematis E

Fence L

Red chokeberry B

'May Night' salvia H

'Magnus' purple coneflower G

Penstemon I

# Plants & Projects

In early spring, cut the wild lilac, Russian sage, and ornamental grasses close to the ground. Shear spent flowers off the salvia to promote repeat bloom. Prune the clematis to control its size.

**A** **'Victoria' wild lilac** (use 1 plant)
This evergreen shrub has shiny and crinkly dark-green foliage and is extremely drought tolerant after it's established. Blooms in spring with small dark-blue flowers at branch ends. See *Ceanothus* 'Victoria', p. 123.

**B** **Red chokeberry** (use 2)
This multi-stemmed bushy shrub is covered with tiny white flowers in spring before bright-red berries appear in summer. Glossy green foliage turns into a stunning display of orange and red in the fall. See *Aronia arbutifolia*, p. 120.

**C** **'Sarabande' Chinese silver grass** (use 3)
This perennial forms a fountain of long thin leaves, each green with a central white stripe. Flower stalks rise above the leaves in late summer or fall, though bloom can be unreliable in the Northwest. See *Miscanthus sinensis*, p. 135.

**D** **'Sunset' rock rose** (use 2)
Magenta-pink flowers cover this mounded evergreen shrub for weeks in summer. Wavy-edged gray-green foliage is attractive year-round. See *Cistus* x *pulverulentus*, p. 124.

**E** **'Elsa Spath' clematis** (use 1)
A deciduous vine with dark-green compound leaves. It bears large violet-blue flowers from late spring into fall. See *Clematis* hybrids, p. 124.

**F** **'Longin' Russian sage** (use 2)
This perennial forms an airy silver-gray clump of upright stems and small leaves. Bears spikes of lavender-blue flowers from summer into fall. See *Perovskia atriplicifolia*, p. 136.

**G** **'Magnus' purple coneflower** (use 7)
A perennial with tall, sturdy stalks that bear rosy pink flowers with dark centers from summer into fall. See *Echinacea purpurea*, p. 126.

**H** **'May Night' salvia** (use 8)
From early summer into fall, spikes of dark indigo-purple flowers rise above this perennial's heart-shaped leaves. See *Salvia* x *superba*, p. 141.

**I** **Penstemon** (use 11)
A clump-forming perennial that blooms in late spring and summer. This variety has dark blue-and-purple flowers on stalks that raise above the foliage. See *Penstemon*, p. 136.

**J** **'Mavis Simpson' geranium** (use 1)
This sprawling perennial has light-green leaves and bears small pink flowers in summer. See *Geranium* x *riversleaianum*, p. 130.

**K** **'Autumn Joy' sedum** (use 3)
A perennial with succulent gray-green foliage. Topped from summer through fall by flat flower heads that turn from greenish-pink to deep russet. See *Sedum*, p. 142.

**L** **Fence**
This easy-to-build fence makes an attractive backdrop for the border. See p. 183.

**M** **Stepping-stones and ornament**
Flagstones lead to an ornamental focal point and provide access for maintaining the deepest part of the planting.

# A border in the shade

If the best spot for a border on your property receives only morning sun, try this design. Like the previous design, this one arranges carefully chosen combinations of shrubs and perennials against a solid background. Here, however, the plants are proven performers in the shade.

Nearest the fence are mid-size shrubs offering a mixture of deciduous and evergreen foliage and a variety of eye-catching flowers from late winter through fall. Lower-growing perennials fill out the front of the bed with no less interesting foliage and flowers. The upright, sword-like leaves of the iris and sweet flag are particularly effective accents here.

1 square = 1 ft.

Lawn

SITE: Shady

SEASON: Summer

CONCEPT: An interesting mix of foliage and flowers, textures, shapes, and colors creates a border of shade-tolerant plants.

## Plants & Projects

**Ⓐ Mexican orange** (use 1 plant)
An evergreen shrub with shiny compound leaves. Clusters of fragrant white flowers bloom in spring and sporadically through summer. See *Choisya ternata*, p. 123.

**Ⓑ 'Cleopatra' camellia** (use 3)
An upright, compact evergreen shrub. In late fall and winter, its glossy green leaves set off rose-pink flowers. See *Camellia sasanqua*, p. 123.

**Ⓒ 'Nikko Blue' hydrangea** (use 1)
This deciduous shrub offers large round leaves and striking clusters of papery blue flowers in summer. See *Hydrangea macrophylla*, p. 132.

**Ⓓ Oregon grape** (use 2)
A spreading evergreen shrub with handsome deeply divided leaves. The showy yellow flower clusters in spring produce blackish-blue berries

later in the year. See *Mahonia aquifolium*, p. 135.

**Ⓔ 'Maiden's Blush' fuchsia** (use 1)
An upright shrub prized for its distinctive pale-pink, pendent flowers. Foliage may be evergreen in mild winters. See *Fuchsia*, p. 129.

**Ⓕ Lenten rose** (use 9)
This perennial forms a clump of shiny green leaves with toothed

Ⓚ **Fence**

Ⓓ **Oregon grape**

Ⓐ **Mexican orange**

Ⓒ **'Nikko Blue' hydrangea**

Ⓑ **'Cleopatra' camellia**

Ⓓ **Oregon grape**

Ⓙ **Variegated sweet flag**

Ⓛ **Stepping-stones and ornament**

Ⓗ **'Green Gold' hosta**

Ⓔ **'Maiden's Blush' fuchsia**

Ⓘ **'Peach Blossom' astilbe**

Ⓖ **Japanese iris**

Ⓗ **'Green Gold' hosta**

Ⓕ **Lenten rose**

Ⓖ **Japanese iris**

edges. In late winter, it bears white, greenish, pink, or purple flowers. See *Helleborus orientalis*, p. 130.

**G** **Japanese iris** (use 3)
A perennial displaying sword-like leaves and spectacular pur-plish-blue flowers in summer. See *Iris ensata*, p. 133.

**H** **'Green Gold' hosta** (use 3)
This perennial makes a clump of large dark-green leaves with yellow borders that fade to cream. In summer, you can remove the lavender flowers to highlight the foliage. See *Hosta*, p. 132.

**I** **'Peach Blossom' astilbe** (use 11)
Striking plumes of tiny flow-ers rise above this perennial's feathery foliage in summer. Flowers are peach colored. See *Astilbe* x *japonica*, p. 121.

**J** **Variegated sweet flag** (use 6)
A perennial, grasslike plant with leaves striped creamy white and green. Spreads to form a patch. See *Acorus gramineus* 'Variegatus', p. 119.

**See p. 67 for the following:**

**K** **Fence**

**L** **Stepping-stones and ornament**

**B** **'Cleopatra' camellia**

**F** **Lenten rose**

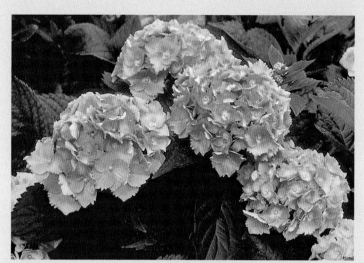

'Nikko Blue' hydrangea (*Hydrangea macrophylla*, p. 132) ▲

# PLANT PORTRAITS

These shrubs and perennials are a welcome sight in borders in sun or shade.

● = First design, pp. 66–67

▲ = Second design, pp. 68–69

'Peach Blossom' astilbe (*Astilbe* x *japonica*, p. 121) ▲

'Elsa Spath' clematis (*Clematis* hybrids, p. 124) ●

Japanese iris (*Iris ensata*, p. 133) ▲

# Create a "Living" Room

## A PATIO GARDEN PROVIDES PRIVACY AND PLEASURE

**A patio** can become a true extension of your living space with the addition of plants to screen views and to create an attractive setting. Such outdoor "rooms" are particularly welcome in the Northwest with the arrival of summer after the rainy season. In this design, plants and a tall louvered fence at one end of the patio form a three-dimensional wall that changes with the seasons. The flagstone paving accommodates a family barbecue or even a large gathering that can spill out onto the lawn. Together, plants and patio nicely mingle the indoors with the outdoors.

From early summer through fall, the plantings provide a colorful accompaniment to your patio

House

1 square = 1 ft.

Lawn

Climbing **D** hydrangea

'Autumn Joy' **E** sedum

**L** Common thyme

**J** 'Munstead' English lavender

Rosemary **I**

**L** Common thyme

**K** 'Berggarten' sage

Hen-and- **F** chicks

'Autumn Joy' **E** sedum

'Edward Goucher' **C** abelia

activities. There are flowers in pink, purple, lilac, rose, blue, and white. Foliage, much of it evergreen, is a subtle palette of silvery grays and greens accented by darker greens and purples.

Next to the house is a kitchen garden that enlivens meals as well as the patio planting. We show plants grown for seasoning and fragrance, with foliage that picks up the garden color scheme. In a warm sunny spot, you could substitute basil, tomatoes, or peppers.

## Plants & Projects

Seasonal pruning will keep these plants looking good. The hydran-gea vine climbs by itself, clinging to the fence. Train the smoke trees to tree form and prune yearly, as well as the other shrubs and the vine, to maintain the desired sizes.

**A** **'Royal Purple' smoke tree** (use 2 plants)
This small deciduous tree is eye-catching for months. The leaves are red in spring and dark-purple in summer. It displays large fluffy pink flower plumes from summer into fall. See *Cotinus coggygria*, p. 125.

**B** **Grey's senecio** (use 6)
The gray-green foliage of this evergreen shrub contrasts strikingly with the smoke tree above it. Bears yellow flowers in summer, but some people shear the flowers (as shown here) to highlight the foliage. See *Senecio greyi*, p. 142.

**C** **'Edward Goucher' abelia** (use 3)
This shrub forms a mound of dark-green foliage that has bronze tones in spring and fall. Rosy pink-purple flowers bloom in summer and attract butterflies. See *Abelia* x *grandiflora* 'Edward Goucher', p. 118.

**D** **Climbing hydrangea** (use 1)
Draping the fence with large glossy leaves from early spring to late fall, this deciduous vine bears lacy clusters of white flowers in summer. The thick stem's peeling bark is attractive in winter. See *Hydrangea petiolaris*, p. 132.

**E** **'Autumn Joy' sedum** (use 16)
Flat clusters of tiny rosy flowers perch atop this perennial's fleshy gray-green leaves in summer. In fall, flowers turn rust-colored. See *Sedum*, p. 142.

**F** **Hen-and-chicks** (use 24)
This charming little evergreen perennial makes rosettes of succulent gray-green leaves. See *Sempervivum tectorum*, p. 142.

**G** **'Silver King' artemisia** (use 2)
A perennial that forms a handsome clump of finely divided, aromatic, woolly silver-gray leaves that turn red in fall. See *Artemisia ludoviciana* var. *albula*, p. 120.

**H** **Moss phlox** (as needed)
This mat-growing perennial edges the flagstones with semi-evergreen dark leaves and stunning masses of blue, pink, purple, scarlet, or white flowers spring through summer. See *Phlox subulata*, p. 136.

**I** **Rosemary** (use 1)
The thin gray-green leaves of this evergreen shrub are aromatic and tasty. Small blue, lilac, or white flowers bloom intermittently through the year. See *Rosmarinus officinalis*, p. 140.

**J** **'Munstead' English lavender** (use 6)
This evergreen shrub forms a mound of fragrant gray-green leaves. Foliage is covered with spikes of fragrant pale-lavender flowers in early summer. See *Lavandula angustifolia*, p. 134.

**K** **'Berggarten' sage** (use 2)
A compact perennial with fragrant gray-green leaves that are used as a culinary seasoning. It bears spikes of small blue flowers in early summer. See *Salvia officinalis*, p. 141.

**L** **Common thyme** (use 13)
This kitchen-garden ground cover produces small, fragrant evergreen leaves that are valued as a seasoning. In summer it is covered with tiny pink, rose, or white flowers. See *Thymus vulgaris*, p. 145.

**M** **Louvered fence**
A cedar fence provides privacy while allowing air to circulate through nearby plants. See p. 181.

**N** **Paving**
Flagstones of varied size and shape make an informal patio. Stones with mottled gray tones will complement the planting's foliage. See p. 157.

SITE: Sunny

SEASON: Summer

CONCEPT: This planting provides privacy and a colorful setting for entertaining guests or enjoying the early-morning air on your own.

'Royal Purple' smoke tree **A**

**M** Louvered fence

**B** Grey's senecio

**N** Paving

**H** Moss phlox

**G** 'Silver King' artemisia

# A patio in the shade

If your patio is already blessed with a cool canopy of after-noon shade, perhaps from a large nearby tree, consider this design. The basics are the same as on the previous pages, but here we feature a garden of shade-loving shrubs and perennials.

As before, the planting creates a sense of privacy on the patio without blocking out the surroundings. The scents of the late-winter-blooming winter hazel and daphne will draw you out of the house early in the year. As summer nears, the winter hazel leafs out to form an ethereal screen.

Bloom continues through the spring into summer in pinks, yellows, and whites. The handsome foliage of shrubs and pe-rennials takes center stage from midsummer into winter. And the striking leaves and flower stalks of the acanthus and the remarkably twisted stems of Harry Lauder's walking stick are guaranteed to serve as conversation pieces at any gathering.

SITE: Shady

SEASON: Spring

CONCEPT: A mixed planting of shrubs and perennials creates privacy and ambience for a shady patio.

House

Lawn     1 square = 1 ft.

A Winter hazel
Japanese painted fern H
'Bow Bells' rhododendron D
F Cascade penstemon
Tassel fern G
E Variegated winter daphne
I Lungwort
'Snow Lady' rhododendron C
K Blue star creeper
C 'Snow Lady' rhododendron
J Moss phlox
B Harry Lauder's walking stick
M Paving
L Moss phlox

## Plants & Projects

**A Winter hazel** (use 3 plants)
A deciduous shrub with vase-shaped habit, it bears clusters of pendulous fra-grant yellow flowers on bare branches in early spring. New leaves are pink, then turn green. See *Corylopsis pauciflora*, p. 125.

**B Harry Lauder's walking stick** (use 1)
The stems and twigs of this deciduous tree are contorted in fantastic shapes. Yellow (male) or red (female) flowers bloom in late winter before leaves appear. In fall, foliage turns yellow. See *Corylus avellana* 'Contorta', p. 125.

**C 'Snow Lady' rhododendron** (use 4)
Clusters of fragrant white flowers bloom on this shrub in spring. Attractive evergreen foliage. See *Rhododendron*, p. 139.

**D 'Bow Bells' rhododendron** (use 3)
This evergreen shrub produces clusters of lovely light-pink flowers in spring. New

leaves are copper-colored. See *Rhododendron*, p. 139.

**E Variegated winter daphne** (use 1)
An evergreen shrub prized for the clusters of intensely fragrant pinkish-white flowers it bears in late winter and early spring. Glossy leaves are edged with yellow. See *Daphne odora* 'Aureomarginata', p. 126.

**F Cascade penstemon** (use 1)
A native perennial with showy tubular dark purple-and-blue flowers on 1- to 2-ft. spikes above its foliage summer through early fall. See *Penstemon serrulatus*, p. 136.

**G Tassel fern** (use 1)
The upright, finely divided fronds of this evergreen fern contrast handsomely with the acanthus. See Ferns: *Polystichum polyblepharum*, p. 128.

**H Japanese painted fern** (use 17)
This small, low-growing fern offers rosettes of lacy leaves in shades of green, silver, and maroon. See Ferns: *Athyrium niponicum* 'Pictum', p. 128.

**I Lungwort** (use 6)
Starting in early spring, this perennial bears numerous tiny pink, red, or violet flowers. Green leaves are spotted with white and look good through fall. See *Pulmonaria saccharata*, p. 139.

**J Moss phlox** (as needed)
A spreading, mat-growing perennial with semi-evergreen dark leaves and masses of blue, pink, purple, scarlet, or white flowers. See *Phlox subulata*, p. 136.

**K Blue star creeper** (as needed)
This low, creeping perennial has tiny bright-green leaves and bears sky-blue, starlike flowers in late spring and then off and on during the summer. See *Pratia pedunculata*, p. 137.

**See p. 71 for the following:**

**L Moss phlox** (as needed)

**M Paving**

# PLANT PORTRAITS

Whether you have sun or shade, these plants create a cozy patio niche with attractive flowers and foliage.
● = First design, pp. 70–71
▲ = Second design, pp. 72–73

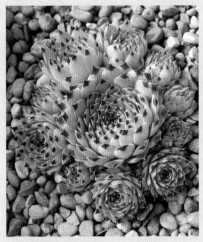

**Hen-and-chicks** (*Sempervivum tectorum*, p. 142) ●

**'Berggarten' sage** (*Salvia officinalis*, p. 141) ●

**Common thyme** (*Thymus vulgaris*, p. 145) ●

**Climbing hydrangea** (*Hydrangea petiolaris*, p. 132) ●

**'Silver King' artemisia** (*Artemisia ludoviciana*, p. 120) ●

**'Munstead' English lavender** (*Lavandula angustifolia*, p. 134) ●

# Garden in the Round

## CREATE A PLANTING WITH SEVERAL ATTRACTIVE FACES

**Plantings in residential landscapes** are usually "attached" to something. Beds and borders hew to property lines, walls, or patios; foundation plantings skirt the house, garage, or deck. Most of these plantings are meant to be viewed from the front, rather like a wall-mounted sculpture in raised relief.

The planting shown here is designed to "float" like an island in the landscape. Because you can walk around the bed, plants can be displayed "in the round," presenting different scenes from different vantage points. This is an excellent option if you want to squeeze more gardening space from a small lot, add interest to a rectangular one, or divide a large area into smaller outdoor "rooms."

Without a strong connection to a structure or other landscape feature, a bed like this requires a sensitivity to scale. To be successful, the bed must neither dominate its surroundings nor be lost in them. And it must relate to other plantings and landscape features, even though it is not connected to them. Here, the large shrubs and massed plants beneath them are attractive from a distance. And there's always something to admire up close as you stroll by.

Lawn

1 square = 1 ft.

SITE: Sunny

SEASON: Midsummer

CONCEPT: Floating on the lawn, this planting looks good from any vantage point: at a distance or as you stroll close by.

'Dawn' **B** viburnum

See site plan for **D**.

'Happy Returns' **G** daylily

'Little Princess' **C** spirea

Blue oat grass **I**

'Mavis Simpson' **H** geranium

# Plants & Projects

The blue, green, silvery, and purple foliage of this planting set each other off, while also making an effective backdrop for the yellow-and-pink flowers. There's bloom in every season—even winter—with the peak in summer. Little more than seasonal pruning and maintenance will keep the planting healthy and attractive.

**A** **'Royal Purple' smoke tree** (use 1 plant)
Very showy throughout the growing season, the leaves of this large deciduous shrub open red and turn purple in summer. Displays equally showy fluffy plumes of pink-brown flowers from summer to fall. See *Cotinus coggygria*, p. 125.

**B** **'Dawn' viburnum** (use 1)
A deciduous shrub that bears fragrant pink flowers in late winter. Dark-green leaves are tinged with red. See *Viburnum* x *bodnantense*, p. 146.

**C** **'Little Princess' spirea** (use 3)
This deciduous shrub forms a mound of dark-green leaves. Flat-topped clusters of tiny rosy pink flowers bloom for weeks in summer. See *Spiraea japonica*, p. 143.

**D** **'Silver Knight' Scotch heather** (use 5)
The silvery gray foliage of this evergreen shrub complements the flowering viburnum in winter. Small mauve-pink flowers bloom in summer, dry out, and remain on stems in winter. See *Calluna vulgaris*, p. 122.

**E** **'Flower Carpet Pink' rose** (use 2)
This spreading deciduous shrub bears numerous pink flowers against shiny green leaves from spring through autumn. See *Rosa*, p. 139.

**F** **'Blue Star' juniper** (use 5)
An evergreen shrub, it forms a low, spreading mass of striking silvery blue foliage. See *Juniperus squamata*, p. 134.

**G** **'Happy Returns' daylily** (use 8)
This perennial bears cheerful lemon-yellow, trumpet-shaped flowers from early summer into fall. Clumps of arching narrow foliage are attractive, too. See *Hemerocallis*, p. 131.

**H** **'Mavis Simpson' geranium** (use 2)
This perennial makes a spreading patch of gray-green leaves covered in summer with pale-pink flowers. See *Geranium* x *riversleaianum*, p. 130.

**I** **Blue oat grass** (use 10)
Grown for its pale-blue foliage, this clump-forming evergreen perennial also bears thin flower spikes that turn beige or tan. See *Helictotrichon sempervirens*, p. 130.

**J** **Cushion spurge** (use 5)
This perennial forms a low mound of green leaves that turn red in fall. Yellow flowers appear in spring and last for months. See *Euphorbia polychroma*, p. 128.

**K** **Blue star creeper** (as needed)
Dotted between and at the edges of the steppingstones, this perennial makes a mat of green foliage that is speckled off and on from spring through summer with light-blue starlike flowers. See *Pratia pedunculata*, p. 137.

**L** **Path**
Flagstones of irregular shapes and random sizes reflect the informality of the planting. See p. 156.

**A** **'Royal Purple' smoke tree**

**E** **'Flower Carpet Pink' rose**

**I** Blue oat grass

**K** **Blue star creeper**

**J** Cushion spurge

**L** Path

**H** **'Mavis Simpson' geranium**

**F** **'Blue Star' juniper**

**G** **'Happy Returns' daylily**

# An anchored island

People in the Northwest love their majestic trees. Builders strive to preserve at least some existing trees on new lots, and mature specimens on older properties are prized. But, like an elephant in a living room, a 50-ft. conifer in the middle of a lawn can be more than a little problematic.

This design shows one way to make a treasured, but awkward, friend more at home in your landscape. As the anchor of an island bed, the tree is no longer marooned on the lawn. And by relating its island planting to other plantings elsewhere on the property, the tree becomes part of a larger whole.

Chosen for their tolerance of dry dappled shade, these plants perform year-round. Spring, shown here, is the season of peak bloom. Foliage of varied colors and textures provides interest in the planting from summer into winter.

## Plants & Projects

**A Winter hazel** (use 1 plant)
This large deciduous shrub blooms on bare wood in the early spring, displaying clusters of small yellow flowers. New leaves are bronze, turning to green. See *Corylopsis pauciflora*, p. 125.

**B Barnes' narrow male fern** (use 3)
The upright semievergreen fronds of this fern have an interesting, slightly ruffled look. See *Dryopteris filix-mas* 'Barnesii', p. 128.

**C Lungwort** (use 4)
A perennial with wide green, white-spotted leaves. In early spring, small stalks bear pink, red, or violet flowers. See *Pulmonaria saccharata*, p. 139.

**D Bigroot geranium** (use 6)
This perennial makes a bushy clump of fragrant light-green leaves. Bears magenta or pink flowers in late spring. It is evergreen in mild winters. See *Geranium macrorrhizum*, p. 130.

**E 'Fröhnleiten' barrenwort** (use 19)
An evergreen perennial whose leaflets turn red-and-purple in cold winters. Rising above the leaves in spring, long stalks bear bright-yellow flowers. See *Epimedium* x *perralchicum*, p. 127.

> SITE: Shady
>
> SEASON: Spring
>
> CONCEPT: An island bed gives a mature tree a more active role in a home landscape as well as adding interest to a lawn-dominated yard.

Existing Douglas fir

Lawn

1 square = 1 ft.

Barnes' narrow male fern **B**

Bigroot geranium **D**

**J** Creeping thyme

Path **K**

'Fröhnleiten' **E** barrenwort

**G** Japanese painted fern

**H** 'Luxuriant' bleeding heart

**E** 'Fröhnleiten' barrenwort

**I** Lenten rose

**G** Japanese painted fern

'Velvet Night' **F** heuchera

**F** **'Velvet Night' heuchera** (use 3)
Grown for its striking deep-purple leaves, this perennial also bears tiny cream-green flowers in summer. Foliage is evergreen in mild winters. See *Heuchera americana*, p. 131.

**G** **Japanese painted fern** (use 6)
This striking deciduous fern has lacy silver-green fronds with maroon veins and stalks. The colors are almost iridescent. See *Athyrium niponicum* 'Pictum', p. 128.

**H** **'Luxuriant' bleeding heart** (use 5)
Forming clumps of soft fernlike leaves, this perennial displays charming heart-shaped pink flowers that dangle on arching stalks above the foliage in late spring. See *Lamprocaprios*, p. 134.

**I** **Lenten rose** (use 3)
In late winter and early spring, the distinctive white, green, pink, or purple flowers of this perennial cluster among the shiny compound foliage at the ends of thick green stalks. See *Helleborus orientalis*, p. 130.

**J** **Creeping thyme** (as needed)
Planted among the flagstones, this evergreen perennial forms a mat of fragrant shiny green leaves that turn maroon in winter. See *Thymus praecox* ssp. *arcticus*, p. 145.

**See p. 75 for the following:**

**K** **Path**

**A** Winter hazel

**Lungwort C**

**Bigroot geranium D**

# PLANT PORTRAITS

In shade or sun, these plants make an island bed attractive when viewed from near or far.

● = First design, pp. 74–75
▲ = Second design, pp. 76–77

'Happy Returns' daylily (*Hemerocallis*, p. 131) ●

Creeping thyme (*Thymus praecox* ssp. *arcticus*, p. 145) ▲

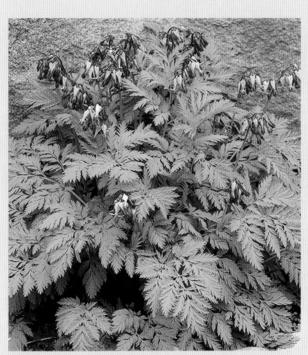

'Luxuriant' bleeding heart (*Lamprocaprios*, p. 134) ▲

'Fröhnleiten' barrenwort (*Epimedium* x *perralchicum*, p. 127) ▲

'Mavis Simpson' geranium (*Geranium* x *riversleaianum*, p. 130) ●

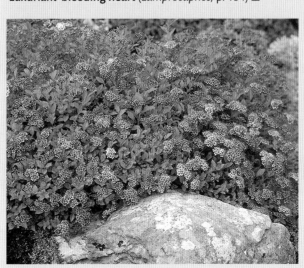

'Little Princess' spirea (*Spiraea japonica*, p. 143) ●

Cushion spurge (*Euphorbia polychroma*, p. 128) ●

# A Shady Hideaway

## BUILD A COZY RETREAT IN A CORNER OF YOUR YARD

**One of life's little pleasures** is sitting in a shady, private spot reading a book or newspaper or just looking out onto your garden, relishing the fruits of your labors. If your property is long on lawn and short on shade or privacy, a bench under a leafy arbor can provide a welcome respite from the cares of the day. Tucked into a corner of the yard and set among attractive shrubs, vines, and perennials, the arbor shown here is a desirable destination in all four seasons.

Shrubs of medium height and a vine overhead help create a cozy sense of enclosure, affording privacy as well as shade. Plantings in front of the arbor and extending along the property lines integrate the hideaway with the lawn (or other plantings) and make a pleasing scene when viewed from the house. The design is equally effective in an open corner or backed by a property-line fence.

There are flowers from late winter through fall in yellow, pink, white, and purple. English lavender adds fragrance by the bench, while thyme releases aroma when underfoot. Attracted to the abelia, butterflies will put on a show. The contorted stems of the small tree, Harry Lauder's walking stick, are an extraordinary sight. Water trickling over the basalt column adds a soothing touch.

## Plants & Projects

The arbor and plants can be installed in a few weekends. Once the plants are established, seasonal maintenance and cleanup should keep this durable planting looking good for years. As the abelia and rhododendron approach maturity, you'll need to prune them to maintain the desired size.

Property line

Lawn

1 square = 1 ft.

Ⓐ **'Edward Goucher' abelia** (use 3 plants)
This shrub forms a loose mound behind the arbor. Clusters of pink-purple flowers bloom in summer. Semievergreen leaves have bronze tints in spring and are purple-bronze in fall. Copper sepals (leaflike structures below the flowers) add winter interest. See *Abelia* x *grandiflora*, p. 118.

Ⓑ **Harry Lauder's walking stick** (use 1)
A deciduous shrub or small tree with spectacularly twisted branches and stems. In late winter it bears tiny red female flowers or pendulous catkins of yellow male flowers. In fall, leaves turn yellow. See *Corylus avellana* 'Contorta', p. 125.

Ⓒ **Fuchsia** (use 1)
This upright, open shrub bears dangling red-and-purple flowers all summer. Leaves are tinged with red. May be evergreen in mild winters. See *Fuchsia magellanica*, p. 129.

Ⓓ **'Gomer Waterer' rhododendron** (use 3)
In late spring, this evergreen shrub bears lovely white flowers with pink margins. Deep-green foliage looks good all year. See *Rhododendron*, p. 139.

Ⓔ **'Hidcote' English lavender** (use 3)
An evergreen shrub, this forms a compact mound of thin, aromatic, gray-green leaves. In early summer, it bristles with spikes of tiny, fragrant, deep-purple flowers. See *Lavandula angustifolia*, p. 134.

Ⓕ **'Vancouver Gold' silky leaf woadwaxen** (use 7)
This deciduous shrub makes a low mat of green, twiggy stems covered with tiny green leaves. It bears a mass of bright-yellow pealike flowers from late spring into summer. See *Genista pilosa*, p. 129.

Ⓖ **Golden clematis** (use 2)
Numerous small, lantern-shaped yellow flowers bloom on this deciduous vine all summer. Fluffy seed heads appear in fall and last into winter. See *Clematis tangutica*, p. 124.

Ⓗ **'Johnson's Blue' geranium** (use 3)
This perennial's pretty blue flowers and attractive foliage are a pleasing sight at the foot of the bench. It blooms from late spring into summer. See *Geranium*, p. 130.

Ⓘ **'Autumn Joy' sedum** (use 3)
A popular perennial grown for its fleshy gray-green foliage and flat clusters of tiny

SITE: Sunny

SEASON: Summer

CONCEPT: Enjoy colorful, eye-catching plants while you relax under a shady arbor.

**M** Arbor

**J** 'Goldsturm' coneflower

**H** 'Johnson's Blue' geranium

**G** Golden clematis

**K** 'Birch Hybrid' bellflower

**A** 'Edward Goucher' abelia

**B** Harry Lauder's walking stick

**O** Ornament

**N** Paving

**L** Creeping thyme

**D** 'Gomer Waterer' rhododendron

**E** 'Hidcote' English lavender

**F** 'Vancouver Gold' silky leaf woadwaxen

**I** 'Autumn Joy' sedum

**C** Fuchsia

flowers that start out pale pink and turn deep rusty red from summer into fall. See *Sedum*, p. 142.

**J** **'Goldsturm' coneflower** (use 5)
Yellow daisylike flowers with a dark "eye" rise on stiff leafy stalks above this perennial's basal mound of coarse green foliage. Blooms summer into fall. See *Rudbeckia*, p. 140.

**K** **'Birch Hybrid' bellflower** (use 12)
This perennial forms a low, spreading mass of green heart-shaped leaves with crinkled

margins. Bears bell-shaped blue flowers in summer. See *Campanula*, p. 123.

**L** **Creeping thyme** (as needed)
Planted among the flagstones, this evergreen perennial has gray-green leaves that release a scent when stepped on. Bears tiny purplish-white flowers in summer. See *Thymus praecox* ssp. *arcticus*, p. 145.

**M** **Arbor**
This simple structure can be built in a weekend. See p. 180.

**N** **Paving**
Flagstones in random sizes and shapes complement the casual feel of the planting. See p. 157.

**O** **Ornament**
A specially bored basalt rock makes a pleasing water feature. Can be bought bored with reservoir, pump, and installation instructions at garden centers and rock suppliers.

# Grow your hideaway

In this design, instead of building your shade, you plant it. Here, the open canopy of a Japanese maple provides dappled shade for the bench and its comfortable occupants. A leafy screen of shrubs and ornamental grasses creates a sense of privacy but not confinement.

As in the previous design, there are flowers almost year-round. Eye-catching flower buds on the viburnum add winter interest. In early spring, fragrant white blossoms entice strollers to the bench. A rhododendron and evergreen candytuft round out the spring bloom. Although flowering picks up again in midsummer, the garden is at its most colorful in fall, with oranges, reds, yellows, and russets supplied by perennial flowers and the foliage of the Japanese maple and ornamental grasses.

See site plan for Ⓓ.

Property line

Bench

Lawn

1 square = 1 ft.

SITE: Sunny

SEASON: Early fall

CONCEPT: Anchored by a shade tree, this hideaway, from ground cover to canopy, is homegrown.

Ⓐ **Japanese maple**

Ⓔ **'Magnus' purple coneflower**

**'Spring Bouquet' viburnum** Ⓑ

Ⓒ **'Purpurascens' Chinese silver grass**

**Ornament** Ⓚ

**'Goldsturm'** Ⓗ **coneflower**

**Creeping thyme** Ⓘ

**'Little Gem' candytuft** Ⓕ

**Paving** Ⓙ

Ⓖ **'Autumn Joy' sedum**

## Plants & Projects

**Ⓐ Japanese maple** (use 1 plant)
This deciduous tree provides dappled shade in summer. Here we've shown a seed-grown plant (not a cultivar) with green summer foliage that turns red-purple in fall. See *Acer palmatum*, p. 118.

**Ⓑ 'Spring Bouquet' viburnum** (use 3)
An upright evergreen shrub with dark-green leaves on reddish stems. Pretty pink buds appear in fall and open in early spring as fragrant white flowers. Metallic-blue berries follow and last for months. See *Viburnum tinus*, p. 146.

**Ⓒ 'Purpurascens' Chinese silver grass** (use 5)
This perennial makes a graceful upright fountain of thin green leaves, each with a pink midrib. Turns orange-red in fall. In late summer and fall, it is topped by fluffy flowers and seed heads. See *Miscanthus sinensis*, p. 135.

**Ⓓ Dwarf rhododendron** (use 3)
This low, spreading evergreen shrub bears dark-purple flowers in spring. Small blue-gray leaves look good the rest of the year. See *Rhododendron impeditum*, p. 139.

**Ⓔ 'Magnus' purple coneflower** (use 3)
In summer, this perennial bears large daisylike flowers on stiff branched stalks above a loose clump of coarse green leaves. Flower petals are purple, centers orange. See *Echinacea purpurea*, p. 126.

**Ⓕ 'Little Gem' candytuft** (use 3)
An evergreen perennial, this makes a low, sprawling mass of thin glossy leaves. Covered with small white flowers in spring. See *Iberis sempervirens*, p. 133.

**See pp. 78–79 for the following:**

**Ⓖ 'Autumn Joy' sedum** (use 3)

**Ⓗ 'Goldsturm' coneflower** (use 3)

**Ⓘ Creeping thyme** (as needed)

**Ⓙ Paving**

**Ⓚ Ornament**

'Purpurascens' Chinese silver grass (*Miscanthus sinensis*, p. 135) ▲

## PLANT PORTRAITS

Privacy, shade, flowers, foliage, and fragrance—these plants provide all the necessities for a relaxing backyard retreat.
● = First design, pp. 78–79
▲ = Second design, pp. 80–81

**'Little Gem' candytuft**
(*Iberis sempervirens*, p. 133) ▲

**Golden clematis**
(*Clematis tangutica*, p. 124) ●

**'Gomer Waterer' rhododendron**
(*Rhododendron*, p. 139) ●

**'Birch Hybrid' bellflower**
(*Campanula*, p. 123) ●

**Harry Lauder's walking stick**
(*Corylus avellana* 'Contorta', p. 125) ●

# Splash Out

## MAKE A WATER GARDEN THE FOCUS OF OUTDOOR ACTIVITIES

**A water garden** adds a new dimension to a home landscape. It can be the eye-catching focal point of the entire property, a center of outdoor entertainment, or a quiet out-of-the-way retreat. A pond can be a hub of activity—a place to garden, watch birds and wildlife, raise ornamental fish, or stage an impromptu paper-boat race. It just as easily affords an opportunity for some therapeutic inactivity; a few minutes contemplating the ripples on the water's surface provides a welcome break in a busy day.

A pond can't be moved easily, so choose your site carefully. Practical considerations are outlined on pp. 164–167 (along with instructions on installation and on planting water plants). In addition to those considerations, contact local authorities to find out if you must follow code requirements. Then consider how the pond and its plantings relate to the surroundings. Before plopping a pond down in the middle of the backyard, imagine how you might integrate it, visually if not physically, with nearby plantings and structures. For example, we've shown this pond bordered by an informal crushed-rock patio.

Foliage is the star of the planting and gives it year-round appeal. Fall and winter are the most colorful seasons, with the bronzy red plume cedar and curly sedge, yellow ocher heather, tawny Chinese silver grass, and bright-red dogwood stems. In spring and summer, the season shown here, flowers accent foliage that comes in a pleasing range of greens.

SITE: Sunny

SEASON: Summer

CONCEPT: A pond is at the center of a versatile and exciting outdoor living area.

# Plants & Projects

Installing a pond is arduous but simple work, involving several weekends of digging. The plants require only seasonal maintenance, but the pond will need regular attention to keep a healthy balance of water plants and fish (if you have them) in order to maintain adequate oxygen levels and to keep algae in check. Consult local or mail-order suppliers to help you get the right mix.

**Ⓐ Plume cedar** (use 1 plant)
This fine-textured evergreen tree is soft gray-green in summer and bronzy red in winter. Peeling cinnamon-colored bark is attractive. See *Cryptomeria japonica* 'Elegans', p. 126.

**Ⓑ 'Elegantissima' variegated Siberian dogwood** (use 3)
An all-season performer, this deciduous shrub displays red stems in winter, white flowers in spring, green-and-white leaves in summer, and bluish-white berries in late summer. See *Cornus alba*, p. 125.

**Ⓒ Winter hazel** (use 1)
A deciduous shrub, this bears yellow flowers on bare wood in early spring that are followed by bronze leaves that turn green in summer. See *Corylopsis pauciflora*, p. 125.

**Ⓓ 'Robert Chapman' Scotch heather** (use 5)
This evergreen shrub forms a low mass of ascending stems. Tiny scalelike leaves are bright-red when new and then turn golden. In summer, small white flowers bloom up and down the stems. See *Calluna vulgaris*, p. 122.

**Ⓔ Spreading English yew** (use 2)
This low evergreen shrub has large dark-green needles. It makes a good ground cover. See *Taxus baccata* 'Repandens', p. 144.

**Ⓕ 'Morning Light' Chinese silver grass** (use 1)
The slender arching leaves of this perennial are green with a white midrib that gives the clump a silvery sheen. In late summer and fall, it bears tall fluffy flower and seed heads. See *Miscanthus sinensis*, p. 135.

**Ⓖ Cascade penstemon** (use 1)
A native perennial blooming from summer through early fall with tubular dark purple-and-blue flowers on 1- to 2-ft. stalks above its foliage. See *Penstemon serrulatus*, p. 136.

**Ⓗ Hosta** (use 1)
This perennial is grown primarily for its foliage. For this design, choose a cultivar that forms a big mound of large blue leaves. See *Hosta*, p. 132.

**Ⓘ Lenten rose** (use 6)
This evergreen perennial bears distinctive purple, pink, white, or green flowers in early spring. Its leathery green leaves are attractive all year. See *Helleborus orientalis*, p. 130.

**Ⓙ Fox red curly sedge** (use 3)
This perennial makes a clump of thin reddish-bronze leaf blades that keep their color year-round. The summer flowers are insignificant. See *Carex buchananii*, p. 123.

**Ⓚ 'Massachusetts' kinnikinnick** (as needed)
Plant this tough evergreen ground cover in open spaces between other plants. Deep-green leaves have a burgundy cast. The small white-to-pink spring flowers produce red berries. See *Arctostaphylos uva-ursi*, p. 120.

**Ⓛ Water plants** (as desired)
You can grow a variety of plants in the pond. We've shown a water lily. See Water plants, p. 147.

**Ⓜ Pond**
You can make this pond with a commercially available liner. The deep end is edged with flagstones. The other rises gradually until water and surrounding "land" are joined by a miniature shore of river rock and large stones. See p. 164.

Ⓒ **Winter hazel**

Ⓘ **Lenten rose**

Ⓐ **Plume cedar**

Ⓕ **'Morning Light' Chinese silver grass**

Ⓖ **Penstemon**

Ⓜ **Pond**

Ⓗ **Hosta**

Ⓚ **'Massachusetts' kinnikinnick**

Ⓓ **'Robert Chapman' Scotch heather**

# PLANT PORTRAITS

Set off by nearby water, these plants combine fresh foliage and lovely flowers for your poolside pleasure.

● = First design, pp. 82–83

▲ = Second design, pp. 84–85

**Black mondo grass** (*Ophiopogon planiscapus* 'Ebony Knight', p. 136) ▲

**'Morning Light' Chinese silver grass** (*Miscanthus sinensis*, p. 135) ●

**'Robert Chapman' Scotch heather** (*Calluna vulgaris*, p. 122) ●

**Fox red curly sedge** (*Carex buchananii*, p. 123) ●

**'Sulphureum' barrenwort** (*Epimedium* x *versicolor*, p. 127) ▲

**Water lily** (Water plants: *Nymphaea*, p. 147) ●

# Mini-pond

This little pond provides the pleasures of water gardening for those without the space or energy required to install and maintain a larger pond. Within its smaller confines, you can enjoy one or more water plants and a few fish. Or you might leave it as a reflecting pool, as shown here.

Pond and plantings can stand alone in an expanse of lawn, but they will look best integrated into a larger scheme. The scale is just right for use as the focal point of a small patio, as shown here, or as part of a larger patio planting.

As in the previous design, the planting displays a delightful collection of foliage textures and colors chosen to complement or contrast with those of their neighbors. Spring is brightened by delicate flowers. And the black mondo grass and colorful pavers are a striking sight throughout the year.

## Plants & Projects

**A** **Redvein enkianthus** (use 1 plant) The blue-green leaves of this slow-growing deciduous shrub turn orange-red in fall. Small bell-shaped flowers that are veined with red bloom in late spring. See *Enkianthus campanulatus*, p. 126.

**B** **Soft shield fern** (use 7) This evergreen fern forms a dense mass of upright-green fronds, each rising from its own brown crown. See Ferns: *Polystichum setiferum*, p. 128.

**C** **'Krossa Regal' hosta** (use 1) This perennial makes a vase-shaped clump of wide, powdery blue-green leaves. Tall stalks bear pale-lilac flowers in summer. See *Hosta*, p. 132.

**D** **'Luxuriant' bleeding heart** (use 7) Lines of dainty heart-shaped pink

1 square = 1 ft.

SITE: Shady

SEASON: Spring

CONCEPT: A miniature pond is the focal point of a small-scale but varied planting.

Lawn

Existing patio

**A** Redvein enkianthus

**F** 'Sulphureum' barrenwort

**C** 'Krossa Regal' hosta

**B** Soft shield fern

**D** 'Luxuriant' bleeding heart

**G** Japanese painted fern

**G** Japanese painted fern

**K** Paving

**I** Foamflower

**J** Pond

**H** Black mondo grass

**E** 'Velvet Night' heuchera

**D** 'Luxuriant' bleeding heart

flowers dangle from thin curving stalks above this perennial's soft, fernlike blue-green foliage. Blooms in late spring. See *Lamprocamprios*, p. 134.

**E** **'Velvet Night' heuchera** (use 3)
A semievergreen perennial prized for its striking purple foliage. Tiny white-green flowers float on thin stalks above the foliage in spring. See *Heuchera americana*, p. 131.

**F** **'Sulphureum' barrenwort** (use 12)
This evergreen perennial bears purple-tinted green leaves on wiry stems. Yellow

flowers rise above the leaves in spring. See *Epimedium* x *versicolor*, p. 127.

**G** **Japanese painted fern** (use 2)
A small deciduous fern with lacy fronds of silver, green, and maroon. See Ferns: *Athyrium niponicum* 'Pictum', p. 128.

**H** **Black mondo grass** (as needed)
This perennial ground cover spreads to form a patch of wide, grassy, purple-black leaves. See *Ophiopogon planiscapus* 'Ebony Knight', p. 136.

**I** **Foamflower** (as needed)
Planted around the bleeding heart and

hosta, this perennial carpets the ground with dark foliage that covered with tiny clusters of pink and white flowers in spring. See *Tiarella cordifolia*, p. 145.

**J** **Pond**
It's easy to make this shallow reflecting pond with a rectangular fiberglass shell and some elbow grease. See p. 164.

**K** **Paving**
Set bright-colored pavers on a sand-and-gravel base after you have installed the shallow pond. See p. 156.

# Easy Pond

## MAKE A HANDSOME WATER GARDEN IN A FEW WEEKENDS

SITE: Sunny

SEASON: Summer

CONCEPT: Water is a welcome presence in the landscape, especially when surrounded by lovely plants.

**The plantings in this design** are intended to settle the pond comfortably into an expanse of lawn. Flagstone paving invites visitors to stroll up to the pond's edge. Framing the pond and path are a small broadleaf evergreen tree and perennial ground covers planted in contrasting waves of color and texture. A full season of flowers in complementary blues, purples, and golds will draw hummingbirds and butterflies as surely as they delight the eye.

Lawn

1 square = 1 ft.

## Plants & Projects

Installing a pond is arduous but simple work, requiring several weekends of energetic digging. Lay out and install the paving at the same time as the pond. Once established, the plants require only seasonal care. The pond will need regular attention to keep a healthy balance of water plants and fish (if you have them) in order to maintain oxygen levels and to keep algae in check. Consult local or mail-order suppliers to help you determine the right mix.

**A Wax myrtle** (use 1 plant)
This small tree adds graceful height to the pond planting. Fragrant leaves are fairly small, smooth, leathery, and evergreen; they won't litter the pond in fall. See *Myrica cerifera*, p. 135.

**B 'Gracillimus' Chinese maiden grass** (use 3)
This ornamenal grass has a weeping habit. Flower plumes rise high above the foliage in late summer and last through winter. See *Miscanthus sinensis* 'Gracillimus', p. 135.

**C Mealycup sage** (use 12)
This perennial's grayish-green foliage is topped with many blue flower spikes visited by hummingbirds and butterflies. To keep it blooming all season, remove flowers as they fade. But don't discard them—they make wonderful dried flowers. See *Salvia farinacea*, p. 141.

**D Oregon grape** (use 5)
A spreading evergreen shrub with handsome deeply divided leaves. The showy yellow flower clusters in spring produce blackish-blue berries later in the year. See *Mahonia aquifolium*, p. 135.

**E 'Stella de Oro' daylily** (use 20)
For small fountains of grassy foliage near the water's edge, plant these perennials en masse. Clusters of golden trumpets open daily in spring and often repeat in fall. See *Hemerocallis* 'Stella de Oro', p. 131.

**F 'Blue Pacific' shore juniper** (use 3)
This evergreen shrub bears bright-blue-

'Little Grapette' daylily **G**

'Stella de Oro' **E**
daylily

green trailing foliage that will fall softly over the flagstone edging and into the pond. See *Juniperus conferta* 'Blue Pacific', p. 134.

**G** **'Little Grapette' Daylily** (use 30)
This reliable and popular short perennial with rosy purple flowers that bloom in early summer will fill in the space after a few years. See *Hemerocallis*, p. 131.

**H** **'Homestead Purple' verbena** (use 6)
This perennial spreads out to form an edging of felty leaves interlaced with bright-purple flowers. Cut back occasionally to encourage a new flush of bloom. See *Verbena* x *hybrida* 'Homestead Purple', p. 146.

**I** **Louisiana iris** (use 3)
This plant forms a tall clump of pale-green swordlike leaves that can survive half-submerged in water. Bright-yellow flowers rise a foot above the leaves in spring. Foliage is attractive year-round. See *Iris* x Louisiana hybrids, p. 133.

**J** **Soft rush** (use 2)
Plant this bold grasslike wetland perennial for its yellow-green flowers and low maintenance requirements. Can survive in up to 4 in. of water. See *Juncus effusus*. p. 133.

**K** **Water lily** (use 1)
No pond is complete without these lovely floating flowers. Pointed petals open in layers above saucer-shaped leaf pads. We've shown a pink-flowering cultivar here. See Water plants: *Nymphaea*, p. 147.

**L** **Pond**
You can make this pond with a commercially available flexible liner. See p. 164.

**M** **Paving**
A flagstone edge widens into a natural path around the front of the pond. See p. 156.

# Down to Earth

## HARMONIZE YOUR DECK WITH ITS SURROUNDINGS

**A backyard deck** is a perfect spot for enjoying the outdoors. Too often, however, the deck offers little connection to its outdoor surroundings. Perched on skinny posts above a patch of lawn, it is a lonely outpost rather than an inviting gateway into the garden.

In this design, a low deck nestles in a planting that provides flowers and foliage for year-round enjoyment. Conceived for a site with a backyard that slopes down from the deck, the planting turns an area that is impractical for play or difficult to maintain as a lawn into a lovely border of foliage and flowers that you can enjoy from house, deck, or yard below. (The planting can be adapted for sites that are steeper or more level than the gradual slope shown.)

The plants are chosen and placed to minimize erosion and to make the most of color, texture, form, and fragrance. Flowering trees frame the bed at both ends, providing blossoms in spring, shade in summer, colorful foliage in fall, and attractive bark in winter. Evergreen and deciduous shrubs, vines, perennials, and grasses extend the colors and textures, as well as sweet scents, from one end of the deck to the other.

Japanese stewartia Ⓐ

SITE: Sunny

SEASON: Summer

CONCEPT: A pleasing mix of durable, often-fragrant plants integrates a low deck with its hillside surroundings.

'Spring Bouquet' viburnum Ⓓ

Compact Korean spice viburnum Ⓔ

'Springwood White' heath Ⓕ

## Plants & Projects

You'll need to water young plants to get them established. But after a year or two, these durable perennials, trees, and shrubs will require infrequent supplemental watering and a minimum of care. Prune the shrubs to keep them from overgrowing their neighbors. Shear the heath each spring. Divide any perennials that become crowded.

Ⓐ **Japanese stewartia**
(use 1 plant)
This deciduous tree is striking in every season. Silky buds and fresh green leaves appear in spring, followed by large white camellia-like flowers in summer, bronze-to-purple foliage in fall, and attractive bare branches with flaking bark in winter. See *Stewartia pseudocamellia*, p. 144.

Ⓑ **Japanese snowbell** (use 1)
This deciduous tree provides dappled summer shade and yellow foliage in fall. Fragrant white flowers will dangle over the deck in spring. See *Styrax japonicum*, p. 144.

Ⓒ **Mexican orange** (use 5)
This dense, glossy, evergreen shrub makes an informal and aromatic hedge along the deck. The light-green leaves are pungent in the hot sun, and the clusters of white flowers that bloom off and on all year look like orange blossoms and smell just as sweet. See *Choisya ternata*, p. 123.

Ⓓ **'Spring Bouquet' viburnum** (use 4)
Beautiful all year, this evergreen shrub has dark-green, red-tinted leaves. Clusters of burgundy-white buds form in fall and last through winter, opening into sweet-scented white flowers in spring. Blue berries appear in late summer. See *Viburnum tinus*, p. 146.

Ⓔ **Compact Korean spice viburnum** (use 2)
A deciduous shrub with clusters of white flowers that add a sweet spicy scent near the steps in spring. Leaves may turn red in fall. See *Viburnum carlesii* 'Compactum', p. 146.

Ⓕ **'Springwood White' heath** (use 20)
This evergreen shrub spreads to form a fine-textured but tough edge along the lawn. Small needlelike foliage is covered with white flowers in early spring. See *Erica carnea*, p. 127.

Ⓖ **'Comtesse de Bouchaud' clematis** (use 2)
Vigorous as well as beautiful, this deciduous vine will cover the rails of the deck with darkgreen leaves from spring through fall. Large rose-pink flowers bloom in summer. See *Clematis* hybrids, p. 124.

Ⓗ **Peony hybrid** (use 3)
A bushy perennial with dark-green glossy leaves that turn shades of purple and gold in autumn. It bears large fragrant flowers in late spring in colors that range from white to pink to rose. See *Paeonia*, p. 136.

Ⓘ **Penstemon** (use 12)
This late-spring-and-summer flowering perennial has showy dark blue-and-purple flowers on stalks towering above the green foliage. See *Penstemon*, p. 136.

Ⓙ **'Monch' Frikart's aster** (use 6)
A carefree perennial with eye-catching, yellow-centered, lavender-blue daisylike flowers above dark-green foliage. It blooms with the penstemon from late summer through fall. See *Aster* x *frikartii*, p. 121.

Ⓚ **'Bright Star' purple coneflower** (use 6)
A summer-blooming perennial that looks fabulous alongside the penstemon. It forms a mound of dark-green leaves. Tall, sturdy stalks bear large dark-pink daisylike flowers above the foliage. See *Echinacea purpurea*, p. 126.

Ⓛ **'Stella de Oro' daylily** (use 15)
Sunny yellow flowers bloom among the arching grassy leaves of this compact perennial from early summer to late fall. See *Hemerocallis*, p. 131.

**B** Japanese snowbell

**G** 'Comtesse de Bouchaud' clematis

**D** 'Spring Bouquet' viburnum

**K** 'Bright Star' purple coneflower

**M** Planter

See site plan for **L**.

**H** Peony hybrid

**I** Penstemon

Penstemon **I**

**N** Stepping-stones

Mexican orange **C**

**J** 'Monch' Frikart's aster

**H** Peony hybrid

**F** 'Springwood White' heath

**M** **Planters**

Large wooden containers on the pads leading to the deck are planted with evergreen shrubs and perennials. One each of the following is shown per box: Black chokeberry (*Aronia melanocarpa*, p. 120) is an upright shrub with bright-red leaves in fall and winter. At its feet are Grey's senecio (see *Senecio greyi*, p. 142) a mounding shrub with woolly leaves, and 'Palace Purple' heuchera (see *Heuchera*, p. 131) a perennial with dark-purplish, maple-shaped leaves.

**N** **Stepping-stones**

A few flagstones are planted among the flowers for quick access to the yard. See p. 156.

House

Deck

1 square = 1 ft.

Lawn

SITE: Shady

SEASON: Spring

CONCEPT: On a shady site, colorful flowers and foliage brighten the view from the deck.

G Crossvine  A Redvein enkianthus

D Variegated winter daphne

M Japanese stewartia

L Planter

C Leucothoe

H Sword fern

N Stepping-stones

I Lenten rose

J Variegated hosta

E 'Bow Bells' rhododendron

B Mountain laurel

F 'Debutante' Japanese andromeda

K 'White Queen' barrenwort

House

Deck

Lawn

1 square = 1 ft.

# Skirting a shady deck

This design also integrates the deck with its surroundings, but it does so in a shadier environment, produced by large trees or the house.

Evergreen shrubs, ferns, and perennials form a lush skirt flowing down the hill from the deck. Flowers in shades of pink bloom from late winter through summer, brightening this shady site. The foliage is as colorful as the flowers and much of it lasts all year. There are variegated leaves, leaves tinted when new, and leaves that blaze with color in fall. Planters offer possibilities for seasonal displays.

Like the previous design, this one catches the eye when viewed from the house, the deck, or the lawn.

## Plants & Projects

**A Redvein enkianthus**
(use 1 plant)
This large deciduous shrub has tiered branches and small blue-green leaves that turn bright-orange-red in fall. Clusters of red-veined flowers bloom in late spring. See *Enkianthus campanulatus*, p. 126.

**B Mountain laurel** (use 5)
This evergreen shrub has glossy leaves and showy pink flowers in early summer. (Cultivar on

facing page has red buds, too.) See *Kalmia latifolia*, p. 134.

**C Leucothoe** (use 3)
Clusters of sweet-scented white flowers line the stems of this evergreen shrub in spring. See *Leucothoe axillaris*, p. 134.

**D Variegated winter daphne** (use 3)
This compact shrub features gold-edged evergreen leaves. In late winter, purple buds open into very sweet-smelling small white flowers with a rosy tint. See *Daphne odora* 'Aureomarginata', p. 126.

**E 'Bow Bells' rhododendron** (use 4)
This delightful evergreen shrub nestles by the bench. Light-pink bell-shaped flowers bloom in spring. New leaves start out coppery and turn green. See *Rhododendron*, p. 139.

**F 'Debutante' Japanese andromeda** (use 4)
In spring, this evergreen shrub bears abundant bell-shaped white flowers, and bright gold or red new leaves mingle with glossy green leaves. See *Pieris japonica*, p. 137.

**G Crossvine** (use 2)
This attractive fast-growing, vigorous evergreen vine will cover the deck railings with stunning trumpetlike reddish-orange flowers with yellow throats that bloom throughout the spring and summer. See *Bignonia capreolata*, p. 121.

**H Sword fern** (use 19)
Native to the Northwest, this dependable fern has long dark shiny fronds that look good all year. See Ferns: *Polystichum munitum*, p. 128.

**I Lenten rose** (use 8)
Large white, pink, purple, or greenish flowers bloom very early in spring on this handsome perennial with leathery evergreen leaves. See *Helleborus orientalis*, p. 130.

**J Variegated hosta** (use 9)
Perennials grown primarily for their foliage, hostas also bear white, lavender, or purple flowers in summer on stalks above the leaves. A cultivar with variegated green-and-white leaves will complement the nearby Lenten rose and barrenwort. See *Hosta*, p. 132.

**K 'White Queen' barrenwort** (use 16)
One of the best shade-loving ground covers, this perennial has attractive heart-shaped foliage that changes color over the seasons. In spring, airy sprays of small white flowers show up among leaves, which have deep-red margins. See *Epimedium grandiflorum*, p. 127.

**L Planters**
Fill these with shade-loving shrubs and ferns. One per planter of the following are shown: 'Valley Fire' Japanese andromeda (see *Pieris japonica*, p. 137) is an evergreen shrub with glossy red leaves and drooping clusters of white flowers. Fragrant sarcococca (see *Sarcococca ruscifolia*, p. 142) is an evergreen shrub with very fragrant flowers in early spring. Japanese painted fern (see Ferns: *Athyrium niponicum* 'Pictum', p. 128) has fronds in shades of green, silver, maroon.

**See pp. 88–89 for the following:**

**M Japanese stewartia** (use 1)

**N Stepping-stones**

**'Debutante' Japanese andromeda** (*Pieris japonica*, p. 137) ▲

**Crossvine** (*Bignonia capreolata*, p. 121) ▲

# PLANT PORTRAITS

These plants can enhance a deck with lovely foliage textures and colors, as well as pretty flowers.
● = First design, pp. 88–89
▲ = Second design, pp. 90–91

**Variegated hosta** (*Hosta*, p. 132) ▲

**Mountain laurel** (*Kalmia latifolia*, p. 134) ▲

**Compact Korean spice viburnum** (*Viburnum carlesii* 'Compactum', p. 146) ●

# A Postal Planting

## MAKE YOUR DAILY MAIL RUN A PERENNIAL PLEASURE

**For some, the lowly mailbox** may seem a surprising candidate for landscaping. But posted like a sentry by the driveway entrance, the mailbox is highly visible to visitors and passersby. And it is one of the few places on your property that you visit nearly every day. A handsome planting like the one shown here pleases the passing public and rewards your daily journey, as well as that of your friendly letter carrier.

Plantings around mailboxes too often suffer from timidity—too few plants in too little space. This design makes a bold display, covering a good-size area with color for many months. The long-blooming perennials here are all well suited to the hot, sunny, and often dry conditions that prevail by most streetside mailboxes.

Mail arrives year-round, and no season is overlooked in this planting. Summer is the most colorful, with cheery flowers in blue, pink, red, and gold, highlighted by the yucca's eye-catching spires of creamy white blossoms. Sage, sedum, and asters continue the show through the fall. Then the evergreen foliage of many of the plants comes into its own, making the planting look fresh for visits through the winter and spring, when pink dianthus and blue phlox begin the cycle anew.

**'Golden Sword' Ⓐ**
**yucca**

**Stone edging Ⓙ**

## Plants & Projects

These are all tough, heat-tolerant plants, but they do best if you add a deep bark mulch to help conserve moisture. Maintenance is minimal. In early spring, cut back the old stems and renew the mulch. Then enjoy your trips to the mailbox.

Ⓐ **'Golden Sword' yucca** (use 1 plant)
This shrubby perennial offers sword-shaped evergreen leaves striped with yellow and gold. Bears showy clusters of creamy flowers on tall stems in summer. See *Yucca filamentosa*, p. 147.

Ⓑ **'Powis Castle' artemisia** (use 1)
This perennial forms a large mound of lacy gray-green aromatic foliage. Can be evergreen in areas with mild winters. See *Artemisia*, p. 120.

Ⓒ **'Cherry Chief' autumn sage** (use 1)
Loose clusters of cherry red flowers cover this bushy perennial from summer through fall. Evergreen in mild winters. See *Salvia greggii*, p. 141.

Ⓓ **'Goldsturm' coneflower** (use 3)
This perennial makes a late-summer show of large, golden-yellow daisylike flowers with black centers, above a mound of dark-green foliage. See *Rudbeckia fulgida*, p. 140.

Ⓔ **'Appleblossom' yarrow** (use 6)
This tough perennial offers aromatic,

delicate-looking gray-green foliage. It bears flat clusters of tiny clear pink flowers through the summer months. A fine companion for the neighboring sedum and autumn sage. See *Achillea*, p. 119.

Ⓕ **'Autumn Joy' sedum** (use 3)
This perennial has interesting fleshy gray-green leaves topped by flat clusters of flowers that appear in August and mature from pink to rusty red as autumn progresses. See *Sedum*, p. 142.

Ⓖ **Stoke's aster** (use 3)
From June to frost, this perennial produces pretty blue flowers atop evergreen foliage. See *Stokesia laevis*, p. 144.

Ⓗ **'Bath's Pink' dianthus** (use 2)
Pick a few of this perennial's fragrant pink flowers on late-spring mail runs; enjoy the grassy evergreen foliage the rest of the year. See *Dianthus*, p. 126.

Ⓘ **Moss phlox** (use 3)
Choose a pale-blue-flowered variety of this evergreen perennial ground cover to creep around the yucca. Blooms prolifically for several weeks in spring. See *Phlox subulata*, p. 136.

Ⓙ **Stone edging**
Keep the lawn and bed separate with an edging of small fieldstones, installed using the method described for installing a brick edging on p. 156.

SITE: Sunny

SEASON: Early summer

CONCEPT: Drought-tolerant perennials enhance your trips to the mailbox.

See site plan for **C** and **G**.

**E** 'Appleblossom' yarrow

**D** 'Goldsturm' coneflower

'Powis Castle' **B** artemisia

**F** 'Autumn Joy' sedum

**H** 'Bath's Pink' dianthus

**I** Moss phlox

1 square = 1 ft.

Lawn

**J**

**C**

**G**

**D**

**B**

**F**

**E**

Driveway

**A**

**I**

**H**

Mailbox

Street

# A Green Space for Recycling

## SCREEN OFF BINS WITH A FENCE, FOLIAGE, AND FLOWERS

**Sometimes the simplest landscaping project** packs a surprisingly big punch. This design hides recycling bins, an increasingly common residential feature, from view, while making access easy and recycling chores more enjoyable. The paving, screen, and plantings can be installed in a weekend. With this small investment of time and money you can turn one of the most frequently visited parts of your property into an eye-catching feature.

A wooden screen angles around a paved area that is roomy enough for several bins, yard-waste containers, and trash cans. Made of thin vertical slats, the screen obscures the area from view, yet allows ventilation. It opens at the driveway, where the bins are most likely to be wheeled out. Against the screen, a simple planting of shrubs, vines, and perennials makes a bold year-round display.

Foliage, flowers, and fruit display warm colors all year. The planting's cheeriness will be especially appreciated during the dreary winter months. As shown here, it offers sweet-scented yellow blossoms of Chinese witch hazel, the oranges and reds of the Scotch heather, and the bright-red twigs of the dogwood.

**'Elegantissima' variegated Siberian dogwood** **B**

**Evergreen clematis** **F**

See site plan for **J**.

**'Emerald 'n Gold' creeping euonymus** **H**

**Gladwin iris** **G**

**Scotch heather** **C**

SITE: Sunny

SEASON: Late winter

CONCEPT: Flowers and foliage along a fence screen and integrate a recycling area into the backyard.

## Plants & Projects

Spend a weekend installing this project. Then keep it looking good with just seasonal care. The clematis can be left alone to cover the screen or pruned to concentrate the foliage on the top. Shear the spent flowers off the heather in late winter, and prune the euonymus to keep it from climbing the dogwood.

**A** **Chinese witch hazel**
(use 1 plant)
The gray-green leaves of this small deciduous tree or large shrub turn yellow in fall. In winter, before leaves appear, it bears very fragrant flowers with yellow straplike petals. See *Hamamelis mollis*, p. 130.

Driveway

Garage

Lawn

1 square = 1 ft.

**I** Screen

**E** Black chokeberry

**A** Chinese witch hazel

**D** Foxberry

**B** 'Elegantissima' variegated Siberian dogwood (use 1)
Colorful all year, this deciduous shrub has white flowers in spring, green-and-white leaves through fall, and bright-red bark in winter. See *Cornus alba*, p. 125.

**C** Scotch heather (use 9)
This evergreen shrub forms a mass of tiny green scalelike leaves that turn red, orange, or yellow in winter. In summer, it bears small white, pink, or purple flowers. The colors of foliage and flower vary with the cultivar. The one shown has warm winter tones. See *Calluna vulgaris*, p. 122.

**D** Foxberry (use 15)
A Northwest-native, this evergreen shrub will fill the space under the tree with glossy dark-green foliage. Clusters of small pinkish-white flowers in late spring are followed by sour red berries that you can share with the birds. See *Vaccinium vitis-idaea*, p. 146.

**E** Black chokeberry (use 1)
This compact, bushy evergreen shrub boasts showy white flowers in mid-spring, dark-purple berries in summer, and green foliage that turns into an eye-catching red in the fall. See *Aronia melanocarpa*, p. 120.

**F** Evergreen clematis (use 1)
A fast-growing evergreen vine has lustrous dark-green leaves. White flowers will cover the foliage and perfume the air in early spring. See *Clematis armandii*, p. 124.

**G** Gladwin iris (use 3)
A perennial with glossy, lance-shaped leaves. Clusters of purple flowers in summer are followed by interesting seedpods that split to reveal striking bright-orange seeds. See *Iris foetidissima*, p. 133.

**H** 'Emerald 'n Gold' creeping euonymus (use 3)
This spreading shrub makes a tough, good-looking ground cover. Small shiny evergreen leaves are gold and green and have a pink tinge in winter. See *Euonymus fortunei*, p. 127.

**I** Screen
A simple structure with narrow vertical "pickets," this screen is as easy to construct as it is attractive to the eye. See p. 182.

**J** Paving
Interlocking precast pavers laid on sand and gravel will accommodate rolling bins. See p. 156.

# Screen for a shady site

The concept here is similar to that in the preceding design—screen your recycling center from view with just a few hours installation labor. The difference is that the plants in this design will do all the screening and thrive in dappled shade.

The foliage makes an effective and attractive screen all year, providing subtle contrasts and complements in color and texture in every season.

Starting in winter, the planting also offers flowers for many months of the year. In mild years, the Christmas rose may be blooming by the drive when you make the trip to recycle holiday wrappings. It may still be in flower when the rhododendrons blossom in spring. There's another show in summer when the foxberry and bunchberry bloom together.

## Plants & Projects

**A Vine maple** (use 1 plant)
Anchoring one end of the planting, this small native tree (or large shrub) has lovely gray bark and light-green deciduous leaves that put on a show in fall when they turn yellow, red, and orange. See *Acer circinatum*, p. 118.

**B Red chokeberry** (use 7)
This multi-stemmed bushy shrub is covered with bright blooms of tiny white flowers in spring before bright-red berries appear in summer. Glossy green foliage turns into a stunning display of orange and red in the fall. See *Aronia arbutifolia*, p. 120.

**C Fragrant sarcococca** (use 3)
This evergreen shrub has glossy green leaves and small white flowers with a welcome sweet scent in late winter. See *Sarcococca ruscifolia*, p. 142.

> SITE: Shady
>
> SEASON: Midsummer
>
> CONCEPT: A living screen of lustrous foliage and fragrant flowers greens up a recycling center.

See site plan for **I** and **J**.

**D** **Spreading English yew** (use 3)
Naturally compact and low-growing in front of the chokeberry, this evergreen shrub is distinguished by large, flat, needlelike leaves that stay dark-green all year. See *Taxus baccata* 'Repandens', p. 144.

**E** **Tassel fern** (use 3)
Stiff, lustrous evergreen fronds add fine texture and contrasting form to the rhododendrons and yews on each side of them. See Ferns: *Polystichum polyblepharum*, p. 128.

**F** **'Snow Lady' rhododendron** (use 3)
This evergreen shrub bears showy white, fragrant blossoms that stand out in spring against its fuzzy green foliage and the red leaves of the chokeberry. See *Rhododendron*, p. 139.

**G** **Bunchberry** (use 14)
A native perennial ground cover, this spreads to form a very low mass of erect stems topped with shiny dark-green leaves that turn red in fall. Small white, dogwood-like flowers cover the plant from late spring into summer. See *Cornus canadensis*, p. 125.

**H** **Bishop's hat** (use 13)
One of the best perennial ground covers for shade, its lovely heart-shaped evergreen leaves turn from coppery to green to maroon over the summer. In spring, they are topped with sprays of small pale-pink or white flowers. See *Epimedium grandiflorum*, p. 127.

**I** **Christmas rose** (use 3)
This evergreen perennial forms a clump of handsome dark, shiny leaves. In winter, large white flowers open at the ends of the stems and last for weeks. See *Helleborus niger*, p. 130.

**J** **Paving**
Irregular flagstones in the storage area are easy to install, and they complement the free-form screen. See p. 156.

**See p. 95 for the following:**

**K** **Foxberry** (use 6)

# PLANT PORTRAITS

A mix of carefree plants creates or complements a colorful screen in all seasons.
● = First design, pp. 94–95
▲ = Second design, pp. 96–97

Scotch heather (*Calluna vulgaris*, p. 122) ●

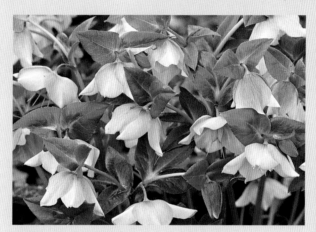

Christmas rose (*Helleborus niger*, p. 130) ▲

Foxberry (*Vaccinium vitis-idaea*, p. 146) ● ▲

'Emerald 'n Gold' creeping euonymus (*Euonymus fortunei*, p. 127) ●

Evergreen clematis (*Clematis armandii*, p. 124) ●

# Gateway Garden

## ARBOR, FENCE, AND PLANTINGS MAKE A HANDSOME ENTRY

**Entrances are an important part** of any landscape. They can welcome visitors onto your property; highlight a special feature, such as a rose garden; or mark the passage between two areas with different character or function. The design shown here can serve any of these purposes.

A contemporary version of the old picket fence makes a friendly and attractive barrier, just enough to signal the confines of the front yard or contain the family dog. The simple vine-covered arbor provides welcoming access.

In this design, the fence is stepped back on both sides of the arbor to create planting niches for small trees, shrubs, and perennials. The picketed enclosures help showcase the blossoms of azaleas and magnolias, which send fragrance over the walkway in spring. Imaginative combinations of shrubs, perennials, and grasses weave through the planting on either side of the fence. The overall effect is slightly formal but comfortable.

Saucer magnolia **A**

'Hardizer's Beauty' azalea **C**

'Vancouver Gold' silky leaf woadwaxen **B**

'Autumn Joy' sedum **F**

'Goldsturm' coneflower **G**

## Plants & Projects

For many people, a picket fence and vine-covered arbor represent old-fashioned neighborly virtues. You can extend the fence and plantings as needed. The shrubs require no more than seasonal pruning to maintain size and shape.

**A Saucer magnolia** (use 2 plants)
In early spring, this deciduous tree puts on a glorious display of large fragrant flowers in white, pinks, or purples. Leaves come out after the flowers fade and are large, attractive, and shiny green. The bare branches are handsome in winter. See *Magnolia x soulangeana*, p. 135.

**B 'Vancouver Gold' silky leaf woadwaxen** (use 11)
Tiny dark-green leaves on this low-growing deciduous shrub make a pretty edge along the pavement. Masses of sunny yellow flowers will brighten the entry in early summer. Gray-green stems give an evergreen look in winter. See *Genista pilosa*, p. 129.

**C 'Hardizer's Beauty' azalea** (use 8)
This striking evergreen shrub nestles beneath the magnolias. Bright-pink flowers bloom in

spring against a background of dark-green leaves. See *Rhododendron*, p. 139.

**D Dwarf rhododendron** (use 5)
This evergreen shrub forms a neat low mound of small blue-gray leaves. In spring, it bears clusters of beautiful deep-purple flowers. See *Rhododendron impeditum*, p. 139.

**E 'The President' clematis** (use 2)
This fast-growing deciduous vine will cover the arbor with a profusion of large violet-blue flowers in early summer. See *Clematis* hybrids, p. 124.

**F 'Autumn Joy' sedum** (use 8)
This favorite offers foliage and fall flowers. It forms an attractive mass of succulent leaves topped in late summer with flat flower heads that start out pink and slowly turn rusty red. See *Sedum*, p. 142.

**G 'Goldsturm' coneflower** (use 5)
This perennial forms a large clump of deep-green leaves. In summer and into fall, dark-eyed, daisylike gold flowers provide sunny color by the arbor. See *Rudbeckia*, p. 140.

**H 'Moonshine' yarrow** (use 7)
Another bright spot along the

fence, this perennial bears clusters of tiny lemony yellow flowers above a mass of gray-green fernlike foliage all summer long. See *Achillea*, p. 119.

**I Dragonfly columbine** (use 6)
This perennial forms a lovely mound of blue-green leaves with scalloped margins. In spring, large flowers with long spurs dangle on slender stalks above the leaves. See *Aquilegia*, p. 119.

**J 'Elijah Blue' blue fescue grass** (use 14)
Tucked between the woadwaxen and yarrow, the bright-blue blades of this clump-forming perennial offer a striking contrast in texture and color. Narrow flower spikes rise above the leaves in summer and turn tan in fall. See *Festuca ovina* var. *glauca*, p. 128.

**K 'Alba' thrift** (use 12)
This evergreen perennial forms a neat cushion of narrow green leaves. In spring, it sends up many stiff green stalks ending

in pom-poms of pure white flowers. Scattered blooms appear through summer and fall. See *Armeria maritima*, p. 120.

**L 'Birch Hybrid' bellflower** (use 23)
This perennial spreads to form a low mass of heart-shaped leaves covered for most of the summer in purple-blue bell-like flowers. See *Campanula*, p. 123.

**M Fence and arbor**
Made of standard dimension lumber, the fence and arbor are easy to build. A simple ladder trellis runs up the sides and over the top of the arbor to support the vines. See p. 184.

**N Paving**
Flagstone, shown here, is ideal for a high-traffic entry. Choose a material to suit your site and needs. See p. 156.

E 'The President' clematis

A Saucer magnolia

M Fence and arbor

H 'Moonshine' yarrow

K 'Alba' thrift

Paving N

'Vancouver Gold' B silky leaf woadwaxen

See site plan for D and I .

J 'Elijah Blue' blue fescue grass

L 'Birch Hybrid' bellflower

C 'Hardizer's Beauty' azalea

SITE: Sunny

SEASON: Summer

CONCEPT: Flowers for many months and attractive foliage year-round complement a simple fence and arbor.

Lawn

Driveway

Sidewalk

1 square = 1 ft.

**'Alba' thrift**
(*Armeria maritima*,
p. 120) ●

**Saucer magnolia**
(*Magnolia* x *soulangeana*,
p. 135) ●

# PLANT PORTRAITS

Combining enticing fragrance, lovely flowers, and handsome foliage, these plants create a distinctive entry.
● = First design,
    pp. 98–99
▲ = Second design,
    pp. 100–101

**'Riccarrtonii' fuchsia** Ⓓ

Ⓕ **'Hidcote' English lavender**

**'Hardizer's Beauty' azalea** (*Rhododendron*, p. 139) ●

**'The President' clematis** (*Clematis* hybrids, p. 124) ●

**'Elijah Blue' blue fescue grass**
(*Festuca ovina* var. *glauca*, p. 128) ●

**'Springwood Pink' heath**
(*Erica carnea*, p. 127) ▲

# A welcoming border

Not every entry calls for a fence. In this simple design, waist-high evergreen shrubs, perennials, and grasses create a deep garden bed that serves as an attractive barrier on either side of a vine-covered entry arbor.

An abundance of evergreen foliage ensures that the planting looks good year-round. The rhododendrons put on a glorious floral show in spring. Their foliage provides a handsome backdrop for the summer blossoms of fuchsias and bellflowers, the fall foliage and plumes of Chinese silver grass, and the winter blooms of the heath.

'The President' **H** clematis

'Goldsturm' **I** coneflower

'Purpurascens' **E** Chinese silver grass

'Birch Hybrid' **J** bellflower

**B** 'Sweet Simplicity' rhododendron

**K** Arbor

See site plan for **G** .

**C** 'Arpege' azalea

**E** 'Purpurascens' Chinese silver grass

**A** 'PJM' rhododendron

**D** 'Riccarrtonii' fuchsia

**F** 'Hidcote' English lavender

**L** Paving

**I** 'Goldsturm' coneflower

**J** 'Birch Hybrid' bellflower

Lawn

Driveway

1 square = 1 ft.

Sidewalk

# Plants & Projects

**A** **'PJM' rhododendron**
(use 3 plants)
Covered with clusters of purple flowers in early spring, the dark-green foliage of this compact evergreen shrub looks good all winter. See *Rhododendron*, p. 139.

**B** **'Sweet Simplicity' rhododendron** (use 3)
White blossoms edged in pink will spill over the walk when this evergreen shrub blooms in late spring. Leaves are dark-green and shiny all year. See *Rhododendron*, p. 139.

**C** **'Arpege' azalea** (use 1)
In spring, the sweet-scented

deep-yellow flowers of this shrub are a treat near the walkway. Leaves are deciduous and dark-green. See *Rhododendron viscosum*, p. 139.

**D** **'Riccarrtonii' fuchsia** (use 6)
Like a hanging basket without the fuss, this upright shrub bears a profusion of small, bright pink-and-purple flowers all summer long. Leaves are dark-green with a bronzy cast. See *Fuchsia*, p. 129.

**E** **'Purpurascens' Chinese silver grass** (use 3)
This graceful arching perennial has purplish-green leaves that

turn orange-red in fall. Flower plumes may rise above the leaves in late summer and turn to fluffy seed heads in winter. See *Miscanthus sinensis*, p. 135.

**F** **'Hidcote' English lavender** (use 8)
A small evergreen shrub with fragrant gray-green leaves. Masses of scented, deep-purple flowers rise on long stalks above the leaves in early summer. See *Lavandula angustifolia*, p. 134.

**G** **'Springwood Pink' heath** (use 12)
From winter to spring this ever-

green shrub makes a carpet of pink blooms along the lawn edge. Very small, green, needle-like foliage brightens the edge of the planting the rest of the year. See *Erica carnea*, p. 127.

**See p. 98 for the following:**

**H** **'The President' clematis** (use 2)

**I** **'Goldsturm' coneflower** (use 8)

**J** **'Birch Hybrid' bellflower** (use 32)

**K** **Arbor**

**L** **Paving**

# Elegant Symmetry

## MAKE A FORMAL GARDEN FOR YOUR BACKYARD

**Formal landscaping** often lends dignity to the public areas around a home (see pp. 16–17). Formality can also be rewarding in a more private setting. There, the groomed plants, geometric lines, and symmetrical layout of a formal garden can help to organize the surrounding landscaping, provide an elegant area for entertaining, or simply be enjoyed for their own sake.

"Formal" need not mean elaborate. This elegant design is really no more than a little perennial border in the shape of a wheel. A small decorative tree at the center and a holly hedge around the edge establish the shapes. Opposing beds of perennials are laid out along the curved hedge in mirror images of each other.

The garden will be in its glory in late summer and fall (as shown here) with a vibrant palette of foliage in reds and purples and flowers in blues, purple, rust, yellows, and golds. The show lasts a long time before the perennials die back. In winter, the holly hedge and the maple will maintain the garden's structure. Even more than other types of landscaping, formal gardens work well only when carefully correlated with other elements in the landscape, including structures and plants. A round garden can be difficult to integrate. Relate it to rectilinear elements, such as a fence or hedges. And repeat plants used in the design elsewhere in your landscape to tie things together.

## Plants & Projects

Of all gardens, a formal garden most obviously reflects the efforts of its makers. After the hedge has filled in, this garden requires attention mostly to keep it looking neat—shearing the hedge, pruning, and seasonal cleanup. Cut the mums back by one-half in June to control their height. Replace them every three or four years. For more spring color, plant bulbs among the hostas and other perennials.

**Ⓐ 'Bloodgood' Japanese maple** (use 1 plant)
A fine filagree of deep-red leaves makes this deciduous tree a beautiful centerpiece. Foliage stays red from spring through fall. Smooth gray bark and a delicate branching habit are attractive in winter. See *Acer palmatum*, p. 118.

**Ⓑ 'Green Island' Japanese holly** (use 32)
This compact evergreen shrub forms a mass of dense twigs and dark-green leaves that are ideal for formal shearing. See *Ilex crenata*, p. 133.

**Ⓒ Bluebeard** (use 2)
This loose, open shrub makes a perfect mound of gray-green stems and foliage. In late summer, the upper parts of the stems are lined with blue flowers that last for many weeks. See *Caryopteris* x *clandonensis*, p. 123.

SITE: Sunny

SEASON: Late summer

CONCEPT: This self-contained planting is formal simplicity at its best.

1 square = 1 ft.

Lawn

Florist's **Ⓗ** chrysanthemum

'Palace Purple' **Ⓖ** heuchera

'Autumn Joy' **Ⓔ** sedum

'Monch' **Ⓕ** Frikart's aster

'Green Island' **Ⓑ** Japanese holly

Bluebeard **Ⓒ**

**D New England aster** (use 2)

This perennial forms a stout clump of dark leaves topped from late summer through fall with masses of pink, purple, or violet flowers. See *Aster novae-angliae,* p. 121.

**E 'Autumn Joy' sedum** (use 12)

A standout in the fall garden, this perennial has succulent gray-green leaves and bears unusual flat clusters of flowers that start out light-pink in late summer and deepen to rusty red. See *Sedum,* p. 142.

**F 'Monch' Frikart's aster** (use 12)

Lavender-blue flowers with bright golden centers cover the dark-green leaves of this carefree perennial and last for many weeks from late summer on. See *Aster* x *frikartii,* p. 121.

**G 'Palace Purple' heuchera** (use 8)

Showy mounds of large, bronzy purple, maple-shaped foliage echo the Japanese maple. Leaves may survive mild winters on these semievergreen perennials. Airy sprays of small white flowers rise on thin stalks above the foliage in summer. See *Heuchera,* p. 131.

**H Florist's chrysanthemum** (use 24)

Autumn wouldn't be as colorful without these old-time favorite perennials, which bear masses of daisylike flowers in fall. Shown here are a mix of purples, oranges, and golds that complement the other fall colors in this scheme. When the plant isn't in bloom, dark-green, lobed leaves are attractive. See *Chrysanthemum* x *morifolium,* p. 124.

**I 'Vera Jameson' sedum** (use 8)

Succulent purple-gray leaves cover the short stems of this carefree perennial, topped in late summer with flat clusters of pink flowers that last through fall. See *Sedum,* p. 142.

**J 'Krossa Regal' hosta** (use 6)

This long-lived perennial will fill the inner circle with vase-shaped mounds of lovely powdery blue-green leaves that contrast beautifully with the red maple. *See Hosta,* p. 132.

**K Edging**

The inner and outer circles are made of bricks laid perpendicular to the beds. See p. 156.

**L Walkway**

Crushed stone is easy to install and suits the simple lines of this design. See p. 156.

**A 'Bloodgood' Japanese maple**

**H Florist's chrysanthemum**

**C Bluebeard**

**G 'Palace Purple' heuchera**

**I 'Vera Jameson' sedum**

**F 'Monch' Frikart's aster**

**L Walkway**  **K Edging**

**J 'Krossa Regal' hosta**

**B 'Green Island' Japanese holly**

**E 'Autumn Joy' sedum**

**D New England aster**

# A formal patio

In this design, a terrace large enough to accommodate a table and chairs is framed by formal beds, creating a lovely spot for an intimate lunch or a restful hour with a book.

A few of the perennials are the same as in the preceding design, but the basic layout has a different look and feel. Four flowering hydrangea trees anchor the corners and provide a sense of enclosure.

White and blue are the dominant colors here, enlivened by the peach, apricot, and orange tones of tea roses, daylilies, and potted marigolds. The blooms will be at their peak in midsummer, when Northwesterners are most likely to linger on the patio. But the roses will treat you to delicious scents and sights all season.

1 square = 1 ft.          Lawn

## Plants & Projects

**Ⓐ Peegee hydrangea**
(use 4 plants)
A deciduous shrub trained to grow as a small single-trunk tree. In midsummer, branch tips burst with huge clusters of creamy flowers that turn pink and age to tan in late fall. Many nurseries sell these shrubs already trained to a single trunk. See *Hydrangea paniculata* 'Grandiflora', p. 132.

**Ⓑ 'Just Joey' rose** (use 2)
A large robust shrub, this rose has glossy deciduous leaves and a profusion of very large fragrant flowers from spring through fall. Frilly-edged, orangy pink petals fade to white. See *Rosa*, p. 139.

SITE: Sunny

SEASON: Late summer

CONCEPT: This formal setting for an intimate gathering is enhanced by small trees and scented flowers.

Peegee Ⓐ
hydrangea

Ⓑ 'Just Joey' rose

Ⓜ 'Palace Purple' heuchera

Ⓓ Daylily

Ⓘ Container

Ⓙ Paving

See site plan for Ⓖ.

Daylily Ⓓ

'Palace Purple' Ⓜ
heuchera

Ⓐ Peegee
hydrangea

'Monch' Ⓛ
Frikart's' aster      Ⓔ Catmint      Ⓓ Daylily      Ⓗ 'Blue Clips'
Carpathian bellflower      'Flower Carpet Ⓒ
White' rose      Bluebeard Ⓚ      'Johnson's Blue' Ⓕ
geranium

**C** **'Flower Carpet White' rose**
(use 4)
Clusters of lightly scented white flowers will blanket the low, arching branches of this deciduous shrub from spring to fall. See *Rosa*, p. 139.

**D** **Daylily** (use 18)
This graceful perennial has grassy leaves and large lilylike flowers in many colors and bloom times. For months of color, plant early-, midseason-, and late-blooming varieties. See *Hemerocallis*, p. 131.

**E** **Catmint** (use 20)
This perennial forms soft mounds of light-green foliage covered with small violet-blue flowers in early summer and off and on through fall. See *Nepeta x faassenii*, p. 135.

**F** **'Johnson's Blue' geranium**
(use 24)
This perennial offers handsome jagged-edged leaves and clusters of blue flowers. It blooms from early summer to fall. See *Geranium*, p. 130.

**G** **Moss phlox** (use 38)
This low-growing perennial spreads to form a mat covering of prickly-textured evergreen foliage and eye-catching pink, magenta, lilac-blue, or white flowers that bloom in spring. See *Phlox subulata*, p. 136.

**H** **'Blue Clips' Carpathian bellflower** (use 32)
This perennial forms a delicate mound of heart-shaped evergreen leaves. Small, purple-blue flowers bloom most of the summer. See *Campanula carpatica*, p. 123.

**I** **Containers**
For bright accents on the terrace, fill the pots with long-blooming annuals. Marigolds and dahlias in bright-oranges and whites are shown here.

**J** **Paving**
Although flagstone is shown here, choose the paving material that complements your home. See p. 156.

**See p. 102–103 for the following:**

**K** **Bluebeard** (use 2)

**L** **'Monch' Frikart's aster** (use 2)

**M** **'Palace Purple' heuchera**
(use 8)

# PLANT PORTRAITS

These well-behaved low-care trees, shrubs, and perennials bring form, texture, flowers, and scent to a formal garden.
● = First design, pp. 102–103
▲ = Second design, pp. 104–105

**'Blue Clips' Carpathian bellflower**
(*Campanula carpatica*, p. 123) ▲

**Creeping phlox**
(*Phlox subulata*, p. 136)▲

**Florist's chrysanthemum**
(*Chrysanthemum* x *morifolium*, p. 124) ●

**'Bloodgood' Japanese maple**
(*Acer palmatum*, p. 118) ●

**New England aster**
(*Aster novae-angliae*, p. 121) ●

**Bluebeard** (*Caryopteris* x *clandonensis*, p. 123) ● ▲

# An Island Retreat

## CREATE A FREESTANDING PATIO GARDEN

**Patios and outdoor entertainment areas** are often right next to the house. While this proximity has many advantages, it isn't always practical or most effective to graft a patio onto the house. The landscaped freestanding patio shown here offers more flexibility in planning and using your landscape. Place it to take advantage of a view or a particularly private spot on your property. Use it as a retreat from household hubbub. If you already have a deck or patio off the family room or kitchen, a freestanding area can help accommodate large gatherings, perhaps as an area for quiet conversation away from more raucous activities.

In this design, a small multitrunked tree and mid-height shrubs provide a sense of place and enclosure without walling out the surroundings. The wispy foliage of the gaura, artemisia, and rosemary, along with the blue fescue grass and the silvery lamb's ears, gives the planting a Mediterranean look. And there are flowers year-round.

A freestanding patio garden like this one looks self-contained on paper, but like all landscape features, it looks and functions best when carefully correlated with other elements on your property. Transitions, both physical and visual, between major landscape features are particularly important. An expanse of lawn, changes of level that separate one area from another, or a planting that screens sight lines can all help different elements in your landscape coexist effectively.

'Marina' **A**
arbutus

Japanese **F**
anemone

'Palace Purple' **H**
heuchera

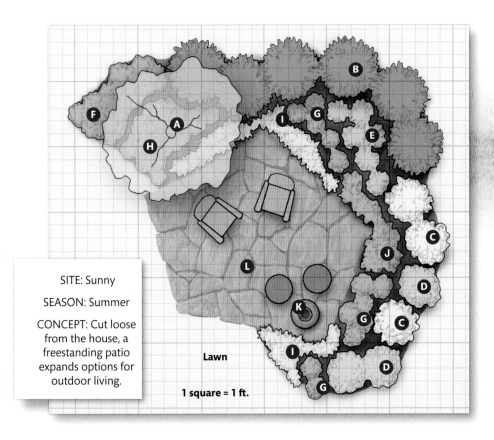

SITE: Sunny

SEASON: Summer

CONCEPT: Cut loose from the house, a freestanding patio expands options for outdoor living.

Lawn

1 square = 1 ft.

# Plants & Projects

Installing the patio and preparing the planting beds are strenuous but not difficult work. (Install the patio first.) The plants can be set out in a weekend. Once the plants are established, you'll have very little to do beyond seasonal pruning, division when the perennials get crowded, and cleanup.

**Ⓐ 'Marina' arbutus** (use 1 plant)
This small multitrunked tree offers bell-shaped pink flowers in fall, red berries, and glossy evergreen leaves. Shiny, reddish bark is eyecatching, too. See *Arbutus*, p. 120.

**Ⓑ 'Majorca Pink' rosemary** (use 6)
An evergreen shrub with fragrant deep-green foliage, it bears lavender-pink flowers in late winter and early spring. See *Rosmarinus officinalis*, p. 140.

**Ⓒ 'Iceberg' rose** (use 3)
This shrub rose displays fragrant white flowers against attractive green foliage. Blooms nearly all year. See *Rosa*, p. 139.

**Ⓓ 'Powis Castle' artemisia** (use 3)
A billowy mass of silver foliage makes this perennial a striking garden accent. See *Artemisia*, p. 120.

**Ⓔ Gaura** (use 6)
Another wispy perennial, it forms a loose clump of small lance-shaped green leaves on arching stems. Pale pink-and-white flowers dot the foliage from spring through fall. See *Gaura lindheimeri*, p. 129.

**Ⓕ Japanese anemone** (use 10)
This perennial forms a low clump of large, dark-green leaves. Tall stems carry small daisylike flowers from late summer into fall. See *Anemone* x *hybrida*, p. 119.

**Ⓖ Pincushion flower** (use 13)
Frilly light-blue flowers adorn this perennial's neat mounds of airy foliage from late spring through summer. See *Scabiosa caucasica*, p. 142.

**Ⓗ 'Palace Purple' heuchera** (use 18)
A perennial grown for its distinctive purple foliage, which is shaped like small maple leaves. It bears tiny white flowers on tall thin stalks from spring into summer. See *Heuchera*, p. 131.

**Ⓘ Blue fescue grass** (use 27)
This perennial forms mounds of thin blue-green leaves at the edge of the flagstones. Narrow flower spikes emerge from the clumps in early summer. See *Festuca ovina* var. *glauca*, p. 128)

**Ⓙ Lamb's ears** (use 9)
Children can't resist touching this perennial's soft silver foliage. Plants form a low mat topped by purple flowers in early summer. See *Stachys byzantina*, p. 144.

**Ⓚ Container plantings**
Plants in pots brighten up the patio with seasonal plantings of annuals or, as shown here, perennial scented geraniums. See *Pelargonium*, p. 136.

**Ⓛ Paving**
Irregular flagstone pavers set on a sand-and-gravel base make a durable, informal patio. See p. 156.

'Majorca Pink' **Ⓑ** rosemary

Blue fescue **Ⓘ** grass

**Ⓔ** Gaura

**Ⓒ** 'Iceberg' rose

Paving **Ⓛ**

Container **Ⓚ** plantings

**Ⓘ** Blue fescue grass

**Ⓖ** Pincushion flower

**Ⓙ** Lamb's ears

**Ⓓ** 'Powis Castle' artemisia

# A Woodland Link

## CREATE A SHRUB BORDER FOR NEARBY WOODS

**The woodlands of the Northwest** are treasured by all who live in the region. Subdivisions, both new and old, often incorporate woodland areas, with homes bordering landscapes of stately trees and large shrubs. And in some older neighborhoods, mature trees on adjacent lots create almost the same woodland feeling.

The planting shown here integrates a domestic landscape with a woodland edge, making a pleasant transition between the open area of lawn and the woods beyond. The design takes inspiration from the buffer zone of small trees and shrubs nature provides at a sunny woodland edge, and it should provide the same attraction to wildlife (and to the people who enjoy wildlife) as a natural edge does.

Trees and shrubs of various sizes mingle in the planting, larger ones toward the back, imitating natural layered growth. Narrow Serbian spruces echo the taller trees in the woods behind. Avenues of geraniums extend from the front center of the planting to each corner. In spring these areas showcase daffodils and other bulbs. From winter through fall there are flowers and attractive foliage. Whether viewed from across the yard or up close, the planting is appealing all year.

SITE: Sunny

SEASON: Early summer

CONCEPT: A layered planting of trees, shrubs, and perennials makes a pleasing transition between lawn and adjacent woodland.

## Plants & Projects

Before planting, dig and improve the soil throughout the entire area (except under the path) with organic matter. A mulch of compost or wood chips and regular watering the first summer will speed establishment. Other than seasonal maintenance, you'll need to divide the bulbs and perennials when they become crowded.

**A** **Chinese witch hazel** (use 3 plants) In winter, fragrant clusters of small yellow flowers cover the bare branches of this small deciduous tree or large shrub. Leaves turn yellow in fall. See *Hamamelis mollis*, p. 130.

**B** **Serbian spruce** (use 3) This spire-shaped conifer has short evergreen needles that are glossy green above and whitish below. See *Picea omorika*, p. 137.

**C** **'Valley Fire' Japanese andromeda** (use 9) A dense bushy evergreen shrub whose glossy green leaves are

**B** Serbian spruce

Garden ornament **L**

**C** 'Valley Fire' Japanese andromeda

Barnes' narrow male fern **F**

Gloriosa daisy **H**

**K** Path

**I** Catmint

**A** Chinese witch hazel

**C** 'Valley Fire' Japanese andromeda

See site plan for **J** .

Existing woodland

1 square = 1 ft.

Lawn

bright-red when new. In spring, an abundant supply of eye-catching buds produce drooping clusters of white flowers. See *Pieris japonica*, p. 137.

**D Holly osmanthus** (use 3)
The toothed, lustrous dark-green leaves of this evergreen shrub resemble holly leaves. In spring, it is covered with small fragrant white flowers. See *Osmanthus burkwoodii*, p. 136.

**E Salal** (use 38)
When grown in full sun, this evergreen shrub spreads to form a low mass of dull-green leaves. Bears pendulous pinkish-white flowers in spring and edible blue-black fruit in fall. See *Gaultheria shallon*, p. 129.

**F Barnes' narrow male fern** (use 31)
Massed in spots at the edges of the planting, this semiever-green fern makes an upright clump of long narrow fronds. See Ferns: *Dryopteris filix-mas* 'Barnesii', p. 128.

**G 'Johnson's Blue' geranium** (use 24)
This perennial makes a wide mound of attractive foliage that is covered from late spring into summer with cup-shaped lavender-blue flowers. See *Geranium*, p. 130.

**H Gloriosa daisy** (use 18)
Cheerful orange-yellow flowers with dark centers rise above this perennial's gray-green leaves for months in summer. See *Rudbeckia hirta*, p. 140.

**I Catmint** (use 3)
A perennial with equally attractive foliage and flowers. Pale-green leaves on sprawling stems are a crinkly heart shape. From early spring into fall, tiny blue flowers line the upper portions of the stems. See *Nepeta* x *faassenii*, p. 135.

**J Bulbs** (as needed)
For a spectacular spring show, plant daffodils, hyacinths, and tulips among the geraniums. Choose your favorite colors and plant a lot of them—if possible, 100 or more of each. See Bulbs, p. 122.

**K Path**
This wood-chip path nicely complements the woodland feeling. See p. 156.

**L Garden ornament**
A piece of architectural salvage, such as the column shown here, or a birdbath can add interest to the planting.

**A** Chinese witch hazel

**D** Holly osmanthus

Serbian spruce **B**

**E** Salal

**H** Gloriosa daisy

**G** 'Johnson's Blue' geranium

**F** Barnes' narrow male fern

**C** 'Valley Fire' Japanese andromeda

**F** Barnes' narrow male fern

# Link for a shadier edge

If an adjacent woodland shades your property, try this design, which features plants tolerant of shady conditions. The layout of the planting bed is similar to that of the previous design. Larger trees and shrubs are underplanted by low shrubs, perennials, and bulbs. Two "avenues" of low plants open from the front center of the planting to the corners. And a meandering path affords up-close viewing as well as access to the woods beyond.

From late winter through spring, the planting is in full bloom. Flowers in whites, pinks, and yellows fill the trees and carpet the ground, creating a lovely sight from a distance and up close, where fragrance enhances the enjoyment. Foliage textures and colors and the shapes of the plants provide interest in summer, accented by swaths of blue Carpathian bellflowers. In fall, the leaves of the serviceberry and oakleaf hydrangea impart a fiery finish to the growing season.

## Plants & Projects

**A** **'Autumn Brilliance' serviceberry** (use 4 plants) This deciduous tree is covered with white flowers in early spring, provides dappled shade in summer, and offers bright-red-orange fall foliage. See *Amelanchier* x *grandiflora*, p. 119.

**B** **Mountain hemlock** (use 3) This slow-growing evergreen conifer makes a handsome irregular cone of blue-green needlelike foliage. See *Tsuga mertensiana*, p. 146.

**C** **Oakleaf hydrangea** (use 5) The leaves of this deciduous shrub turn from pale-green, to dark-green, to red-and-purple from spring to fall. It bears striking clusters of long-lasting papery flowers in summer. See *Hydrangea quercifolia*, p. 132.

**D** **Low sarcococca** (use 8) This low, spreading evergreen shrub is a good ground cover. In late winter, small fragrant white flowers nestle at the bases of the glossy green leaves. See *Sarcococca humilis*, p. 142.

**E** **Leucothoe** (use 8) This compact evergreen shrub is wider than it is tall, with a dense growth of shiny narrow leaves. Bears fragrant white flowers in spring. See *Leucothoe axillaris*, p. 134.

**F** **Carpathian bellflower** (use 30) This perennial forms a patch of heart-shaped green leaves that are covered for most of the summer with bell-shaped violet-blue flowers. See *Campanula carpatica*, p. 123.

> SITE: Shady
>
> SEASON: Late spring
>
> CONCEPT: Evergreen trees and shrubs guarantee color year-round at this shady woodland edge.

1 square = 1 ft.

Lawn

**A** 'Autumn Brilliance' serviceberry

**M** Garden ornament

**C** Oakleaf hydrangea

**B** Mountain hemlock

**A** 'Autumn Brilliance' serviceberry

**F** Carpathian bellflower

**J** Daffodils

**D** Low sarcococca

**G** Bleeding heart

**L** Path

**I** Lungwort

**K** Barnes' narrow male fern

**G Bleeding heart** (use 7)
This perennial offers soft, blue-green fernlike foliage. In late spring, pink heart-shaped flowers dangle from thin arching stalks. See *Lamprocamprios spectabilis*, p. 134.

**H 'Magnificum' leopard's bane** (use 24)
This perennial spreads to form a low patch of heart-shaped leaves. Yellow asterlike flowers bloom in spring. See *Doronicum orientale*, p. 126.

**I Lungwort** (use 6)
A perennial with attractive gray-green foliage spotted with white. In spring, many tiny pink, red, or violet flowers float on stalks above the leaves. See *Pulmonaria saccharata*, p. 139.

**J Daffodils** (as needed)
A mix of white and yellow daffodils planted with the Carpathian bellflowers make a lovely spring show. Plant several hundred if possible. See Bulbs: *Narcissus*, p. 122.

**See p. 109 for the following:**

**K Barnes' narrow male fern** (use 30)

**L Path**

**M Garden ornament**

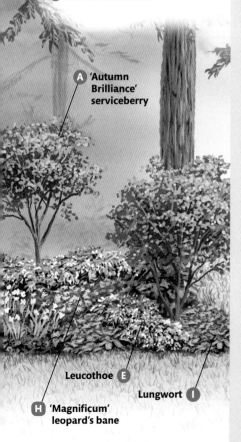

A **'Autumn Brilliance' serviceberry**

**Leucothoe** E

**Lungwort** I

H **'Magnificum' leopard's bane**

# PLANT PORTRAITS

With handsome foliage and flowers, these plants are effective against a woodland backdrop.

● = First design, pp. 108–109
▲ = Second design, pp. 110–111

**Gloriosa daisy**
(*Rudbeckia hirta*, p. 140) ●

**'Magnificum' leopard's bane**
(*Doronicum orientale*, p. 126) ▲

**Serbian spruce**
(*Picea omorika*, p. 137) ●

**Mountain hemlock**
(*Tsuga mertensiana*, p. 146) ▲

**Hyacinth**
(Bulbs: *Hyacinthus*, p. 122) ●

**Salal** (*Gaultheria shallon*, p. 129) ●

**Bleeding heart** (*Lamprocamprios spectabilis*, p. 134) ▲

# Plant Profiles

**Plants are the heart of the designs** in this book. In this section you'll find descriptions of all the plants used in the designs, along with information on planting and maintaining them. These trees, shrubs, perennials, grasses, bulbs, and vines have all proven themselves as dependable performers in the Northwest. They offer a wide spectrum of lovely flowers and fruits, handsome foliage, and striking forms. Most contribute something of note in at least two seasons. You can use this section as an aid when installing the designs in this book and as a reference guide to desirable plants for other home landscaping projects.

## Using the Plant Profiles

All of these plants are proven performers in many of the soils, climates, microclimates, and other conditions commonly found in the Northwest. But they will perform best if planted and cared for as explained in the Guide to Installation, beginning on p. 140. In the following descriptions and recommendations, "full sun" means a site that gets at least eight hours a day of direct sun throughout the growing season. "Partial sun" and "partial shade" both refer to sites that get direct sun for part of the day but are shaded the rest of the time by a building, fence, or tree. Plants preferring partial sun or shade often do best with morning sun and afternoon shade. "Full shade" means sites that don't receive direct sunlight.

The plants are organized here alphabetically by their scientific name. If you are browsing, page references direct you to the designs in which the plants appear. Numbers in **_bold italic_** type indicate the page where you can find a photo of the plant.

## Northwest Hardiness Zones

This map is based on one developed by the U.S. Department of Agriculture. It divides the Northwest into hardiness zones based on average minimum winter temperatures. Plants described in this book are given hardiness designations corresponding to a USDA Hardiness Zone on the map. A Zone 8 plant, for example, can be expected to survive winter temperatures as low as 5°F. However, cold hardiness is not the only climate factor that determines whether a plant is adapted to specific western climates. Most notably, high summer temperatures, intense sunlight, and aridity often limit plant adaptation in desert areas. Even when USDA Zone designations seem to indicate a plant will do well in your area, it is always good advice to double check final plant lists with a knowledgeable local nursery staff member. Your local water department and cooperative extension service are also good sources of information on plant adaptation.

**Average Annual Extreme Minimum Temperature 1976-2005**

| Temp (F) | Zone | Temp (C) | Temp (F) | Zone | Temp (C) |
|---|---|---|---|---|---|
| -40 to -35 | 3a | -40 to -37.2 | -5 to 0 | 6b | -20.6 to -17.8 |
| -35 to -30 | 3b | -37.2 to -34.4 | 0 to 5 | 7a | -17.8 to -15 |
| -30 to -25 | 4a | -34.4 to -31.7 | 5 to 10 | 7b | -15 to -12.2 |
| -25 to -20 | 4b | -31.7 to -28.9 | 10 to 15 | 8a | -12.2 to -9.4 |
| -20 to -15 | 5a | -28.9 to -26.1 | 15 to 20 | 8b | -9.4 to -6.7 |
| -15 to -10 | 5b | -26.1 to -23.3 | 20 to 25 | 9a | -6.7 to -3.9 |
| -10 to -5 | 6a | -23.3 to -20.6 | | | |

**This is not an official USDA Plant Hardiness Zone Map.**

# Climate Change and the Impact on Northwest Home Landscaping

As the climate of the Northwest changes, new home land-scaping challenges are on the rise. In recent years, the area has struggled with an increase in wildfires, destruction from new pests and diseases, extreme weather events, and general shifts in precipitation and temperature. Climate change also impacts the pollinators that you rely on to keep your landscape growing. A shift in the migration patterns of birds and life cycles of insects due to weather changes or events could lead to arrivals in our area too early or late for the plants they've grown to rely on. It could also mean that the habitats of neighboring pests extend or shift to your area, creating a new host of problems. Heavy storms can lead to an increase in moisture, mold, and fungal diseases on plants or cause the outright destruction of habitats found in trees, shrubs, and plants in your home landscape.

Changes in temperatures greatly impacts the growth rate of plants, so even an occasional period of intense heat or increased precipitation can cause plants to experience too much growth too quickly and become leggy, bloom prematurely, or not meet the necessary growing conditions at all. Nationwide, we have begun to see shifts in hardiness zones, meaning the plants you've had in your landscape for years might not thrive the way they used to.

Staying conscious of the plants you choose for your yard is a good way to make the most of your home landscape. By using attractive native or regionally adapted plants, you can get ahead of the negative impacts of climate change and reduce the amount of maintenance or replacements needed in the future. Choosing plants that thrive in the Northwest is beneficial for pollinators and can help build a stronger, more resilient natural world around you.

Choosing plants that are native to the Northwest like the sword fern shown here will help your garden thrive as climate change deepens.

# Removing Invasive Species and Planting Natives for a Healthy Ecosystem

When deciding which plants to keep, remove, or add to your home landscape, it is crucial to make sure that none are invasive species or noxious or banned weeds. Invasive species are non-native plants that aggressively spread and choke out any other species around them, including important plants that native pollinators rely on to survive. Typically, these unwanted plants are from another region or habitat but easily adapt to new areas by producing mass quantities of seeds, having difficult to remove root systems, monopolizing water, and other available resources, or having allelopathic tendencies (producing chemicals that prevent other plants from being able to grow nearby). These invasive plants thrive in their new environments and destroy the natural areas where they settle. Because of their resiliency, removing them can sometimes be a challenge, but if you stay on top of it and plant native alternatives, you'll be able to help your entire region starting at home.

The USDA and different states have their own lists of noxious weeds that should be removed or not planted because of their harmful impacts. Check with your state's extension office for a list of undesirable plants you should be on the lookout for in your area.

Fortunately, there are many native or localized plants that you can substitute in your home landscape. While these plants might need water and attention during the first season or two, many are extremely low maintenance after they become established. When it is time to create your dream landscape, take the time to do research and find the perfect native plant alternatives that are attractive and offer valuable habitats for pollinators and birds. Visit your local nursery to see available options or order plants online. Plant those beneficial ecosystem additions whenever possible to help rebuild and strengthen your natural environment.

Replace invasive heavenly bamboo with black chokeberry, shown here, for a similar look that keeps your garden healthy.

# Plants to Avoid in the Home Landscape

The following plants are either considered invasive species or have invasive tendencies and should be removed or avoided whenever possible in the home landscape. Consider using a native plant as a replacement.

- *Acanthus mollis* (BEAR'S BREECHES)
- *Acer ginnala* (AMUR MAPLE)
- *Ailanthus altissima* (TREE-OF-HEAVEN)
- *Ajuga reptans* (AJUGA)
- *Akebia quinate* (AKEBIA)
- *Amorpha fruticose* (INDIGO BUSH)
- *Buddleia davidii* (BUTTERFLY BUSH)
- *Cortaderia selloana* 'Pumila' (DWARF PAMPAS GRASS)
- *Cyperus alternifolius* (UMBRELLA SEDGE)
- *Cytisus scoparius* (SCOTCH BROOM)
- *Daphne laureola* (SPURGE LAUREL)
- *Fallopia sachalinensis* (KNOTWEED)
- *Galium odoratum* (SWEET WOODRUFF)
- *Hypericum (ST.-JOHN'S-WORT)*
- *Lamium maculatum* 'Pink Pewter' (LAMIUM)
- *Liriope muscari* 'Big Blue' (LILYTURF)
- *Lonicera japonica* 'Halliana' (HALL'S JAPANESE HONEY-SUCKLE)
- *Nandina domestica* (HEAVENLY BAMBOO)
- *Pennisetum (FOUNTAIN* GRASS)
- *Phyllostachys aurea* (GOLDEN BAMBOO)
- *Phytolacca americana* (POKEWEED)
- *Prunus laurocerasus* (CHERRY LAUREL)
- *Rubus bifrons* (HIMALAYAN BLACKBERRY)
- *Verbena bonariensis* (VERBENA)
- *Wisteria sinensis* (CHINESE WISTERIA)

*Buddleia davidii*
BUTTERFLY BUSH

*Galium odoratum,*
SWEET WOODRUFF

*Nandina domestica*
'Wood's Dwarf'
heavenly bamboo

### *Abelia* x *grandiflora* 'Edward Goucher'

'EDWARD GOUCHER' ABELIA. A dependable semi-evergreen shrub that bears countless small rosy pink-purple flowers in the summer and attracts butterflies. The sepals, small leaflike structures below the flower, turn copper in late summer through fall and are very showy even after the flowers have dropped. Lustrous pointed leaves are bronzy green in spring, dark-green in summer, and purple-bronze in winter. This cultivar grows 3 to 5 ft. tall. It needs full or partial sun and is drought tolerant. To keep the plants compact, cut new shoots in half in summer. Then each year in late winter to early spring cut a third of the old stems close to the ground. **Hardy to Zone 6.** Pages: 51, 71, 78.

### *Acer circinatum*

VINE MAPLE. This Northwest-native can be a large, spreading, bushy, multistemmed deciduous shrub or a small single-stemmed tree growing up to 30 ft. tall. Leaves are green in summer and turn yellow, red, and orange in fall. Grows in full sun to shade. Plants in sunnier spots have more intense fall color. Tolerant of a wide range of soils, vine maples thrive in moist areas. Can be shaped as a large multitrunked shrub or tree. **Hardy to Zone 5.** Pages: 24, 30, 96.

### *Acer davidii*

STRIPEBARK MAPLE. A deciduous tree with a rather narrow habit, reaching 20 to 30 ft. tall. Showy chainlike clusters of greenish-yellow flowers in spring are followed by chains of small winged seeds that drop in summer. Fall color is yellow, red, and orange. The bark, especially showy in winter, is green with obvious white striping. Prefers partial shade. Carefree. **Hardy to Zone 5.** Pages: 44, *45*.

### *Acer palmatum*

JAPANESE MAPLE. A small- to medium-size deciduous tree with delicate-looking serrated leaves. There are many kinds with leaves that are green, bronze, or red in summer. All are colorful in fall. Plants are sold as seed-grown or as named cultivars. Seed-grown plants often grow faster. Named cultivars are more expensive but have more dependable traits. 'Bloodgood' (pp. 102, *105*) grows to 20 ft. tall and stays dark red spring through fall. Coralbark maple (*A. p.* 'Sango Kaku', pp. 62, *62*) grows 15 ft. or taller and has foliage that is reddish in spring, light-green in summer, and yellow in fall. Twigs turn bright coral-red in winter and early spring. Red laceleaf Japanese maple (*A. p.* 'Dissectum Atropurpureum', pp. 61, *62*) is a short spreading tree with deeply cut red leaves. Mature height varies from 3 to 8 ft. Japanese maples grow slower than some trees, so buy the biggest tree you can afford. Plants are sold balled-and-burlapped or in containers. All grow best in full sun to partial shade and in rich, moist soil covered with mulch. Prune to preserve the tree's natural shape. **Hardy to Zones 5–8.** Pages: 42, 81.

*Abelia* x *grandiflora* 'Edward Goucher' ABELIA

*Acer circinatum* VINE MAPLE

### Achillea

YARROW. Long-blooming perennials with flat clusters of small flowers on stiff stalks 2 to 3 ft. tall and
finely divided gray-green leaves that have a pungent aroma. 'Appleblossom' (p. 92) has pink flowers. 'Moonshine' (p. 98) has lemon-yellow flowers.
All need full sun. Cut off old flower stalks when the
blossoms fade. Divide every few years in spring or
fall. **Hardy to Zone 3.**

### Acorus gramineus 'Variegatus'

VARIEGATED SWEET FLAG. A perennial grasslike plant
that grows 1 ft. tall and spreads by rhizomes. Looks
good near water. Leaves are striped creamy white
and green. Flowers bloom in midsummer but are
inconspicuous. Prefers constantly moist soil in full
or partial shade but will adapt to drier, fertile soils.
**Hardy to Zone 6.** Page: 69.

### Amelanchier x grandiflora 'Autumn Brilliance'

'AUTUMN BRILLIANCE' SERVICEBERRY. A small deciduous tree up to 25 ft. tall. Masses of white flowers
in early spring are followed by blue or purplish
summer berries loved by birds, and bright-red-
orange fall foliage. Smooth gray bark adds winter
interest. Full or partial sun. **These serviceber-
ries are very hardy (to at least Zone 4) and
are best adapted to the Pacific Northwest
and high elevation areas of the West.** Pages:
33, 110.

### Anemone x hybrida

'JAPANESE ANEMONE'. A perennial with small daisylike flowers and large, soft-textured, dark-green
leaves. Blooms for several weeks in late summer
into fall. Needs partial shade and rich, moist soil.
Plants grow 3 to 4 ft. tall and spread at least as
wide. **Hardy to Zone 4.** Page: 107.

### Aquilegia

COLUMBINE. Delicate flowering perennials with
spurred flowers in many single and multicolored
shades. Plants bloom in spring and early summer
and form neat mounds of blue-green, scalloped
leaves. Flower stalks range from 12 to 48 in. tall.
The Dragonfly hybrids (p. 98) have strong stems
and large flowers with long spurs. Columbines
grow best in light shade but can take full sun.
Carefree, they are short-lived but self-seed easily.
**Hardy to Zone 3.** Pages: 28, **31.**

*Acorus gramineus* 'Variegatus'
VARIEGATED SWEET FLAG

*Acer palmatum*
JAPANESE MAPLE

*Achillea* 'Moonshine'
YARROW

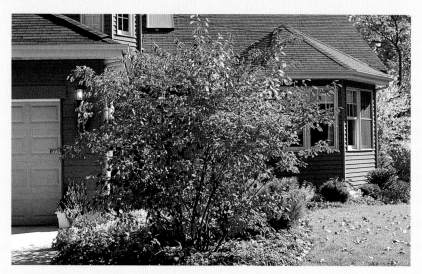

*Amelanchier* x *grandiflora*
'Autumn Brilliance'
SERVICEBERRY

### Arbutus

ARBUTUS. Striking evergreen trees with shiny red to orange bark and small, bell-shaped flowers followed by red fruits. Leaves are shiny green. 'Marina' (p. 107) can grow to 40 ft. but is usually smaller, with larger leaves and pinkish flowers in fall. Plant in full sun or partial shade and well-drained soil. **Hardy to Zone 7.**

### Arbutus unedo 'Compacta'

COMPACT STRAWBERRY TREE. Evergreen shrub with multiple trunks, shiny green leaves, and peeling bark. White bell-shaped flowers bloom in fall around the time the previous year's fruit is turning orange-red. Prefers well-drained soil in sun or shade. Prune only to expose the beautiful bark. **Hardy to Zone 7.** Page: 28.

*Arctostaphylos uva-ursi*
'Massachusetts'
KINNIKINNICK

### Arctostaphylos uva-ursi 'Massachusetts'

'MASSACHUSETTS' KINNIKINNICK. One of a group of native evergreen ground covers with shiny brown bark and deep-green foliage. Small white to pink spring flowers produce berries that are red in the fall. This cultivar is an excellent ground cover less than a foot tall and spreading to 6 ft. wide. Plant in full sun or part shade. **Hardiness varies.** Pages: 17, 61, 83.

### Armeria maritima 'Alba'

'ALBA' THRIFT. A perennial that forms a tuft of narrow evergreen leaves and bears spherical white flower heads on stiff stalks up to 1 ft. tall. Blooms generously in spring, with scattered blossoms in summer and fall. Needs full sun and well-drained soil. Looks best with occasional water. **Hardy to Zone 4.** Pages: 98, *100*.

### Aronia arbutifolia

RED CHOKEBERRY. A multi-stemmed shrub that grows 5 to 12 ft. tall and 4 to 8 ft. wide. In late spring, small white flowers bloom heavily. In fall, the flowers become clusters of bright-red fruits. Glossy green leaves turn orange and red in fall. Can tolerate a wide variety of soils if it's well-drained. Grows in full sun or part shade, but there are more flowers and vibrant red leaves in fall in full sun. Very popular with native pollinators. A. melanocarpa, black chokeberry, (pp. 21, 28, *31*, 36, *39*, 95) is smaller and typically tops out at 1 to 2 ft. tall and wide. Dark-green leaves turn bright red in the fall. Mid-spring, white flowers appear at the end of the branches and drop in summer for black-purple berries that last until fall. It can grow in almost any landscape in full sun, part shade, or full shade. Tolerates most soil types and is heat and drought tolerant. **Hardy to Zone 4.** Pages: 23, 27, 44, *45*, 53, 67, 89, 96.

### Artemisia

ARTEMISIA. Shrubby perennials, woody at the base, with fragrant, gray-green, finely divided leaves. Beautiful accent plants. They rarely flower. A. 'Powis Castle' (pp. 33, *35*, 92, 107) forms a dome-shaped mound of deeply cut silver foliage 2 to 3 ft. tall and 3 to 6 ft. wide. A. *ludoviciana* 'Silver King' (pp. 71, *73*) has smaller, lance-shaped, woolly silver-gray leaves that turn red in the fall. Plant in full sun. Will tolerate dry soil but grows faster with watering. **Hardiness varies but generally widely adapted.**

## Aster

ASTER. Carefree clump-forming perennials that bear daisylike flowers from summer through fall, most having a vibrantly colored ring of rays surrounding a yellow or orange center. Frikart's aster (*A. x frikartii* 'Monch', pp. 42), grows 2 to 3 ft. tall and bears light-purple flowers. *A. x f.* 'Monch' (pp. 51, 88, 103) has lavender-blue flowers. New England aster (*A. novae-angliae*, pp. 103, **105**) bears large sprays of pink, purple, or violet flowers. Asters thrive in full sun and well-drained soil and are drought tolerant. Prune to the ground in early spring. Cut new stems back by one-third in late spring to keep plants from getting floppy. Divide every few years in early spring.

## Astilbe

ASTILBE. Among the best perennials for shady or partly shady sites. In early to midsummer, fluffy plumes of tiny flowers stand high above glossy compound leaves. Foliage is attractive all season. There are many hybrids that grow from 6 to 60 in. tall and bear white, pale-pink, rose, purple, or deep-red flowers (pp. 41, 45, **45**). *A. x arendsii* 'Cattleya' (p. 49), reaching 3 ft. tall, has large open crimson-pink flowers. *A. x japonica* 'Peach Blossom' (pp. 69, **69**) grows about 2 ft. tall and has peach-pink flowers. All astilbes prefer rich, moist, well-drained soil. Grow in full or partial shade, or in full sun if you can water them regularly. **Generally hardy to Zones 3 or 4 but are short lived in areas with hot dry summers.**

## Aucuba japonica 'Variegata'

GOLD DUST AUCUBA. An evergreen shrub with thick, erect stems. Grows 6 to 10 ft. tall and at least 5 ft. wide. Large, toothed, leathery leaves are dark-green, speckled with yellow dots. Small maroon flowers bloom in early spring. Female plants bear cherry red berries if there's a male plant nearby. One of the best shrubs for dark shady sites. **Hardy to Zone 6.** Pages: 45, **45**.

## Bergenia cordifolia 'Bressingham White'

'BRESSINGHAM WHITE' BERGENIA. A perennial with large, thick, glossy leaves that are green in summer and turn garnet in winter. Clusters of white flowers show above the foliage for a few weeks in late spring. Forms a clump about 1 ft. tall and 2 ft. wide. Prefers partial shade and moist soil but tolerates sun and garden soil. **Hardy to Zone 3.** Pages: **56**, 57.

## Betula nigra

RIVER BIRCH. A deciduous tree with beige, tan, or coppery bark that peels loose and curls back. The leaves are glossy green all summer and turn tan or gold in the fall. Grows 1 to 2 ft. a year, reaching 60 ft. tall and almost that wide when mature. Needs full sun. Prefers moist soil but adapts to drier sites. Page: 65.

## Bignonia capreolata

CROSSVINE. A fast-growing, vigorous evergreen vine that grows up to 20 ft. tall and wide. Stunning trumpetlike reddish-orange flowers with yellow throats bloom throughout the spring and summer and the dark-green foliage makes it an attractive plant year-round. Tendrils make it an excellent cover for walls, trellises, and fences. Requires little care or water. **Hardy to Zone 6**. Pages: 91, **91**.

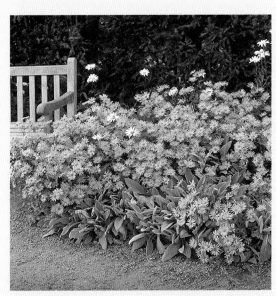

*Aster x frikartii* 'Monch'
FRIKART'S ASTER

*Aster x frikartii*
FRIKART'S ASTER

## Recommended bulbs

### Crocus, Crocus
Cup-shaped flowers on 4-in. stalks in April. Available in white, yellow, lilac, and purple. Plant in masses of 15 to 20 bulbs for a showy display. Plant bulbs 3 in. deep, 3 in. apart. Pages: 37, **39**.

### Hyacinthus, Hyacinth
Very fragrant bell-shaped flowers on a spike rising from a cluster of narrow bright-green leaves. Colors range from white to pink, red, or lavender. Plant 4 to 6 in. deep and 6 in. apart in the fall. Page: **111**.

### Narcissus, Daffodils and jonquils
Bright-yellow, white, or bicolor flowers, often-fragrant, on stalks 6 to 24 in. tall. Different kinds bloom in sequence from early February through early May.

Leaves die down in July. Plant bulbs 4 to 6 in. deep, 4 to 6 in. apart, depending on their size. Very reliable, carefree, and long-lived. Use dwarf daffodils such as 'February Gold' and 'Tête à Tête' close to the house because after they bloom their short leaves are less conspicuous. Use larger daffodils such as 'King Alfred' and 'Mt. Hood' for plantings viewed from a distance. Most narcissus naturalize well. Pages: 37, 38, 111.

### Tulipa, Tulip
Large flowers in bright or pastel shades of all colors but blue, held on stalks 6 to 20 in. tall. Different kinds bloom between February and April. Plant bulbs 4 to 6 in. deep, 4 to 6 in. apart. For the best display, every fall divide and replant existing bulbs, add new ones, and fertilize. Pages: 23, **24**.

### Bulbs
The bulbs recommended in this book are all perennials that bloom in late winter, spring, or early summer. After they flower, their leaves continue growing until sometime in summer, when they gradually turn yellow and die down to the ground. Buy bulbs from a garden center or catalog in late summer or fall. Plant them promptly in a sunny or partly sunny bed with well-prepared, well-drained soil. As a rule, plant bulbs at a depth two to three times the bulb's height. In subsequent years, you need only pick off the flowers after they fade and remove (or ignore, if you choose) the old leaves after they turn yellow in summer. Most bulbs can be divided every few years if you want to grow them elsewhere. Dig them as the foliage is turning yellow; shake or pull them apart; and replant them right away. For more information on specific bulbs, see the box, left.

### Calamagrostis × acutiflora 'Karl Foerster'
'KARL FOERSTER' FEATHER REED GRASS. A showy, cool season grass with 2- to 3-ft. tall foliage and stalks with red-bronze feathery heads that reach 6 ft. tall midsummer. Stalks turn tan and stay standing fall through winter. Thrives in full sun or part shade, especially in hot climates. Prefers rich, well-drained moist soil but can tolerate clay soils. Heat and drought tolerant once established. Growth starts in spring, so cut to the ground in late winter to avoid damaging new growth. Divide clumps in fall or spring. Pages: 48, **49**.

### Calluna vulgaris
SCOTCH HEATHER. An evergreen shrub that is often confused with heath. Ranging from a few inches to 2 ft. tall, its many ascending branches bear tiny scalelike leaves. Depending on cultivar, summer and winter foliage can be colorful. Small bell-shaped flowers bloom on new wood in summer. Because the dried flowers remain on the stems, heathers can appear to be in bloom through the winter. 'Robert Chapman' (pp. 83, **84**) grows to 18 in. tall, has bright-red new growth in winter, and bears purple flowers in summer. 'Silver Knight' (p. 75) grows to 18 in. and bears mauve-pink flowers and silvery gray foliage. Heathers prefer full sun to partial shade and moist, well-drained acidic soil with lots of organic matter. To ensure that you get plants with the winter foliage color you want, shop for plants in winter. Shear in early spring to encourage new growth. **Hardy to Zone 4.** Pages: 95, **97**.

*Camellia sasanqua*
SASANQUA CAMELLIA

*Camellia sasanqua* 'Cleopatra'
'CLEOPATRA' CAMELLIA

## Camellia

CAMELLIA. Evergreen shrubs with glossy foliage and large, lovely white, pink, or rose flowers. There are hundreds of cultivars, differing mostly in flower color, size, and form (single or double) as well as in overall plant habit, mature size, and hardiness. Camellias are also excellent container plants; ask at your nursery for reliable varieties. Japanese camellia (*C. japonica*, pp. 45, **45**) is the most popular camellia, usually ranging in height from 6 to 12 ft. and blooming in late winter to spring. Sasanqua camellias (*C. sasanqua*, pp. 48, 53, 56) are generally smaller plants that range in height from 2 to 3 ft. upward to 10 ft. They bloom in late fall and winter. Lower growers are useful as understory plants. Favorite varieties include 'Setsugekka' (pp. **24**, 25), which has white flowers borne on an upright plant. 'Apple Blossom' (pp. 35, **35**) is a spreading plant with single white flowers that are blushed with pink. 'Cleopatra' (p. 68) forms a more upright, compact plant and bears rose-pink flowers. Camellias need moist, well-drained, acid soil with a layer of mulch and a site that is shaded from midday sun. If needed, prune and fertilize immediately after flowering. **Hardy to Zone 7.**

## Campanula

BELLFLOWER. A large group of useful flowering perennials (a few are annuals) that vary in plant habit and flower form. Plant in flower beds, rock gardens, or containers. Spreading types are useful as small-scale ground covers. The ones used in our designs bloom for many weeks in the summer. Carpathian bellflower (*C. carpatica*, pp. 46, 110) is a short, compact perennial, about 1 ft. tall and wide, with light-blue blooms. 'Blue Clips' (pp. 105, **105**) has sky-blue flowers and medium-green foliage. 'Birch Hybrid' (pp. 79, **81**, 98) is a very low, spreading plant with abundant violet-blue, open bell-shaped flowers. Campanulas grow best in partial shade but can take full sun. Water regularly. Cut back after bloom. Divide as necessary in fall or early spring. **Hardy to Zones 4–8.**

## Carex buchananii

FOX RED CURLY SEDGE. A grasslike plant that grows in clumps 2 to 3 ft. tall. Leaves curl at the tip and keep their striking reddish-bronze color all year, providing texture and color contrast in the garden through the seasons. Summer flowers are insignificant. Grow in full sun or partial shade. Unlike some sedges, it does well in hot sun and well-drained soil. Self-sows to form a patch. **Hardy to Zone 5.** Pages: 83, **84**.

## Caryopteris x *clandonensis*

BLUEBEARD. A small deciduous shrub that blooms for weeks in late summer. Bright- or dark-blue flowers contrast with the soft gray-green foliage and gray-green stems. 'Blue Mist' bears flowers that are powdery blue. 'Dark Knight' has dark-blue flowers among silvery gray foliage. Plants need full sun and well-drained soil and thrive in a warm, dry spot. Cut bluebeard close to the ground each spring for compact growth and maximum bloom. Will grow 2 to 3 ft. wide by fall. Pages: 102, **105**.

## Ceanothus 'Victoria'

'VICTORIA' WILD LILAC, CEANOTHUS. An evergreen shrub useful in dry landscapes, especially on slopes. Leaves are small, dark-green, shiny, and crinkly. Blooms in spring with a profusion of small, deep-blue flowers at branch ends. Plant in full sun and well-drained soil. No need to water once established. Grows 5 ft. or more tall and wide. **Hardy to Zone 7 and not adapted to desert climates.** Pages: 18, 33, 46, 66, 67.

## Chamaecyparis obtusa 'Nana Gracilis'

'NANA GRACILIS' DWARF HINOKI CYPRESS. A slow-growing conifer with graceful, glossy, emerald-green foliage. Its habit is naturally open and sculpted with short sprays of scalelike foliage. No pruning necessary. Prefers full to partial sun and moist, well-drained soil. Buy the largest plant you can afford. It may someday reach 8 ft. or taller and spread 3 to 4 ft. wide. **Hardy to Zone 4.** Pages: 23, 42, 48.

## Choisya ternata

MEXICAN ORANGE. An evergreen shrub reaching 8 ft. tall with glossy leaves that are very aromatic in the hot sun. Blooms in the spring and sporadically throughout the summer with terminal white clusters of flowers that smell somewhat like an orange-tree blossom. Plant in full sun to partial shade. It is not picky about soil conditions but will not tolerate standing water on its roots. Prune after flowering to encourage a rebloom. May die back in cold winters but will usually resprout from the roots. **Hardy to Zone 7.** Pages: 65, 68, 88.

*Chamaecyparis obtusa* 'Nana Gracilis' DWARF HINOKI CYPRESS

*Choisya ternata* MEXICAN ORANGE

*Ceanothus* 'Victoria' 'VICTORIA' WILD LILAC

*Coreopsis verticillata*
'Moonbeam'

## Chrysanthemum x morifolium

FLORIST'S CHRYSANTHEMUM. An old-time favorite perennial offering hundreds of cultivars, some growing 3 to 4 ft. tall and blooming in many colors from late summer into fall. Attractive dark-green lobed leaves die back each winter. All bloom best in full sun and well-drained soil. Cut old stems to the ground in early spring. To keep the plant short and less floppy when it blooms, cut new growth in half one or two times before July. **Hardiness varies.** Pages: 103, **105**.

## Cistus x pulverulentus 'Sunset'

'SUNSET' ROCK ROSE. A compact evergreen shrub reaching 2 to 3 ft. tall and 3 to 8 ft. wide, with interesting wavy gray-green leaves. Bears many magenta-pink flowers for a long period in summer. Plant in full sun and well-drained soil. Very little pruning is needed. **Hardy to Zone 8.** Page: 67.

## Clematis

CLEMATIS. Deciduous or evergreen vines that climb or sprawl, forming a tangle of leafy stems adorned with masses of flowers, which can be tiny or large. See the box below for information on specific kinds. Plant in partial or full sun; be sure to mulch to keep the roots cool. Because Northwest soils are acidic, add a cup or so of ground limestone to the planting area and mix it thoroughly into the soil. Dig a planting hole deep enough to allow you to cover the root-ball and base of the stem with about 2 in. of soil. Cut the stem back to the lowest set of healthy leaves to encourage the plant to branch near the base. Clematis climbs by twining petioles. Guide the new stems toward a trellis, wire, or other support, and secure them with twist-ties or other fasteners. Prune to control size. Some clematis bloom on old growth, some on new. An easy rule of thumb is to prune right after flowering. It takes most clematis a few years to cover a fence or trellis 6 to 8 ft. tall. Many can eventually climb 10 to 15 ft. **Hardiness varies.**

# Recommended clematis

### Clematis armandii, Evergreen clematis

In early spring, displays fragrant white flowers against glossy evergreen leaves. Climbs 15 to 20 ft. Prune after bloom. Pages: 95, **97**.

### Clematis hybrids

Include many mostly deciduous cultivars. Large-flowered types produce blooms from 3 to 8 in. across. 'Comtesse de Bouchaud' (p. 88) bears rosy pink flowers in summer. 'Elsa Spath' (pp. 67, **69**) has mauve-blue flowers from late spring into fall. 'The President' (pp. 98, **100**) bears deep violet-blue flowers in early summer. Small-flowered types (p. 42) bloom from summer to late autumn, producing flowers in sizes from less than 1 in. to 4 in. across. Early-flowering types may bloom on last year's growth, then again later in the season on new growth. Late-flowering types bloom on new growth. Page: 54.

### C. tangutica, Golden clematis

Small yellow flowers bloom throughout the summer on this deciduous vine, followed by fluffy, silvery seed heads that last throughout fall and into winter. Prune in early spring, removing older shoots and cutting others back by one-third. Pages: 78, **78**.

*Clematis x jackmanii*
'Comtesse de Bouchaud'

*Clematis vitacella* 'Polish Spirit'

## Coreopsis verticillata 'Moonbeam'

'MOONBEAM' COREOPSIS. Long-blooming perennial that bears hundreds of small, lemon-yellow daisylike blossoms from summer to fall. The dark-green leaves are short and threadlike. Spreads by rhizomes to form a patch 1 to 3 ft. wide and tall. Prefers full sun. Remove spent flower heads to extend bloom. Cut back to a few inches above ground in fall or early spring. **Hardy to Zone 3.** Pages: 51, 54, **56**.

*Cornus alba*
'Elegantissima'
VARIEGATED
SIBERIAN DOGWOOD

*Cornus canadensis*
BUNCHBERRY

*Corylopsis pauciflora*
WINTER HAZEL

*Cotinus coggygria*
'Royal Purple'
'ROYAL PURPLE' SMOKE TREE

*Cotoneaster dammeri*
BEARBERRY COTONEASTER

*Cotoneaster horizontalis*
ROCKSPRAY COTONEASTER

## *Cornus alba* 'Elegantissima'

VARIEGATED SIBERIAN DOGWOOD. A deciduous shrub with four-season interest. It has bright-red stems in winter, white flowers in spring, variegated green-and-white leaves from spring through fall, and white berries in late summer. Forms a vase-shaped clump 6 to 8 ft. tall with many erect or arching stems. Plant in full sun or partial shade. Does well in most soils and thrives in soils that stay moist. Cut all the stems down close to the ground every few years (or every year, if you prefer) in early spring. After a few weeks, the plant will send up vigorous new shoots. In fall, these young shoots sport brightly colored bark. **Hardy to Zone 2.** Pages: 83, 95.

## *Cornus canadensis*

BUNCHBERRY. A semievergreen to deciduous perennial that spreads by rhizomes to form a mass of 4- to 9-in.-tall stems topped with whorls of shiny dark-green leaves. Blooms from late spring into summer with small flowers that look just like dogwood blossoms. Foliage turns red in fall. A Northwest-native, it grows best in shade in soil amended with generous amounts of organic matter. Can be difficult to establish but very hardy and drought tolerant thereafter. Pages: 31, 97.

## *Corylopsis pauciflora*

WINTER HAZEL. A deciduous shrub known for its early-spring show of pendulous, primrose-yellow flower clusters blooming on bare wood. New leaves start bronze and turn green. Grows to 6 ft. tall and has a dense and spreading habit. Blooms best in full sun to partial shade. Prune right after flowering. **Hardy to Zone 6.** Pages: 72, 76, 83.

## *Corylus avellana* 'Contorta'

HARRY LAUDER'S WALKING STICK. A deciduous shrub or small tree with stems twisted and contorted in interesting swirls. Named after a vaudeville star who carried a crooked cane on stage. The green leaves, also a bit contorted, turn yellow in fall. Blooms on bare wood in late winter. Male flowers are yellow and pendulous; female flowers are tiny, red, and star shaped, and after pollination produce a small nut that squirrels love. Typically grows to 10 ft. Plant in full sun to partial shade. Prune after flowering to remove suckers and to keep the tree open. Pages: 72, 78, *81*.

## *Cotinus coggygria* 'Royal Purple'

'ROYAL PURPLE' SMOKE TREE. A deciduous shrub with rounded leaves that open red and turn dark-purple for the summer. Following the blooms of small yellow flowers are fluffy hairs that start pink and turn into a purplish-pink that look like smoke rising from the foliage. Grows about 10 ft. tall and wide if unpruned, or you can prune it hard every year to have a smaller shrub with larger leaves—a very dramatic specimen. Needs full sun for good color; turns green if shaded. Pages: 60, 71, 75.

## *Cotoneaster dammeri*

BEARBERRY COTONEASTER. An evergreen ground cover with small white flowers in spring, followed by red berries that hold on through winter. Quickly forms a solid mass. Grows about 1 ft. tall and 6 ft. wide. Plant in full sun to partial shade. Needs very little watering once established. No pruning necessary. Page: 19.

*Crocosmia* 'Lucifer'
CROCOSMIA

*Cryptomeria japonica*
'Elegans'
PLUME CEDAR

*Daphne odora*
'Aureomarginata'
VARIEGATED WINTER DAPHNE

*Echinacea purpurea* PURPLE CONEFLOWER

### Cotoneaster horizontalis

ROCKSPRAY COTONEASTER. A deciduous shrub with branches arrayed in layered sprays. Blooms in the spring with white-tinged pink flowers. Fruit follows, turning red in the fall. Plant in full sun or partial shade. Grows 2 to 3 ft. tall and 5 ft. or more wide. Page: 18.

### Cotoneaster salicifolius 'Repens'

CREEPING WILLOWLEAF COTONEASTER. A shrub often used as ground cover, with evergreen leaves that turn purple in cold weather, white flowers in spring, and red berries in fall. Needs full sun. Page: 65.

### Crocosmia 'Lucifer'

'LUCIFER' CROCOSMIA. A perennial with long sword-like leaves. Red-orange flowers bloom from summer into fall. Hummingbirds love them. Takes full sun to partial shade and needs little water once established. Grows to 4 ft. **Hardy to Zone 6.** Pages: 19, 23, 33.

### Cryptomeria japonica 'Elegans'

PLUME CEDAR. A slow-growing conifer that forms a cone-shaped tree with soft needlelike foliage that is blue-green in summer and bronzy red in winter. The cinnamon-colored bark peels off in strips. Grows to 30 ft. tall. If height will eventually be a problem, 'Elegans Compacta' grows only 6 to 12 ft. tall. Both cultivars need full sun. **Hardy to Zone 6.** Pages: 23, 83.

### Daphne odora 'Aureomarginata'

VARIEGATED WINTER DAPHNE. A compact evergreen shrub with glossy leaves that have an irregular thin gold stripe around the edges. In late winter and early spring, purple buds open into small rose-tinged white flower clusters that have a powerful sweet fragrance. Grows 4 ft. tall and wide. Plant in a location with morning sun, afternoon shade, and well-drained soil. Prune after flowering if desired. **Hardy to Zone 7.** Pages: 25, 56, 61, 73, 90.

### Dianthus 'Bath's Pink'

'BATHS' PINK' DIANTHUS. This low-growing perennial forms a dense, grassy mat of gray-green foliage 6 to 12 in. tall and 1 to 2 ft. wide. Fragrant flowers like tiny pink carnations carpet the plant during the spring. Needs full sun and well-drained soil. Water only when the soil is dry. Pages: 58, 92.

### Dianthus plumarius

COTTAGE PINK. Low-growing perennial with very fragrant flowers that look like small carnations. They bloom in shades of pink and white from late spring into summer. The grassy, blue-green, evergreen foliage forms a dense mat about 6 to 24 in. high and 1 to 2 ft. wide. Flower stalks are about 1 ft. tall. Needs full sun and well-drained soil. **Hardy to Zone 4.** Page: 21.

### Doronicum orientale 'Magnificum'

'MAGNIFICUM' LEOPARD'S BANE. A perennial that forms a mound of heart-shaped green leaves with bright-yellow daisylike flowers rising on long stems in the spring. Plant in partial shade in well-drained soil amended with organic matter. Page: 111, *111*.

### Echinacea purpurea

PURPLE CONEFLOWER. A summer-blooming perennial that attracts bees and butterflies. Large daisylike blossoms with large center "cones" are held high on stiff branching stalks above a basal mound of dark-green foliage. Grows about 3 to 4 ft. tall and 2 ft. wide. Normally this plant has pink-purple flowers, but there are a few cultivars with white flowers. 'Bright Star' (p. 88) has dark-pink flower heads and grows about 30 in. tall. 'Magnus' (pp. 19, 67, 81) bears large purple flowers with orange cones. Plants need full sun. **Hardy to Zone 3.**

### Enkianthus campanulatus

REDVEIN ENKIANTHUS. Clusters of creamy flowers with reddish-pink streaks hang bell-like beneath the leaves in late spring. Foliage turns a brilliant orange-red in the fall. Plant in full sun or partial shade. Likes well-drained soil amended with compost and then mulched. Grows 10 ft. or more in 10 years. **Hardy to Zone 5.** Pages: 53, 84, 90.

*Enkianthus campanulatus*
REDVEIN ENKIANTHUS

*Epimedium pinnatum*
'Colchicum'
BARRENWORT

## Epimedium

BISHOP'S HAT. A long-lived perennial with heart-shaped foliage. Excellent ground cover under trees or shrubs. Leaves change from burgundy to green to maroon over the course of the summer. Small flowers bloom in spring on thin stems above the foliage in red, pink, yellow, or white. Bishop's hat, *E. grandiflorum* (pp. 45, 97), bears sprays of small pale-pink or white flowers in early spring. Slowly forms a patch about 1 ft. tall and up to several feet wide. A number of species and cultivars are known by the common name "barrenwort" (pp. **56**, 57). *E.* x *perralchicum* 'Fröhnleiten' (pp. 76, **77**) has long spiny leaflets and 1-in. yellow flowers. *E. pinnatum* subsp. 'Colchicum' (pp. 35, 53) is a shorter plant with less-spiny leaflets and yellow flowers. *E. grandiflorum* 'White Queen' (p. 91) has foliage with deep-red margins in early spring and small white flowers. *E.* x *versicolor* 'Sulphureum' (pp. **84**, 85) blooms dark yellow above many-leafleted compound leaves. All epimediums need partial or full shade. Provide regular water to get them started. Shear off all foliage to the ground in early spring to encourage a good show of flowers and new foliage. **Generally hardy to at least Zone 5.**

*Epimedium grandiflorum* BISHOP'S HAT

## Escallonia rubra 'Newport Dwarf'

'NEWPORT DWARF' ESCALLONIA. A compact evergreen shrub densely clothed in shiny dark-green leaves. In summer, small upright clusters of red flowers bloom at the ends of the branches. Prefers hot sun and well-drained soil. In cold winters, it may freeze to the ground but will usually resprout from the base. Needs very little pruning. Grows about 2 to 3 ft. tall. **Hardy to Zone 7.** Pages: 38, 54, 63.

## Euonymus fortunei

CREEPING EUONYMUS. A versatile small shrub or ground cover with glossy evergreen leaves. There are many fine cultivars. 'Emerald 'n Gold' (pp. 95, **97**) is very popular, with yellow-edged bright-green leaves that take on a pink tinge in the cold of winter. 'Silver Queen' (pp. 17, 35, 38) bears white-edged bright-green leaves that also turn pinkish in winter. Adapts to sun or shade and needs well-drained soil. Shear or prune at any time to control size or shape. **Generally hardy to at least Zone 6.**

## Erica carnea

HEATH. An evergreen shrub that grows about 1 ft. tall and spreads to form a mass of small needle-like leaves. Blooms profusely in winter and early spring, bearing small, urn-shaped, and long-lasting flowers. 'Springwood White' (p. 88) has white flowers. 'Springwood Pink' (pp. 61, **100**, 101) has pink. Heath does well in full sun or partial shade and well-drained soil with lots of organic matter. Space 18 in. apart for ground cover.

*Erica carnea*
HEATH

*Euonymus fortunei*
Emerald Gaity

# Recommended ferns

### Athyrium niponicum
### 'Pictum' Japanese painted fern
A colorful fern that forms rosettes of finely cut fronds marked in shades of green, silver, and maroon. They look almost iridescent. Deciduous, but can be evergreen when planted in spots where conditions are mild in winter. Grows about 1 ft. tall, 2 ft. wide. **Hardy to Zone 4.** Pages: 31, 53, 73, 77, 85, 91.

### Dryopteris x complexa
### 'Robust' male fern
A thick, lush evergreen fern growing over 3 ft. tall. Divided fronds with slightly arched tips give it a lacy look. Once established it is very drought tolerant. **Hardy to Zone 5.** Page: 35.

### Dryopteris filix-mas 'Barnesii'
### Barnes' narrow male fern
A narrowly upright semievergreen fern with slightly ruffled pinnules (small leaflets). Can reach over 3 ft. tall over time. Does best in well-drained soil. **Hardy to Zone 4.** Pages: 23, 49, 76, 109.

### Polystichum munitum
### Sword fern
A Northwest-native fern with shiny, 2- to 4-ft.-long evergreen fronds. One of the most dependable ferns for shady areas, it will also tolerate quite a bit of sun. Needs little water once established. **Hardy to Zone 4.** Pages: 31, 91.

### Polystichum polyblepharum
### Tassel fern
An evergreen fern with stiff, glossy, finely divided fronds. Needs moist soil. Forms a clump about 2 ft. tall, 3 to 4 ft. wide. **Hardy to Zone 6.** Pages: 57, 73, 97.

### Polystichum setiferum
### Soft shield fern
An evergreen fern with soft, gray-green to green fronds that can form a dense crown. It grows 2 to 3 ft. wide and prefers morning sun. **Hardy to Zone 5.** Pages: 25, 45, 84.

*Athyrium niponicum* 'Pictum'
JAPANESE PAINTED FERN

*Polystichum munitum*
SWORD FERN

*Polystichum polyblepharum*
TASSEL FERN

*Polystichum setiferum*
SOFT SHIELD FERN

### Euonymus japonicus
### 'Microphyllus Variegatus'
VARIEGATED BOXLEAF JAPANESE EUONYMUS. Tough, dependable evergreen shrub with a compact habit and small shiny white-and-green leaves. Grows 1 to 2 ft. tall and wide. Plant in full sun and well-drained soil. Shear or prune at any time to control size or shape. **Generally hardy to at least Zone 6.** Pages: 51, **53**.

### Euphorbia polychroma
CUSHION SPURGE. Upright stems bear whorls of dark-green leaves, forming a dome-shaped clump 1 to 2 ft. tall and wide. From spring into summer, it bears long-lasting bright-yellow flowers. Leaves turn red in fall. Needs full sun or partial shade. Cut the stems back partway after bloom to keep the clump compact and tidy. **Hardy to Zone 9.** Pages: 46, 75, **77**.

### Ferns
Many ferns prefer shade, but some do well in partial shade or even full sun. They grow best in well-drained soil that's been amended with extra organic matter. If you want to keep the foliage very fresh and green, you can cut all the fronds off at the crown each spring before the new fiddle-heads start to unfurl. See the box at left for more information on specific ferns.

### Festuca ovina var. glauca
BLUE FESCUE GRASS. A neat, compact perennial that forms a dense tuft about 1 ft. tall and wide of very slender, blue-green leaves. Narrow flower spikes appear in early summer and soon turn tan. 'Elijah Blue' is one of several cultivars with especially blue-colored foliage. Mass-planted in small areas, it makes a handsome, fine-textured, clumpy display. Takes full sun or partial shade; can take some drought. For fresh foliage, cut the plant close to the ground in early spring. Pages: 98, **100**, 107.

### Forsythia x intermedia
FORSYTHIA. A large, fast-growing deciduous shrub whose arching limbs are covered with bright-yellow flowers for a few weeks in early spring, followed in summer by soft green foliage that turns purple before dropping in late fall. Typically grows 8 to 10 ft. tall, 10 to 12 ft. wide. Needs full or partial sun. Page: 65.

### Fragaria 'Pink Panda'

'PINK PANDA' ORNAMENTAL STRAWBERRY. A compact evergreen ground cover with pink flowers and small edible strawberry fruit in the spring. Dark-green three-toothed leaves turn red in winter. Grows fast, enjoys full sun, and tolerates any soil. Grows 6 in. tall. Pages: 36, **39**.

### Fuchsia

HARDY FUCHSIA. Evergreen and deciduous shrubs in a variety of flower colors, often with different-colored sepals and petals. The petals may be single or double (many ruffled layers). Hummingbirds are attracted to the single-petaled flowers because they can reach the nectar better. Fruits are purple and edible. The fuchsias selected for this book are hardy in the Northwest and may remain evergreen in mild winters. In cold winters they may lose their leaves or die back to the ground, but the crown will resprout. *F. magellanica* (pp. 62, **62**, 78) is an upright open shrub reaching 3 ft. tall that bears many small flowers with red sepals and purple petals all summer long. *F.* 'Riccarrtonii' (p. 101) is an upright, hardy shrub also reaching 3 ft. and has dark-green, bronzy leaves and flowers with rosy pink sepals and dark-purple petals. *F.* 'Maiden's Blush' (p. 68) has small pink flowers covering an upright shrub that grows 3 ft. tall. Fuchsias love partial shade but will do fine in full sun with some summer watering. **Hardy to Zone 9.**

### Garrya elliptica

SILK-TASSEL BUSH. A striking evergreen shrub or small tree that reaches about 10 ft. tall. Leaves are gray-green and wavy along the margins. Masses of long, slender, pendulous gray-green male catkins grace the tree in late winter. Plant in full sun and well-drained soil. Prune only to enhance the shape or open the center to air and light. Pages: 30, 42.

### Gaultheria procumbens

WINTERGREEN. A rhizomatous evergreen ground cover with upright stems and glossy green leaves that crowd together at the tips. Small white urn-shaped flowers appear in summer, followed by red fruit in fall and winter. Foliage turns red-and-purple in winter. Both the leaves and the fruit smell like wintergreen when crushed. Best when protected from the afternoon sun and mulched with organic matter. Grows 6 in. tall. Pages: 28, **31**.

### Gaultheria shallon

SALAL. A Northwest-native evergreen shrub often used as a ground cover. Its leathery leaves are used in floral arrangements. Bell-like clusters of pinkish-white flowers appear in the late spring, followed in the fall by blue-black edible fruit. Grows 6 ft. or more in the shade or 1 ft. in the sun. Spreads by underground stems and does best in soil amended with organic matter. Drought tolerant once established. No pruning necessary. Pages: 109, **111**.

### Gaura lindheimeri

GAURA. A perennial wildflower that forms a loose clump of graceful arching stems and bears pale-pink-and-white flowers from spring through fall. Needs full sun, well-drained soil, and just a little water. Cut to the ground in winter. Grows 2 to 4 ft. tall and wide. **Hardy to Zone 5.** Page: 107.

### Gelsemium sempervirens

CAROLINA JESSAMINE. Evergreen vine beloved for its extremely fragrant and showy display of small bell-shaped yellow flowers in late winter and early spring. The small lancelike leaves are neat and green all year. Needs full sun or partial sun. **Hardy to Zone 7.** Page: 27.

### Genista pilosa 'Vancouver Gold'

'VANCOUVER GOLD' SILKY LEAF WOADWAXEN. A low deciduous ground cover that forms a mat of green twiggy stems with tiny dark-green leaves. In late spring and early summer, a profusion of bright-yellow pealike flowers cover the entire mass. Likes full sun and tolerates drought once established. Needs very little care. **Hardy to Zone 5.** Pages: 33, 61, 78. 98.

*Garrya elliptica*
SILK-TASSEL BUSH

*Genista pilosa*
'Vancouver Gold'
SILKY LEAF WOADWAXEN

### Geranium

GERANIUM, CRANESBILL. Unlike the common geraniums that are grown as bedding plants and in pots, these are hardy perennials that form a compact or sprawling mound of attractive leaves with jagged edges. (See the box below for information on specific kinds.) They bloom in spring or early summer and sporadically until fall with clusters of flowers in various shades of pink, purple, blue-purple, and white. Plant in full sun or partial shade and well-drained soil. Cut off flower stalks when the blossoms fade. If plants look tattered or get floppy in midsummer, cut them back partway and they will bush out again. Otherwise wait until late fall or early spring and cut them to the ground.

## Recommended geraniums

### Geranium x cantabrigiense
A compact mass of light-green, lobed evergreen leaves bearing many light-purple flowers in the summer. Pages: 42, 53.

### G. 'Johnson's Blue'
Popular and dependable, it forms a large sprawling mound, about 1 ft. tall and 2 ft. wide, with medium-size leaves and blue-purple flowers from late spring to fall. **Hardy to Zone 4.** Pages: 54, 78, 105, 109.

*Geranium* 'Johnson's Blue'

### G. macrorrhizum
**Bigroot geranium**
A short, compact plant that forms bushy clumps of fragrant, light-green semievergreen foliage, with magenta or pink flowers in late spring. Makes a good ground cover for partial shade and dry soil. Grows up to 1 ft. tall, 18 to 24 in. wide. **Hardy to Zone 4.** Pages: 35, 45, 51, 76.

*Geranium macrorrhizum*
BIGROOT GERANIUM

### G. x riversleaianum
**'Mavis Simpson' geranium**
A sprawling plant with gray-green leaves and light-pink flowers in summer. **Hardy to Zone 6.** Pages: 67, 75, **77**.

*Geranium x riversleaianum*
'Mavis Simpson' GERANIUM

### Hamamelis mollis
CHINESE WITCH HAZEL. A slow-growing deciduous shrub or small tree that is known for its fragrant, straplike, fall- and winter-blooming yellow flowers. The branches have a slight zigzag appearance. The long gray-green leaves turn yellow in fall. Prefers full sun and well-drained soil but will bloom well in partial shade. Prune suckers and crossing branches after flowering. May grow to 15 ft. tall. Pages: 42, 94, 108.

### Hamelia patens
FIREBUSH. This colorful shrub can grow up to more than 10 ft. tall but usually grows 1 to 4 ft. tall and wide. Firebush bears red-orange tubular flowers from summer to frost against red-tinged leaves that turn maroon as cool temperatures set in. Hummingbirds adore this plant. Extremely heat tolerant, it also has very few pests. Cut to the ground after the first frost. In northern areas, mulch the crown heavily or consider growing it as a wonderful summer annual. **Hardy to Zone 9.** Page: 27.

### Helictotrichon sempervirens
BLUE OAT GRASS. A clump-forming perennial with thin, wiry, pale-blue evergreen leaves. Blooms sparsely, with thin flower spikes that turn beige or tan. Plant in full sun. Simply comb your fingers or a garden "scratching" tool through the clump to pull out any loose, dead leaves. Old clumps may die out in the middle; if so, divide them in fall or early spring. Grows 2 to 3 ft. tall and wide. Pages: 33, **35**, 75.

### Helleborus
HELLEBORE. A clump-forming evergreen perennial with dark leathery leaves and round flowers that bloom for many weeks in late winter and early spring. Christmas rose (*H. niger*, pp. 57, 97, **97**) has white flowers 3 to 4 in. wide that open some years as early as Christmas. Lenten rose (*H. orientalis*, pp. 25, 53, 56, 68, 77, 83, 91) has pink, purple, white, or greenish flowers 2 to 3 in. wide in early spring. Corsican hellebore (*H. argutifolius*, pp. 46, **49**) has sharp-toothed leaves and pale-green flowers in late winter. All need partial shade and rich, well-drained soil. Hellebores are slow-growing, but they self-sow, gradually spreading to form a patch. Once established, all are carefree and long-lived. Groom once a year by cutting off any dead leaves when the flower buds appear. Established clumps are typically about 18 in. tall, 18 to 24 in. wide. **Hardiness and adaptation varies.**

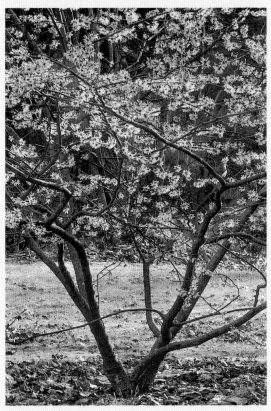

*Hamamelis mollis*
CHINESE WITCH HAZEL

*Helleborus*
HELLEBORE

*Hemerocallis* 'Stella de Oro'
DAYLILY

*Hemerocallis* 'Little Grapette'
DAYLILY

*Heuchera* 'Palace Purple'
HEUCHERA

## Hemerocallis

DAYLILY. One of the most reliable and popular perennials, with large lilylike flowers in summer, held above dense clumps or patches of grassy arching leaves. Most daylilies sold today are hybrids (pp. 65, 105) comprising thousands of named cultivars. Some are evergreen; others die back in winter. Some are low-growing; others have flower stalks reaching 5 ft. Flowers last only a day but are abundant. They come in many shades of white, yellow, orange, red, and purple. Plants bloom from several weeks to several months or more. Mix early-blooming, midseason, and late-blooming varieties to ensure months of color. 'Happy Returns' (yellow flowers; pp. 75, **77**) and 'Stella de Oro' (gold-orange flowers; pp. 21, 86, 88) bloom from early June until October and are compact plants 12 to 24 in. tall. 'Little Grapette' (rosy purple flowers; p. 17, 87) blooms in early summer and grows 2 ft. tall and wide. All 'Black Eyed Stella' (gold flowers with a dark reddish eye; p. 58) grows 1½ ft. tall and wide and blooms similarly to 'Stella de Oro'. All daylilies prefer full sun and well-drained soil. Water regularly during bloom. Pinch off spent flowers; cut off flower stalks after blooming is finished. Divide every few years in late summer or early spring. When planting, space shorter daylilies about 1 ft. apart, taller kinds 2 ft. apart. They will fill in a few years. **Hardy to Zone 3.**

## Heuchera

CORALBELLS. Perennials that form low clumps of almost evergreen foliage and bloom from spring into summer, bearing clouds of tiny red, coral, pink, or white flowers on slender stalks about 18 in. tall. They're fine accent plants or small-scale ground covers. The fresh or dried flowers are also attractive in floral arrangements. Often sold as *H. x brizoides* or *H. sanguinea;* there are a number of other species and a variety of hybrids. *H.* 'Palace Purple' (pp. 51, 89, 103, 107) has dark bronzy purple, maplelike leaves on long stalks. Grown primarily for its foliage, it also forms sprays of tiny white flowers in summer. *H. americana* 'Velvet Night' (pp. 49, 77, 85) has deep-purple leaves and greenish-white flowers in spring. Heucheras do best in partial shade; leaves tend to scorch or fade in full sun. They prefer well-drained soil and some summer water. Remove flower stalks as the blossoms fade. Divide every few years, replanting the divisions an inch or two deeper than they were growing before. **Generally hardy to at least Zone 4.**

Hosta

Hosta 'Green Gold'

Hosta 'Krossa Regal'

### Hosta

HOSTA. A long-lived, carefree, shade-tolerant perennial with beautiful leaves in a wide variety of colors and sizes. Plants form dome-shaped clumps or spreading patches of foliage that look good from spring to fall and die down in winter. Lavender, purple, or white flowers bloom on slender stalks in mid- to late summer. 'Krossa Regal' (pp. 84, 103) has medium-size powdery blue-green leaves and forms vase-shaped clumps 3 ft. tall, 3 to 6 ft. wide, with pale-lilac flowers on stalks 5 ft. tall. Variegated hostas make striking accents. 'Green Gold' (p. 69) forms a mound about 2 ft. tall and wide of large dark-green leaves with yellow borders fading to cream and lavender flowers. Some hostas tolerate full sun, but most grow best in partial or full shade. All need fertile, moist, well-drained soil. Cut off flower stalks before seedpods ripen. Clumps can be divided in late summer or early spring if you want to make more plants; otherwise leave them alone. Snails and slugs can ravage some hostas. Talk to nursery staff about which varieties are most resistant to these pests. **Generally hardy to Zone 3.** Pages: 25, 45, 49, *49*, 53, 83, 91, *91*.

### Hydrangea macrophylla

BIGLEAF HYDRANGEA. A medium-size deciduous shrub with large round leaves and very showy clusters of papery-textured blue, pink, or white flowers in summer. Grows up to 10 ft. tall and equally wide. There are many varieties. 'Nikko Blue' (pp. 68, *69*) is a popular cultivar with blue flowers. It grows only 4 to 6 ft. tall and wide. 'Preziosa' (pp. 16); also sold as *H. serrata*) bears smaller flowers that start out white and turn deep red, blue, or mauve. Grows 5 ft. tall. Hydrangeas are usually grown in partial shade but can be planted in full sun if regularly watered. Avoid late afternoon sun. Bigleaf hydrangea needs fertile, moist, well-drained soil. In early spring cut to the ground one-half of the stalks that have bloomed. Head back the others by cutting off their tips. You may need to add lime to the soil to produce pink flowers or aluminum sulfate to produce blue ones. **Hardy to Zone 6.** Pages: *19*, 28, 53.

### Hydrangea paniculata 'Grandiflora'

PEEGEE HYDRANGEA. A deciduous shrub often trained to grow as a small, single-trunk tree. It has light-green leaves and big clusters of papery flowers at branch tips in mid- to late summer. Flowers open white and gradually turn pink, then tan in late fall. The dried flowers last at least partway through the winter; prune them off in spring. Can reach 15 to 20 ft. tall and wide over time or be kept smaller by annual pruning. Plant in full or partial sun. A vigorous, trouble-free plant. Both specimens in this book are trained as single-trunk trees. You can train them yourself, but purchasing already trained plants from a nursery is much easier. Pages: 28, 104.

### Hydrangea petiolaris

CLIMBING HYDRANGEA. A long-lived deciduous vine that has a thick trunk with peeling bark, large glossy leaves, and lacy clusters of white flowers in June. Clings to a tree or wall and climbs by itself. Tolerates sun or shade; prefers moist, well-drained soil. Grows slowly for the first few years, then climbs several feet a year, eventually to 40 ft. or more. Prune only to keep it in bounds. Pages: 71, *73*.

### Hydrangea quercifolia

OAKLEAF HYDRANGEA. A deciduous shrub with large lobed leaves emerging pale-green in spring, turning dark in summer, and displaying wine-like shades of red-and-purple in fall. The stems have wonderful peeling, cinnamon-colored bark that's attractive in winter. Clusters of papery white flowers top the stems in early summer, then turn beige or pink-tan, lasting through summer and fall. Enjoy the flowers on the plant and in floral arrangements. 'White Queen' has larger-than-average flowers, and 'Snowflake' has double flowers. This species adapts to sun or shade. Water regularly during long dry spells. Grows fairly quickly, reaching at least 6 ft. tall and wide. Pages: 42, 110.

Hydrangea macrophylla
BIGLEAF HYDRANGEA

Hydrangea paniculata 'Grandiflora' PEEGEE HYDRANGEA

Hydrangea quercifolia OAKLEAF HYDRANGEA

## Iberis sempervirens

EVERGREEN CANDYTUFT. A bushy perennial that forms a low or sprawling mound, about 1 ft. tall and 1 to 2 ft. wide, of slender, glossy evergreen foliage. Bears clusters of bright-white flowers for several weeks in March or April. 'Little Gem' (pp. 21, 23, 81, **81**) is a compact plant growing 6 to 8 in. tall. Candytuft can be used as a ground cover. Needs full or partial sun and well-drained soil. Shear off the top of the plants after they bloom. Needs no other care. Don't try to divide it; buy new plants if you want more. **Hardy to Zone 3.** Pages: 61, **62**, 87.

## Ilex x attenuata 'Savannah'

'SAVANNAH' HOLLY. A slim columnar or conical tree growing about 25 ft. tall and 10 to 15 ft. wide, with shiny leaves and lots of red berries. Page: 65.

## Ilex crenata

JAPANESE HOLLY. A compact shrub with dense twiggy growth and small evergreen leaves. Some cultivars spread wider than tall; others grow upright and conical. 'Green Island' (pp. 16, 102) can grow 5 to 8 ft. tall and wide. 'Helleri' (p. 17) is a tight compact shrub 2 to 4 ft. tall. 'Compacta' (p. 41) grows about 6 ft. tall and wide. Plants adapt to full sun or partial shade; need well-drained soil.

## Ilex vomitoria

YAUPON HOLLY. With small, shiny spineless leaves and juicy red berries, it grows about 15 to 20 ft. tall, usually with multiple trunks, and is easily trained and pruned into a picturesque specimen. Page: 41.

## Iris ensata

JAPANESE IRIS. A perennial that forms a clump of dark-green swordlike leaves about 2 ft. tall and produces spectacular 3- to 6-in. flowers on stalks about 3 ft. tall in summer. The broad, ruffled petals have a fragile, velvety texture and come in bright shades of blue, purple, yellow, or white. Needs full sun and rich, fertile, moist soil. **Hardy to Zone 4.** Pages: 69, **69**.

## Iris foetidissima

GLADWIN IRIS. A vigorous perennial with slender shiny leaves and clusters of purple flowers in summer. Large green seedpods split open to reveal bright-orange-red seeds that last for months. This species does well in full sun or shade and is very drought tolerant once established. Grows 2 ft. tall. **Hardy to Zone 4.** Pages: 35, **35**, 95.

## Iris x germanica

BEARDED IRIS. Blooms in spring, with large elegant flowers in shades of blue, lavender, pink, yellow, or white on stalks 2 ft. tall. Flowers open above an attractive clump of stiff, bladelike, gray-green leaves. It needs full sun and extremely well-drained soil. Grows best with little to no irrigation. **Hardy to Zone 3.** Page: 58.

## Iris x Louisiana hybrids

LOUISIANA IRIS. This cool-season perennial forms a clump of straplike foliage 2 ft. tall and 3 ft. wide. Flowers on 3-ft. stalks in early spring. Cultivars come in many colors. Tolerates wet soil or well-drained soil with winter and spring moisture. **Hardy to Zone 5.** Page: 87.

## Iris reticulata 'Harmony'

'HARMONY' RETICULATA IRIS. A miniature iris that grows only 6 in. tall. In early spring, before the swordlike leaves emerge, it bears fragrant purple-and-yellow flowers. Needs full sun and well-drained soil. Page: 28.

## Iris sibirica

SIBERIAN IRIS. A carefree perennial that forms a large, vase-shaped clump of slender green leaves up to 2 ft. long and bears scores of showy flowers in late spring on stalks 2 to 4 ft. tall. 'Caesar's Brother' (pp. **62**, 63) is a popular cultivar with very dark blue-purple flowers. 'Tropic Night' (pp. 17, 49) is a 2-ft. cultivar with deep-purple flowers. Other cultivars have indigo, sky-blue, or yellow flowers. Plants need full or partial sun. After several years, divide clumps in early fall. **Hardy to Zone 3.**

## Juncus effusus

SOFT RUSH. This native grass-like wetland perennial forms clumps 2 to 4 ft. tall with a 5 ft. wide spread. Yellow-green flowers appear in early summer on upright green stems. Spreads easily but can also be divided in mid-spring to early summer. Cut back in early spring. It grows well in moist soil and can tolerate water up to 4 in. deep. Good low-maintenance plant for ponds. **Hardy to Zone 4.** Page: 87.

*Iris reticulata* 'Harmony'

*Iris sibirica* 'Tropic Night'
SIBERIAN IRIS

*Juncus effusus*
SOFT RUSH

Juniperus squamata
'Blue Star' JUNIPER

Lavandula LAVENDER

Leucothoe axillaris

Leucothoe fontanesiana
'Rainbow'

### Juniperus conferta
'BLUE PACIFIC' JUNIPER. An evergreen shrub that is tough and hardy for exposed sites. It makes a good ground cover, staying about 1 ft. tall and spreading 5 to 6 ft. wide. It has short, soft blue-green needles and prefers full sun and excellent drainage. Page: 87.

### Juniperus squamata 'Blue Star'
'BLUE STAR' JUNIPER. A small, slow-growing evergreen shrub that makes an irregular mound of silver-blue, prickly-textured foliage. Needs full sun and well-drained soil. Reaches 1 to 3 ft. tall, 2 to 4 ft. wide after many years. Pages: 46, 75.

### Kalmia latifolia
MOUNTAIN LAUREL. An evergreen shrub with smooth leaves and white, pale-pink, or rosy flowers in late spring and early summer. Adapts to shade but blooms more profusely in partial or full sun; needs moist, well-drained soil. Snap off flower stalks as soon as the petals drop (if you let the seedpods form, the plant will bloom only every other year). Normally reaches 8 ft. tall and wide after. Some cultivars with brighter flowers are more compact and only about 4 ft. tall. Newer compact cultivars have smaller leaves and reach only 2 ft. tall. Pages: 90, **91**.

### Lagerstroemia
CRAPEMYRTLE. A popular deciduous shrub or small tree usually grown with multiple trunks. It blooms for several weeks in the heat of summer, with large clusters of papery flowers at the end of each stem. Exfoliating bark reveals smooth mottled trunks in winter. 'Catawba' (*L. indica*, p. 27) is a purple-flowered cultivar that grows a standard 12 ft. tall and 6 ft. wide. It has excellent fall color and resists mildew. All crapemyrtles need full sun and well-drained soil. **Hardy to Zone 7.**

### Lamprocapnos spectabilis
BLEEDING HEART. Perennials that form rounded clumps of soft-textured, lacy, blue-green foliage. In late spring heart-shaped flowers dangle from delicate stalks. Leaves will die down in summer heat. Common bleeding heart (pp. 110, **111**), is a large showy plant growing 1 to 2 ft. tall and wide with rose-pink flowers. L. s. 'Alba' (pp. 31, **31**) has white flowers. L. 'Luxuriant' (pp. 77, **77**, 84) is smaller and bears pink-and-red flowers on 18-in. stalks rising above a 1-ft.-tall mass of foliage. Bleeding hearts need partial shade and fertile, moist, well-drained soil. **Hardy to Zone 3.**

### Lavandula
LAVENDER. Choice evergreen shrubs ideal for dry sunny locations. They form bushy mounds of fragrant gray-green foliage topped in early summer with countless long-stalked spikes of very fragrant flowers. English lavender, *L. angustifolia*, generally grows 1 to 3 ft. tall, with 1- to 2-ft. flower spikes. 'Munstead' (pp. 71, 78, **73**) reaches about 14 in. and has pale-lavender flowers. 'Hidcote' (pp. 18, 46, 54, 61, 78, 101) grows about 1 ft. tall and wide, with gray-green foliage and dark-purple flowers. *L. x intermedia* 'Provence' (pp. 54, **56**) grows 2 to 3 ft. and has very deep-purple flowers. All lavenders need full sun, well-drained soil, and little water. **Lavenders vary in hardiness with English lavender being the hardiest (Zone 5). Most others are hardy to Zone 7 or 8.**

### Leucothoe
LEUCOTHOE. Evergreen shrubs with arching stems and glossy leaves. In spring, fragrant white flowers line the stems. Drooping leucothoe, *L. fontanesiana*, grows up to 6 ft. tall and wide. 'Rainbow' (p. 44) has leaves that are cream, green, and pink. *L. axillaris* (pp. 30, 90, 110) is a more compact shrub that grows 2 to 4 ft. tall by 3 to 5 ft. wide. Leucothoes need full or partial shade and moist soil.

### Lindera benzoin
SPICEBUSH. A slow-growing deciduous shrub that can reach 6 to 12 ft. tall, often multi-stemmed. Bears clusters of tiny fragrant greenish-yellow flowers in spring. Red berries follow. In fall, the light-green leaves turn a vibrant yellow in fall. Both the leaves and fruit have spicy fragrance when crushed. There are male and female plants, so if you want cross-pollination, request one of each from your local nursery. Prefers full or partial sun but can tolerate full shade. Leaves have best fall color in full sun. Needs moist, well-drained soils. Not adapted to desert areas. **Hardy to Zone 4.** Pages: 23, **24**.

### Lonicera ciliosa
ORANGE HONEYSUCKLE. A deciduous twining vine that can grow 10 to 20 ft. tall and 20 to 30 ft. wide. Dark-green leaves contrast with clusters of bright-orange tubular flowers that bloom from spring to mid-summer. Prune after flowering to encourage more blooms. Edible orange-red berries follow. Serves as a great ground cover or it can be trained up structures. It prefers partial shade but will tolerate full sun as long as it has rich, well-drained soil. Drought tolerant once established. **Hardy to Zone 5.** Pages: 33, **35**.

*Miscanthus sinensis* Chinese silver grass

*Lindera benzoin*
Spicebush

*Lonicera ciliosa*
Orange honeysuckle

## Magnolia x soulangeana

SAUCER MAGNOLIA. Deciduous tree with large leaves. Huge fragrant flowers in white, pink, or purple are borne on leafless stems in early spring. Often the inside and the outside of the flower differ in color. Grows 15 to 25 ft. tall and spread as wide, usually with multiple trunks. Needs full sun, well-drained soil, and regular water. **Hardy to Zone 5.** Pages: 98, **100**.

## Mahonia aquifolium

OREGON GRAPE. Spreading evergreen shrub with handsome deeply divided leaves. Showy yellow flower clusters in spring produce blackish-blue berries later in the year. Grows about 6 ft. tall and has glossy green leaves that are tinged red when new, purplish in cold winters. 'Compacta' grows only 2 to 3 ft. tall but spreads to form a mid-height ground cover. Mahonias can be grown in sun or shade but usually look their best with some shelter. They grow well among tree roots. Water occasionally. Prune to open the center and expose the stems. Hardy to Zone 6. Not well adapted to low elevation desert areas. **Hardy to Zone 6.** Pages: 42, 68, 86.

## Mahonia repens

CREEPING MAHONIA. Spreading evergreen shrub with handsome, deeply divided, blue-green leaves; showy yellow flower clusters in spring; blackish-blue berries in fall; and purple leaf tones in winter. Grows 1 to 3 ft. tall and wide, spreads by rhizomes. Mahonias can be grown in sun or shade. Pages: 31, **31**.

## Malus 'Snowdrift'

'SNOWDRIFT' CRABAPPLE. A small deciduous tree with showy white flowers in late spring that start out red in the bud. Orange-red fruits ripen in early fall and last into winter. Grows 20 to 25 ft. tall. Does best in full sun and well-drained soil. Pages: 51, **53**.

## Miscanthus sinensis

CHINESE SILVER GRASS. A showy grass that forms vase-shaped clumps of long arching leaves. Blooms in late summer or fall, and the fluffy seed heads last through the winter. Bloom is unreliable in the Northwest. For best flowering results, plant in hot sunny spots. 'Morning Light' (pp. 83, **84**) and 'Sarabande' (pp. 17, 67) have very slender, white-striped leaves that look silvery from a distance. Both form a clump of foliage 4 to 5 ft. tall, with flower stalks about 6 ft. tall. 'Purpurascens' (pp. 81, **81**, 101) has leaves that in summer are purplish-green with a pink midrib and in fall are orange-red. All miscanthus need full sun. Cut to the ground in early spring. Pages: 27, 86.

## Myrica cerifera

WAX MYRTLE. An evergreen shrub that grows upright and bushy, with slender twigs and glossy leaves that have a delicious spicy aroma. Clusters of small gray berries line the stems of female plants in fall and winter. Needs full or partial sun. Grows quickly and can reach 30 ft. tall. **Hardy to Zone 7.** Pages: 65, 86.

## Nepeta x faassenii

CATMINT. A perennial that forms a bushy mound of soft pale-green foliage about 18 in. tall and wide topped with clusters of small violet-blue flowers. Blooms most in early summer but continues or repeats throughout the season. Needs full sun and well-drained soil. Shear plants back halfway after the first blooming to keep them tidy and to promote new growth. Pages: 105, 109.

*Nepeta x faassenii*
CATMINT

*Mahonia aquifolium*
Oregon grape

*Osmanthus burkwoodii*
HOLLY OSMANTHUS

*Oxydendrum arboreum*
SOURWOOD

*Paeonia* hybrid
PEONY

### Ophiopogon planiscapus 'Ebony Knight'

'EBONY KNIGHT' BLACK MONDO GRASS. A small perennial with grassy evergreen foliage in an unusual shade of purple-black. Spreads gradually by rhizomes to form a patch under 1 ft. tall. Prefers partial sun and moist, well-drained soil. A patch fills in better if you start with several small plants instead of a few large ones. Mow or shear off the top of the old foliage in early spring. Fresh new growth will look neat the rest of the year. Pages: **84**, 85.

### Osmanthus burkwoodii

HOLLY OSMANTHUS. A slow-growing evergreen shrub that has dark-green leaves with toothed margins. In the spring it bears a profusion of small, fragrant, tubular white flowers. Grows in full sun to shade but flowers best in sun. Can be pruned as a hedge. Grows up to 8 ft. tall. **Hardy to Zone 8.** Pages: 51, 109.

### Oxydendrum arboreum

SOURWOOD. A slow-growing, multitrunked deciduous shrub or single-trunked small tree with light-green, slightly folded leaves. In summer, cream-colored flowers hang from the branches. Small creamy seedpods that follow the flowers and persist well into fall, when the leaves turn shades of yellow, orange, red, or purple. Does well in sun or shade and well-drained soil. Grows up to 20 ft. tall or more. Page: 28.

### Paeonia

PEONY. Long-lived perennials that form a bushy clump of many stems, with spectacular large, fragrant flowers in late May or June and dark glossy foliage that turns purple or gold before it dies down in fall. Choose from a wide variety of hybrids offering single or double flowers in white, pale-pink, or rose. Peonies need full sun and deep, well-drained, fertile soil. Plant in early spring, positioning the thick rootstock so that the pink buds are no more than 1 in. deep. Established clumps are typically 2 to 3 ft. tall, 3 to 4 ft. wide. Pages: 17, 88.

### Parrotia persica

PERSIAN IRONWOOD. A slow-growing, deciduous multistemmed shrub or single-trunked small tree. Bears small clusters of spiderlike red flowers in early spring on bare wood. Leaves are oval with wavy margins and dark-green in summer, changing in fall to yellow, then red, and finally purple. The gray and peeling mature bark is attractive when exposed in winter. Needs full sun and well-drained soil. Grows around 20 ft. tall. Pages: 36, **39**.

### Pelargonium

GERANIUM. Flowering perennials loved for their round flower clusters and long season of bloom from spring into fall. (For hardy geraniums, see *Geranium*.) Flowers come in many single and bi-colored shades of white, pink, red, and purple. All geraniums grow best in full or partial sun. Water regularly. Remove spent flowers. Geraniums are ideal container plants and are often grown as annuals. **Generally hardy to Zone 8 or 9 but grown as annuals anywhere.** Page: 107.

### Penstemon

BEARDTONGUE. Late spring and summer-flowering perennial with showy tubular flower spikes in a wide range of colors and height ranging from 6 in. to several feet tall. Many varieties and hybrids available, including dozens of native species. Most need full or partial sun and look best with regular watering but can be drought tolerant. *P. serrulatus* (pp. 45, 48, 73, 83) is an 8 to 28 in. shade-tolerant Northwest native with dark blue-and-purple flowers from June through August that can grow in moist soil. Cut back to encourage additional blooms and foliage growth. **Hardy to Zone 7.** Pages: 18, 45–48, 66–67, 72–73, 83, 88–89.

### Perovskia

RUSSIAN SAGE. A shrubby perennial that forms an open, vase-shaped clump of straight, fairly stiff stems with sparse silver-gray foliage and tiny but abundant lavender-blue flowers. Blooms for weeks in summer and into fall. *P. atriplicifolia* 'Longin' (pp. 38, 67) has the same graceful lavender flowers but a more upright form. Grow in full sun and well-drained soil. Needs little water. Cut old stems down to 6-in. stubs in spring. Grows 3 to 5 ft. tall and wide by fall. **Hardy to Zone 5.** Pages: 41, 38, 41, 46, 63, 67.

### Phlox subulata

MOSS PHLOX. A low perennial that forms dense mats of prickly-textured evergreen foliage. Pink, magenta, lilac-blue, or white flowers completely cover the foliage for a few weeks in spring. Grows about 6 in. tall and spreads to form a patch 2 to 3 ft. wide. Needs full or partial sun. Tolerates dry sites. To promote neat, compact growth, shear the plants back halfway after they bloom. **Hardy to Zone 3.** Pages: 17, **19**, 41, 51, 71, 73, 92, 105, **105**.

## Phormium tenax

NEW ZEALAND FLAX. A perennial prized for its bold evergreen foliage. Stiff, straplike leaves form a fanlike clump about 6 ft. tall and at least as wide. Stalks bearing reddish flowers rise high above the leaves in summer. Because of the Northwest's cool summers, bloom is unreliable. Many varieties with colorful foliage are available, including 'Rubrum' (p. 51), which has brownish red leaves. All are excellent accent plants, but large types need lots of room. Smaller varieties, better suited to small gardens, are also available. Needs full sun. May not be hardy in colder parts of the Northwest or in colder microclimates. **Hardy to Zone 9.** Pages: 46, **49**.

## Picea abies 'Nidiformis'

BIRD'S-NEST NORWAY SPRUCE. A dwarf conifer with sharp, dark-green needles. Grows wider than tall, typically reaching about 2 to 3 ft. tall and 3 to 5 ft. wide, and is flat or slightly concave on top—hence its common name. Grow in full sun or light shade and well-drained soil. Grows slowly, so buy the biggest plant you can afford. **Hardy to Zone 3.** Pages: 24, **24**.

## Picea omorika

SERBIAN SPRUCE. A narrow, evergreen tree that may eventually reach 50 ft. tall but only 8 to 20 ft. wide. Its needles are dark-green above and whitish below. Mature bark is brown and platelike. Grows best in full sun and well-drained soil. Pages: 108, **111**.

## Pieris japonica

JAPANESE ANDROMEDA, LILY-OF-THE-VALLEY SHRUB. An evergreen shrub with neat, glossy green foliage; beadlike flower buds that are conspicuous all winter; and drooping clusters of white or pink blooms in late winter and early spring. Even young plants bloom abundantly. The new leaves that form after bloom are often bright gold or red and contrast beautifully with the older green leaves. Can grow to 12 ft. tall. There are many fine cultivars. Most eventually reach 4 to 8 ft. tall and wide, and some get larger. 'Mountain Fire' (pp. 53, **53**) has bright-red new growth and white flowers. 'Debutante' (pp. 90, **91**) grows 3 ft. tall and bears white flowers. 'Valley Fire' (pp. 91, 108), whose new growth is also bright red, has white flowers. All need partial shade, preferably afternoon shade, and rich, moist, well-drained soil. Container-grown plants transplant easily, but because the root system is very fibrous, be sure before you plant to slit and tease apart the roots. Prune right after flowering, removing spent flowers and trimming any wayward shoots.

## Pinus mugo

MUGO PINE. A slow-growing pine that forms an irregular shrubby mound, not a conical tree. Needles are dark-green. Needs full sun and well-drained soil. Named cultivars can stay less than 3 ft. tall. Plants grown from seedlings can exceed 10 ft. tall and wide after many years. **Hardy to Zone 3.** Pages: 38, **39**.

## Pinus strobus 'Nana'

DWARF EASTERN WHITE PINE. A very slow-growing evergreen shrub or small tree that makes a nice container plant or point of interest in the garden. It may eventually reach 3 to 7 ft. tall and wide. The needles are blue-green and very soft to the touch. The bark is smooth and gray and has resin blisters. Grows in full sun to partial shade and well-drained soil. Page: 18.

## Pratia pedunculata

BLUE STAR CREEPER. A very low (less than 3 in.) creeping, spreading perennial ground cover with small oval green leaves. Bears tiny sky-blue starlike flowers in late spring and sporadically throughout the summer. Looks great among stepping-stones and withstands light foot traffic. Plant in full sun and well-drained soil. Pages: 49, 73, 75.

*Phormium tenax* 'Rubrum'
NEW ZEALAND FLAX

*Pinus strobus* 'Nana'
DWARF EASTERN WHITE PINE

*Perovskia atriplicifolia*
RUSSIAN SAGE

*Pratia pedunculata*
BLUE STAR CREEPER

# Recommended rhododendrons

Rhododendron 'Bow Bells'

Rhododendron 'Snow Lady'

Rhododendron 'Cilpinense'

Rhododendron 'PJM'

**R. 'Bow Bells'** Bell-shaped pink flowers bloom in spring on an open-habit shrub. Grows about 4 ft. tall and 5 ft. wide. Rounded leaves are green; new growth is coppery. Pages: 72, 90.

**R. 'Cilpinense'** Light-pink flowers bloom in very early spring on a compact, small-leaved shrub. Grows about 3 ft. tall and wide. Pages: 42, 56.

**R. 'Dora Amateis'** White flowers with green spots bloom in a loose open fashion from early to mid spring on this compact semidwarf shrub. Grows about 2 ft. tall and wide. Pages: 31, **31**.

**R. 'Gomer Waterer'** White flowers flushed pink on the petal margins bloom in late spring. Grows up to 5 ft. tall and wide. Very tolerant of sun and drought. Pages: 78, **81**.

**R. 'Gumpo' azaleas** Low, spreading shrubs, 2 to 3 ft. tall and wide, with small evergreen leaves and large pink or white flowers in late spring. Page: 41.

**R. 'Hardizer's Beauty'** Strikingly pink mid-spring flowers bloom on this compact plant with small dark-green leaves. Grows about 2 ft. tall and 3 ft. wide. Pages: 98, **100**.

**R. impeditum** Dark-purple flowers bloom in early to mid spring on this compact plant with very small gray-green leaves. Tolerates sun well. Grows 1 ft. tall. Pages: 61, 81, 98.

**R. 'PJM'** Purple flowers in very early spring on a compact shrub about 4 ft. tall and 3 ft. wide. Has small dark-green leaves. Very hardy and drought tolerant. Page: 101.

**R. 'Ramapo'** Violet flowers bloom in early to mid spring on this low-growing shrub with gray-green leaves. Grows 2 ft. tall. Pages: 16, **19**.

**R. 'Snow Lady'** Clusters of fragrant white flowers with black stamens bloom in early spring on this 3-ft.-tall plant. The fuzzy light-green leaves are attractive. Page: 72, 97.

**R. 'Sweet Simplicity'** White flowers edged in pink bloom in late spring. Has shiny dark leaves. Grows 4 ft. tall. Page: 101.

**R. viscosum 'Arpege'** A deciduous azalea with very fragrant, deep-yellow flowers in early spring. Has hairy stems and dark-green leaves. Page: 101.

## Pulmonaria saccharata

LUNGWORT. A perennial that blooms for many weeks in early spring, with masses of tiny pink, red, or violet flowers. The large, white-spotted leaves make a good ground cover throughout the summer and fall. There are many cultivars with smaller leaves and other flower colors. Needs partial shade. Prefers rich, moist, well-drained soil but will tolerate drier conditions in shade. Cut off flower stalks when the petals fade. Divide every few years in fall. **Hardy to Zones 4–8.** Pages: 57, 73, 76, 111.

## Punica granatum

POMEGRANATE. This is a very ornamental deciduous fruiting shrub. Bronze new growth turns green in summer and bright-yellow in fall. Vibrant orange flowers are held among the shiny leaves in spring. The widely grown cultivar 'Wonderful' (p. 58) has a fountainlike shape and reaches 6 to 12 ft. tall or more. Its flowers are followed by large, bright-red, edible fruit. Plant pomegranates in full sun and well-drained soil. **Hardy to Zone 7.**

## Rhododendron

RHODODENDRON AND AZALEA. An especially diverse and popular group of shrubs with very showy flowers between early spring and early summer. The leaves can be small or large, deciduous or evergreen. The plants can be short, medium-size, or tall, with spreading, mounded, or erect habits. (See the box at left for information on specific varieties. Note: All plants mentioned are evergreen, except for *Rhododendron viscosum* 'Arpege'.)

All rhododendrons and azaleas do best with partial shade and need fertile, moist, well-drained soil. Plant in spring or fall, mixing compost into the planting bed. Be sure not to plant too deep—the top of the root-ball should be level with, or a little higher than, the surrounding soil. Azaleas are usually sold in containers. To ensure that they root well in the surrounding soil, make a few deep cuts down the root ball and tease apart some of the roots before planting. Treat container-grown rhododendrons the same way. Large rhododendron plants are often sold balled-and-burlapped; the roots were cut when the plants were dug and need no further attention. They will grow out through the burlap in time. (Remove any synthetic material.)

Azaleas and rhododendrons are shallow rooted, so mulch with a layer of compost to keep the soil cool and damp. For the first few years, water during any dry spell. Snap off spent flower heads as soon as the petals fade to prevent seed formation (which can reduce the following year's flowering) and to tidy up the plants. Prune right after flowering to control the size and shape of the plant. Deer sometimes eat rhododendrons; spraying the plants with a deer repellent offers some protection.

## Rosa

ROSE. Fast-growing deciduous shrubs with glossy compound leaves, thorny stems or canes, and showy—often-fragrant—flowers. *R.* 'Just Joey' (p. 104) is a vigorous tea rose with an open habit 3 to 5 ft. tall. Flowers are prolific, rounded, double, and fragrant and bloom summer to fall. They open orangish pink and turn white. *R. rugosa* 'Dwarf Pavement' (p. 62) grows only 2 to 3 ft. tall and has very thorny stems. Flowers are semidouble and pink and bloom spring to fall. *R.* 'Flower Carpet' (pp. 16, 54, 75, 105) is a ground-cover rose, 2 to 3 ft. tall and 3 to 4 ft. wide, with shiny leaves and profuse flower clusters from spring through autumn. Available in pink, white, and apple blossom. *R.* 'Iceberg' (p. 107) is a white floribunda 3 to 5 ft. tall.

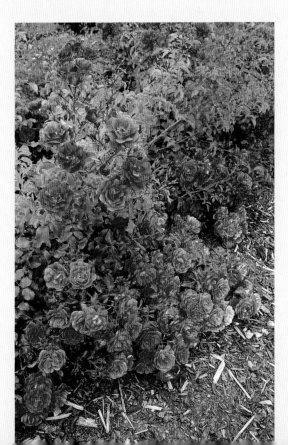

*Rosa* 'Flower Carpet Pink'
ROSE

*Rosa* 'Just Joey'
ROSE

In winter and early spring, many garden centers stock bare-root roses, with the roots packed in moist wood shavings wrapped in a plastic bag. These are a good investment if you buy them right after they arrive in the stores and plant them promptly, but their quality deteriorates as the weather warms and they begin to grow in the bag. Nurseries may also sell bare-root roses in early spring. If you buy a potted rose, you can plant it anytime, but if the rose has already leafed out, be careful not to disturb the roots in the transplant process.

All roses grow best in full sun and fertile, well-drained soil topped with a few inches of mulch. Once established, the roses recommended in this book require no more care than many other shrubs. Prune them once a year in early spring, before new growth starts. (See p. 192 for more on pruning.) The roses recommended here have good resistance to various fungal diseases but may have problems during especially moist years. To control fungal diseases such as powdery mildew or black spot, try some of the new baking soda derivatives available at nurseries. Follow label directions carefully. Aphids—soft-bodied insects the size of a pinhead—may attack new growth. Wash them away with plain or soapy water. Deer eat rosebushes, despite the thorns. Where deer are a problem, consider planting lilacs, spireas, clematis, or other plants instead. **Hardiness varies greatly, but types or varieties can be grown almost anywhere in the Northwest.**

## *Rosmarinus officinalis*

ROSEMARY. Classic Mediterranean evergreen shrub with gray-green needlelike leaves that combine a lovely fragrance with a tasty flavor. Small blue, lilac, or white flowers bloom in late winter and early spring and sporadically throughout the year. Grows upright or spreading, 2 to 5 ft. tall. 'Tuscan Blue' (pp. 33, 54, **56**) is upright, grows up to 6 ft. tall, has deep-blue flowers, and can be grown as a low hedge. 'Majorca Pink' (pp. 36, **39**, 107) is a smaller upright shrub, 2 to 4 ft. tall, with lavender-pink blooms. Rosemaries are tough plants. They do best in full sun and well-drained soil. Need little water once established. Prune or shear in spring or summer. **Hardy to Zone 8.** Pages: 27, 71.

## *Rudbeckia*

CONEFLOWER, BLACK-EYED SUSAN. A popular perennial wildflower that bears daisylike flowers with bright-colored petals and large conical centers in late summer. *Rudbeckia fulgida* var. *sullivantii* 'Goldsturm' (pp. 27, 33, 79, 92, 98) bears hundreds of cheerful yellow black-eyed flowers for several weeks in summer and into fall. Forms a robust clump 2 to 3 ft. tall and wide, with large dark-green leaves at the base and stiff, erect, branching flower stalks. Gloriosa daisy (*R. hirta*, pp. 109, **111**) has large orange-yellow flowers with black centers. Grows 2 to 4 ft. tall, with upright stems. Can be grown as an annual. Some varieties are much smaller. Plant in full sun and well-drained soil. Plants look best with regular watering. Remove spent flowers. Cut down the stalks in fall or spring. **Hardy to at least Zone 4.**

## *Sagina subulata*

IRISH MOSS. A very low-growing, dense ground cover with tiny, linear, emerald-green leaves. Miniature white flowers stand just above the foliage in spring. Not a true moss, it grows best in well-drained soil and partial shade. Looks great between rocks or steppingstones. Pages: 49, **49**.

*Rudbeckia* 'Goldsturm'
CONEFLOWER

*Salvia officinalis*
COMMON SAGE

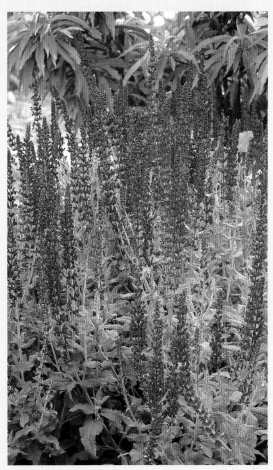

*Salvia* x *superba*
'Blue Queen'

## Salvia farinacea

MEALYCUP SAGE. Clusters of medium-blue flower spikes are borne on upright plants that grow vigorously to 3 ft. tall and wide. Flowers top the gray-green foliage in spring and continue through fall. Improved cultivars are purple, blue, or white and grow to a compact 1½ ft. tall and wide. Pages: 58, 86.

## Salvia greggii

AUTUMN SAGE. It produces small, oval, sage-scented leaves and a profusion of two-lipped flowers, especially in spring and fall. Flowers are white, pink, red, and other colors, depending on the cultivar. 'Cherry Chief' offers bright-red flowers. Autumn sage generally grows 2½ ft. tall and wide. Plant autumn sage in full sun and well-drained soil. Pages: 58, 92.

## Salvia officinalis

COMMON SAGE, GARDEN SAGE. A shrubby perennial with fragrant, gray-green, oval leaves and spikes of lovely blue flowers in June. Leaves are often used in cooking. Ideal for containers and small spaces near the kitchen. Grows 1 to 2 ft. tall, 2 to 3 ft. wide. 'Berggarten' (pp. 71, **73**) has a more compact habit, rounded leaves, and purple flowers. Plants need full sun and well-drained soil.

## Salvia x superba

SALVIA. A long-blooming perennial that forms a patch of dark-green foliage topped with countless flower spikes. (This salvia is also sold as *S. nemorosa* and *S.* x *sylvestris.*) 'May Night' (pp. 19, 67) has dark indigo-purple flowers. Salvias start blooming in June and continue through summer and fall. Shear or trim old flower stalks to keep the plants blooming. They prefer full sun and well-drained soil. Plants grow 18 to 24 in. tall, spread 2 ft. wide. Page: 28.

## Santolina chamaecyparissus

GRAY SANTOLINA. A bushy little shrub grown for its soft, fragrant, fine-textured silver-gray foliage. **Hardy to Zone 6.** Page: 58.

*Salvia* x *superba* 'May Night'

*Sarcococca humilis*
LOW SARCOCOCCA

*Sarcococca ruscifolia*
FRAGRANT SARCOCOCCA

### Sarcococca

SARCOCOCCA. Low sarcococca (*S. humilis*, pp. 35, 56, 110) is a slow-growing evergreen shrub with small, leathery, pointed leaves that are glossy green all year. Blooms in February and March; the small white flowers cluster at the bases of the leaves and are very sweet-scented. Grows 12 to 18 in. tall and 2 to 3 ft. wide. Spreads by rhizomes and can be used as a ground cover. Fragrant sarcococca (*S. ruscifolia*, pp. 25, 44, 53, 91, 97) has glossy green, wavy leaves. Small white flowers in late winter and early spring are also strongly scented. Grows about 3 ft. tall and wide. Plant sarcococcas in full or partial shade. **Hardy to Zones 6 and 7.**

### Scabiosa caucasica

PINCUSHION FLOWER. A perennial that forms a clump of gray-green leaves. Thin stalks about 2 ft. tall bear clusters of usually blue but sometimes white flowers from late spring through summer. Plant in full sun and water regularly. **Hardy to Zone 4.** Page: 107.

### Sedum

SEDUM. Perennials that form clumps of succulent foliage on thick stems topped with flat clusters of tiny flowers. 'Autumn Joy' (pp. 19, 27, 28, 38, 63, 67, 71, 78, 92, 98, 103) grows 2 to 3 ft. tall, with erect stems and gray-green foliage. The flowers change color from pale to deep salmon-pink to rusty red over many weeks in late summer and fall as they open, mature, and go to seed. 'Vera Jameson' (pp. 54, 103) grows about 1 ft. tall, with

floppy stems, rounded leaves in an unusual shade of purple-gray, and pink flowers in August. *S. spurium* 'Dragon's Blood' (pp. 46, **49**) is evergreen, forming a low mat of fleshy bronze leaves covered in summer with clusters of tiny rosy red flowers. Sedums need full sun. Cut down old stalks in winter or early spring. Divide clumps every few years in early spring. **Hardy to at least Zone 3.**

### Sempervivum tectorum

HEN-AND-CHICKS. An evergreen perennial ground cover forming a rosette of succulent leaves with spikes of pink or mauve flowers in summer. Produces numerous plantlets (the "chicks") attached by runners. There are many species and cultivars. They grow best in full hot sun and well-drained soil. Very drought tolerant. Pages: 71, **73**.

### Senecio greyi

GREY'S SENECIO. A mound-forming evergreen shrub with woolly stems and leaves that are soft to the touch. (Also sold as *Brachyglottis greyi*.) New leaves are covered with white hairs and become dark-green and hairless. Yellow daisylike flowers bloom from summer to fall. *S. g.* 'Sunshine' grows 5 ft. tall and wide and has leaves with scalloped edges. Grow senecio in full sun or partial shade. Very drought tolerant once established. Most are grown for their gray foliage, so shear off the flowers if the leaf color is what you're after. Every few years prune older stems by two-thirds in the early spring to encourage new vibrant gray-green growth. Pages: 18, 33, 46, 54, 71, 89.

*Sedum*
'Vera Jameson'

*Sedum*
'Autumn Joy'

*Senecio greyi*
GREY'S SENECIO

## Sorghastrum nutans

INDIAN GRASS. This native ornamental perennial grass has tall clumps of upright blue-green foliage that turns orange and yellow in fall and keeps tones of those colors through winter. Can grow 3 to 7 ft. tall and 1 to 2 ft. wide. In late summer, light brown flowers rise above the foliage to 5 to 6 ft. tall and remain through winter. Drought tolerant and does best in poor, dry soil. Too much water or rich and wet soil will cause grass to flop over. In spring, you can cut back to the ground and divide. **Hardy to Zone 4.** Page: 18.

## Spiraea japonica

JAPANESE SPIREA. A deciduous shrub that forms a low mound of thin, graceful, arching stems, with sharply toothed leaves and round flat clusters of tiny flowers in summer. 'Goldflame' (pp. 28, 61, **62**; sometimes listed under the species *S.* x *bumalda*) has bright-gold leaves tinged with orange in spring and turning red in fall. Flowers are pink-red. 'Little Princess' (pp. 75, **77**) has dark-green leaves and rosy pink flowers. 'Shirobana' (p. 42) has attractive dark-green leaves and mixed white, pink, and deep-rose flowers throughout the summer. All of these cultivars grow about 2 to 3 ft. tall and wide and need full or partial sun. Prune every year in spring, removing some of the older stems at ground level and cutting others back partway. In summer, shear off faded flowers to promote reblooming. Powdery mildew can be a problem late in the summer.

*Sorghastrum nutans*
INDIAN GRASS

*Spiraea japonica* 'Shirobana'
JAPANESE SPIREA

*Styrax japonicum*
JAPANESE SNOWBELL

### Stachys byzantina

LAMB'S EARS. A perennial whose large oval leaves are densely covered with soft white fuzz. Typically the leaves are 3 to 4 in. long, and the plant spreads about 18 in. wide. Blooms in early summer, with small purple flowers on thick stalks about 1 ft. tall. Needs full or partial sun, well-drained soil, and occasional water. **Hardy to Zone 4.** Page: 107.

### Stewartia pseudocamellia

JAPANESE STEWARTIA. A medium-size deciduous tree with a slightly zigzag branching pattern and four-season appeal: silken pointed buds in spring, white camellia-like flowers in midsummer, colorful fall foliage, and flaking bark that's conspicuous in winter. Prefers fertile, moist, well-drained soil and partial or full sun. Water periodically the first summer. Usually sold in small sizes, which transplant best. Prune and train carefully, making sure the main trunks and limbs diverge at wide angles. Grows 30 to 40 ft. tall, about 20 ft. wide. Pages: 16, 53, 88.

### Stokesia laevis 'Blue Danube'

STOKE'S ASTER. A perennial wildflower that blooms June to frost. It has blue flowers on stalks 12 to 18 in. tall. The basal foliage is evergreen. Adapts to full sun or partial shade. Needs well-drained soil. Page: 92.

### Styrax japonicum

JAPANESE SNOWBELL. A deciduous single-trunked tree or large multistemmed bush that puts out a profusion of fragrant white pendulous flowers in spring. Oval green leaves appear while the tree is still in bloom and turn yellow in fall. Plant in full sun to shade. The tree may eventually reach 20 to 30 ft. tall. Pages: 60, 88.

### Taxus baccata 'Repandens'

SPREADING ENGLISH YEW. A low-growing, spreading evergreen shrub with dark-green needles. Grows about 2 to 4 ft. tall and more than 10 ft. wide after many years. This is a female plant, producing attractive red berries with a poisonous hard seed. Adapts to full sun, partial sun, or shade but must have well-drained soil. Prune individual branches as needed to maintain the desired shape. **Hardy to Zone 7.** Pages: 62, 83, 97.

### Tecoma stans 'Gold Star'

'GOLD STAR' ESPERANZA. This shrub may be grown as a perennial in most of the region, pruned to the ground after the first hard freeze. It bears green pecanlike leaves, clusters of yellow bell-shaped flowers from summer until frost, and green bean pods after the flowers fade. Grows to a bushy 5 ft. tall and wide. It requires full hot sun and only occasional watering. Plant it in a protected area or mulch heavily to protect it from freezing. Page: 27.

*Stewartia pseudocamellia*
JAPANESE STEWARTIA

*Taxus baccata* 'Repandens'
SPREADING ENGLISH YEW

## Thymus

THYME. A shrubby perennial that forms a tangle of wiry twigs covered with tiny fragrant evergreen leaves. Blooms profusely in July or August, with pink, mauve, rose, or white flowers. Woolly thyme (*T. pseudolanuginosus*, p. 19) has fuzzy gray leaves and forms a low mat a few inches tall and 1 ft. or more wide. It tolerates light foot traffic and smells good when you step on it. Creeping thyme (*T. praecox* ssp. *arcticus*, pp. 46, 77, **77**, 79) has shiny green leaves that turn maroon in cold weather, grows very low, and withstands light foot traffic. Mother-of-thyme (*T. serpyllum*, pp. 42, **45**) is a bushier plant that grows 6 to 8 in. tall and about 1 ft. wide and bears purple flowers in summer. Common thyme (*T. vulgaris*, pp. 71, **73**) is another bushy type, 8 to 12 in. tall, with purple to white flowers in summer. The leaves are often used in cooking. All thymes need full sun and well-drained soil. **Hardy to Zone 5.**

## Tiarella cordifolia

FOAMFLOWER. A semi-evergreen perennial that forms low-growing patches of glossy heart shaped leaves with burgundy veins in fall and winter. Leaves turn reddish brown in winter. In late spring, pink-and-white flowers bloom on stems that shoot up above the foliage. Grows up to 1 ft. tall and 1 to 2 ft. wide. Needs well-drained soil and partial or full shade. Cut back and divide in spring. **Hardy to Zone 4.** Pages: 84, **85**.

*Tiarella cordifolia*
FOAMFLOWER

# Recommended viburnums

**Viburnum x *bodnantense* 'Dawn'** An upright deciduous shrub with dark-green leaves—scarlet in fall—and peely brown bark. Clusters of fragrant pink flowers bloom on bare wood in late winter but can begin as early as October. Blooms best in full sun. Grows 8 to 10 ft. tall and 6 ft. wide. **Hardy to Zone 5.** Pages: 35, **35**, 75.

**V. *carlesii* 'Compactum', Compact Korean spice viburnum** A deciduous shrub with pink buds that open into spicy-scented white flowers in April. Leaves may be red or green in fall. Grows about 4 ft. tall and wide. Pages: 88, **91**.

**V. *davidii*, David viburnum** A compact evergreen shrub with leathery, veined, dark-green leaves. Flat-topped clusters of white flowers are borne on branch tips in late spring and sporadically into summer. Metallic blue fruit ripens in late fall. Each plant will produce more fruit when there are several plants in the same area. Grows 3 ft. tall in sun, 5 ft. tall in shade. **Hardy to Zone 7.** Pages: 23, 35, 51.

**V. *tinus* 'Spring Bouquet'** A compact evergreen shrub with dark-green leaves borne on reddish stems, clusters of fragrant white flowers in spring, and metallic-blue berries in late summer. Flower buds are set in fall and stay a beautiful burgundy-white all winter. Grows 6 ft. tall and about 4 ft. wide. **Hardy to Zone 8.** Pages: 21, 81, 88.

*Viburnum davidii*
DAVID VIBURNUM

*Viburnum tinus*
'Spring Bouquet'

## Trachelospermum jasminoides

STAR JESSAMINE. This is an evergreen vine with woody, twining steams lined with pairs of small green leaves. It bears dangling clusters of sweetly scented creamy white flowers in spring. It can climb 10 to 15 ft. but is also useful as a sprawling ground cover, 1 to 2 ft. tall. Plant in full sun or partial shade and water during periods of drought. **Hardy to Zone 8.** Page: 58.

### Tsuga canadensis 'Pendula'

WEEPING HEMLOCK. Needlelike leaves are green on top and white below. Grows slowly and spreads wider than tall, reaching 4 to 5 ft. tall and 8 to 10 ft. wide. Will eventually grow twice as tall and wide but will take many years to do so. Start with the largest specimen you can afford. Takes sun or shade but needs moist, well-drained soil. **Hardy to Zone 4.** Pages: 24, *24*.

### Tsuga mertensiana

MOUNTAIN HEMLOCK. The leaves are small blue-green needles arranged in spirals around the stem. Grows slowly, and forms an irregular cone. Likes moist, well-drained soil with some protection from the hot late-afternoon sun or reflected heat. Pages: 110, *111*.

### Vaccinium

VACCINIUM. Evergreen and deciduous shrubs native to the Northwest. They all bear small, pinky white, urn-shaped flowers in the spring, followed by edible fruits, some red, some blue-black, that birds also enjoy. Evergreen huckleberry (*V. ovatum*, pp. 30, *31*) has leaves that start out bronze in spring and turn glossy green; small, sweet, and blue-black fruit; and branches that are attractive in floral arrangements. Grows 2 to 3 ft. tall in the sun and 8 to 10 ft. in the shade. Foxberry (*V. vitis-idaea*, pp. 95, *97*) is an evergreen shrub or ground cover with leaves that begin red-tinged and turn glossy green. Late-spring flowers are followed by small sour red berries. Grows 1 ft. tall and spreads by rhizomes.

### Verbena x hybrida

VERBENA. These are sprawling perennials with ever-green leaves and round clusters of showy flowers. 'Blue Princess' (p. 27) has lightly fragrant lavender-blue flowers. 'Homestead Purple' has vibrant purple flowers. Plant them in full sun. Grows about 1 ft. tall and spreads 3 ft. **Hardy to Zone 7.** Page: 87.

### Viburnum

VIBURNUM. Deciduous or evergreen shrubs with many outstanding features—showy foliage, flowers, fragrance, or fruits, or all of the above. (For more information on specific plants, see the box at right.) All need full or partial sun and moist, well-drained soil. Prune after flowering. Insect and disease free.

### Vitex agnus-castus

CHASTE TREE. A fast-growing deciduous shrub that can be trained as a single-trunk tree that can grow up to 20 ft. tall. Fragrant lavender-colored lilac-like clusters bloom summer through early fall. Gray-green leaves also fragrant when bruised. Prefers well-drained soil and full sun. Drought tolerant once established. Beneficial pollinator plant: flowers attract butterflies and serve as food for butterfly larvae. Heavily prune after flowering for more blooms. **Hardy to Zone 6.** Pages: 18, *19*.

*Vitex agnus-castus*
CHASTE TREE

## Water plants

The plants named here are all tender to frost, but you can overwinter them indoors in a pot or aquarium. There are three main groups of water plants: marginal, floating, and oxygenating. Choose one or more of each for an interesting and balanced effect.

Marginal, or emergent, plants grow well in containers covered with 2 in. or more of water; their leaves and flower stalks stand above the water surface. Dwarf papyrus (*Cyperus haspan*) has leaves that branch out like umbrella spokes; it grows 18 in. tall.

Floating plants have leaves that rest on the water and roots that dangle into it. Water lettuce (*Pistia stratiotes*) forms wide rosettes of pale-green leaves.

Oxygenating, or submerged, plants grow underwater; they help keep the water clear and provide oxygen, food, and shelter for fish. Anacharis (*Elodea canadensis*) is popular; it has tiny dark-green leaves.

Water lilies (*Nymphaea* species, pp. 83, **84**, 87) are the most popular plant for pools and ponds. There are two main groups of water lilies. Hardy water lilies survive outdoors from year to year and bloom in midsummer. Tropical water lilies need warm water and bloom over a longer season from summer through fall, but are treated as annuals. All water lilies need full sun. (See p. 157 for more information on planting.)

## Weigela Florida 'Java Red'

'JAVA RED' WEIGELA. A deciduous shrub with a fountainlike habit, purple-green foliage, and deep-pink tubular flowers beginning in early summer. Hummingbirds enjoy the flowers. Blooms best in full sun and well-drained soil. Grows 6 ft. tall. Pages. 51, **53**

## Wisteria frutescens

AMERICAN WISTERIA. A native deciduous woody vine with dense deep-green foliage full of dangling clusters of fragrant pea-like purple-and-blue flowers from early summer to early fall. It can be trained to climb a trellis, fence, or other vertical structures. Needs well-drained soil and prefers full sun but will tolerate partial shade. More sun results in more flower blooms. It typically grows 15 to 20 ft. tall but can get up to 40 ft. tall if left unchecked. This wisteria is not an aggressive spreader. Prune regularly to control the size and shape and heavily in spring to remove dead foliage and encourage new growth. **Hardy to Zone 5.** Page: 41.

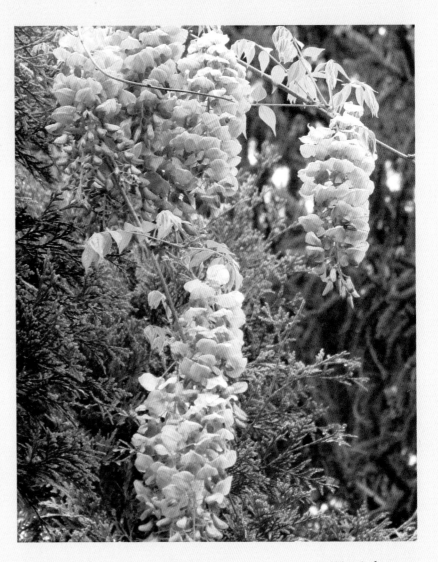

*Wisteria frutescens*
AMERICAN WISTERIA

## Yucca filamentosa 'Golden Sword'

'GOLDEN SWORD' YUCCA. An unusual perennial with evergreen daggerlike leaves, 2 to 4 ft. long, that stick out in all the directions from a short thick trunk. Leaves have a broad yellow stripe down the middle and green edges. Blooms in June, with large creamy white flowers on stiff branching stalks 4 to 6 ft. tall. Needs full or partial sun. Page: 92.

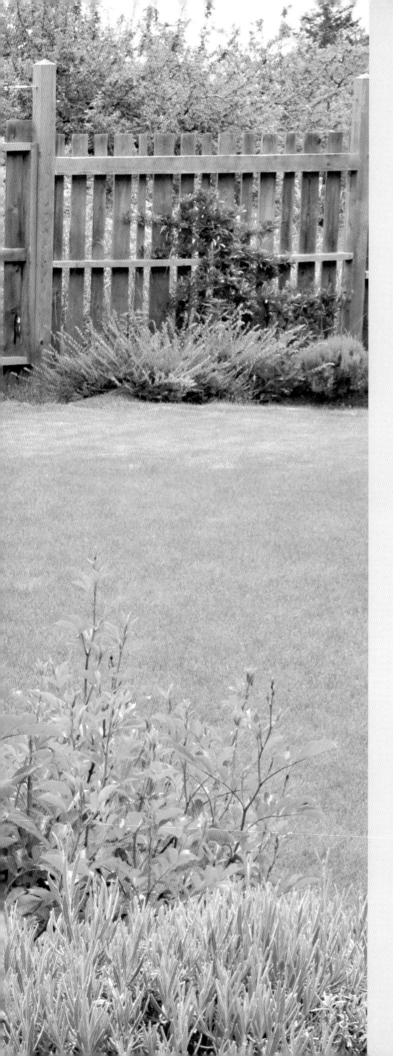

# Guide *to* Installation

**In this section,** we introduce the hard but rewarding work of landscaping. Here you'll find the information you need about all the tasks required to install any of the designs in this book, organized in the order in which you'd most likely tackle them. Clearly written text and numerous illustrations help you learn how to plan the job; clear the site; construct paths, patios, ponds, fences, arbors, and trellises; prepare the planting beds; and install and maintain the plantings. Roll up your sleeves and dig in. In just a few weekends you can create a landscape feature that will provide years of enjoyment.

# Organizing Your Project

**If your gardening experience** is limited to mowing the lawn, pruning the bushes, and growing some flowers and vegetables, the thought of starting from scratch and installing a whole new landscape feature might be intimidating. But in fact, adding one of the designs in this book to your property is completely within reach if you approach it the right way. The key is to divide the project into a series of steps and take them one at a time. This is how professional landscapers work. It's efficient and orderly, and it makes even big jobs seem manageable.

On this and the facing page, we explain how to think your way through a landscaping project and anticipate the various steps. Subsequent topics in this section describe how to do each part of the job. Detailed instructions and illustrations cover all the techniques you'll need to install any design from start to finish.

### The step-by-step approach
**Choose a design and adapt it to your site.** The designs in this book address parts of the home landscape. In the most attractive and effective home landscapes, all the various parts work together. Don't be afraid to change the shape of beds; alter the number, kinds, and positions of plants; or revise paths and structures to bring them into harmony with their surroundings.

To see the relationships with your existing landscape, you can draw the design on a scaled plan of your property. Or you can work on the site itself, placing wooden stakes, pots, or whatever is handy to represent plants and structures.

**Lay out the design on site.** Once you've decided what you want to do, you'll need to lay out the paths and structures and outline the beds. Some people are comfortable pacing off distances and relying on their eye to judge sizes and relative positions. Others prefer to transfer the grid from the plan full size onto the site, using garden lime (a white powder available at nurseries) like chalk on a blackboard to "draw" a grid or outlines of planting beds.

**Clear the site.** (See pp. 144–145.) Sometimes you have to work around existing features—a nice big tree, a building or fence, a sidewalk—but it's usually easiest to start a new landscaping project by removing unwanted structures or pavement and killing, cutting down, or uprooting all the plants. This can generate a lot of debris to dispose of, but it's often worth the trouble to make a fresh start.

**DIGGING POSTHOLES**

**AMENDING SOIL**

**Make provisions for water.** (See pp. 146–147.) While water is in plentiful supply during the rest of the year, summer in the Northwest is usually a time of extended drought. Newly installed plantings will require regular summer irrigation for a year or two. Although drought-tolerant plants are increasingly popular, many plantings often require some summer watering even after the plants are well established. To grow healthy plants and conserve water during summer droughts, plan for irrigation from the start of your project.

**Build the "hardscape."** (See pp. 156–161.) Hardscape includes landscape structures such as fences, trellises, arbors, retaining walls, walkways, edging, and outdoor lighting. Install these elements before you start any planting.

**Prepare the soil.** (See pp. 178–181.) On most properties, it's uncommon to find soil that's as good as it should be for growing plants. Typically, the soil around a new house is shallow, compacted, and infertile. Some plants tolerate such poor conditions, but they don't thrive. To grow healthy, attractive plants, you need to improve the quality of the soil throughout the entire area that you're planning to plant.

**Do the planting and add mulch.** (See pp. 182–188.) Putting plants in the ground usually goes quite quickly and gives instant gratification. Mulching the soil makes the area look neat even while the plants are still small.

**Maintain the planting.** (See pp. 189–199.) Most plantings need regular watering and occasional weeding for the first year or two. After that, depending on the design you've chosen, you'll have to do some routine maintenance—watering, pruning, shaping, cutting back, and cleaning up—to keep the plants looking their best. This may take as little as a few hours a year or as much as an hour or two of your time every week throughout the growing season.

TRANSPLANTING

SETTING FLAGSTONES

# Clearing the Site

**The site you've chosen** for a landscaping project may or may not need to be cleared of fences, old pavement, construction debris, and other objects. Unless your house is newly built, the site will almost certainly be covered with plants.

Before you start cutting plants down, try to find someone to identify them for you. As you walk around together, make a sketch that shows which plants are where, and attach labels to the plants, too. Determine if there are any desirable plants worth saving—mature shade trees that you should work around, large shrubs that could be pruned to complement the design. You can move or give away plants that don't fit into the new scheme. Smaller shrubs can be dug up and relocated, worthwhile perennials and ground covers can be divided and replanted, healthy sod can be lifted and laid elsewhere. Likewise, decide which plants have to go—diseased or crooked trees, straggly or overgrown shrubs, weedy brush, invasive ground covers and tattered lawn.

You can clear small areas yourself, bundling the brush for pickup and tossing soft-stemmed plants on the compost pile, but if you have lots of woody brush or any trees to remove, you might want to hire someone else to do the job. A crew armed with power tools can turn a thicket into a pile of wood chips in just a few hours. Have them pull out the roots and grind the stumps, too. Save the chips; they're good for surfacing paths, or you can use them as mulch.

### Working around a tree

If there are any large, healthy trees on your site, be careful as you work around them. It's okay to prune off some of a tree's limbs, as shown on the facing page, but respect its trunk and roots. Keep heavy equipment from beneath the tree's canopy, and don't lower the level of the soil there or raise it more than a few inches. Try never to cut or wound the bark on the trunk (don't nail things to a tree), because that exposes the tree to disease organisms.

### Killing perennial weeds

Some common weeds that sprout back from perennial roots or runners are dandelion, bindweed, blackberry, dock, plantain, and creeping buttercup. Once they get established, perennial weeds are hard to eliminate. You can't just cut off the tops, because the plants keep sprouting back. You need to dig the weeds out, smother them, or kill them with an herbicide, and it's better to do this before you plant a bed.

## Smothering weeds

This technique is easier than digging, particularly for eradicating large infestations, but much slower. First, mow or cut the tops of the weeds as close to the ground as possible ❶. Then cover the area with sections from the newspaper, overlapped like shingles ❷, or flattened-out cardboard boxes. Top with a layer of mulch, such as compost, straw, grass clippings, or wood chips, spread several inches deep ❸.

Smothering works by excluding light, which stops photosynthesis. If any shoots reach up through the covering and produce green leaves, pull them out immediately. Wait a few months, until you're sure the weeds are dead, before you dig into the smothered area and plant there.

SMOTHERING WEEDS

❶ Smothering kills weeds by depriving them of light. Cut the tops off close to the ground.

❷ Cover with thick newspaper or cardboard.

❸ Top with several inches of mulch. Wait a few months to be sure weeds are dead, and then till rotted newspaper and mulch into the soil.

**Digging.** You can often do a good job of removing a perennial weed if you dig carefully at the base of the stems, find the roots, and follow them as far as possible through the soil, pulling out every bit of root that you find. This is relatively easy with taprooted plants such as dandelions. Plants with roots that go deeper than you can dig or those that spread by runners are difficult to eradicate all at once.

**Spraying.** Herbicides are chemicals that kill weeds. They can be fast and effective but must be chosen and applied with care. Ask at the nursery for those that break down quickly into less toxic substances, and make sure the weed you're trying to kill is listed on the product label. Apply all herbicides as directed by the manufacturer. Take care to keep herbicides off desirable plants. After spraying, you usually have to wait one to four weeks for the weed to die completely, and some weeds need to be sprayed a second or third time. Some weeds just "melt away" when they die, but if there are tough or woody stems and roots, you'll need to dig them up and discard them.

## Replacing turf

If you're planning to add a landscape feature where you now have lawn, you can "recycle" the turf to repair or extend the lawn elsewhere on your property.

The drawing below shows a technique for removing relatively small areas of strong healthy turf for replanting elsewhere. First, with a sharp spade, cut it into squares or strips about 1 to 2 ft. square ❶. Then slice a few inches deep under each square and lift the squares, roots and all, like brownies from a pan ❷. Quickly transplant the squares to a previously prepared site. If necessary, level the turf with a water-filled roller from a rental business. Water well until the roots are established. You can rent a sod-cutting machine for larger areas.

If you don't need the turf anywhere else, or if it's straggly or weedy, leave it in place and kill the grass. Cover it with a tarp or a sheet of black plastic for about four weeks during the heat of summer. A single application of herbicide kills some grasses, but you may need to spray vigorous turf twice. After you've killed the grass, dig or till the bed, mixing it into the soil.

## Removing large limbs

If there are large trees on your property now, you may want to remove some of the lower limbs so you can walk and see underneath them and so more light can reach plantings you're planning beneath them. Major pruning is a job for a professional arborist, but you can remove limbs smaller than 4 in. in diameter and less than 10 ft. above the ground yourself with a bow saw or pole saw.

Use this three-step procedure. First, saw partway through the bottom of the limb, approximately 1 ft. out from the trunk ❶. This keeps the bark from tearing down the trunk when the limb falls. Then make a corresponding cut an inch or so farther out down through the limb ❷. Finally, remove the stub ❸. Undercut it slightly or hold it as you finish the cut, so it doesn't fall away and peel bark off the trunk. Note that the cut is not flush with the trunk but is just outside the thick area at the limb's base, called the branch collar. Leaving the branch collar helps the wound heal quickly and naturally. Wound dressing is considered unnecessary today.

**MOVING TURF**

❶ With a sharp shovel, cut healthy turf into squares or strips of manageable size.

❷ Slice a few inches deep under each square, lift it, and place as soon as possible in a new spot.

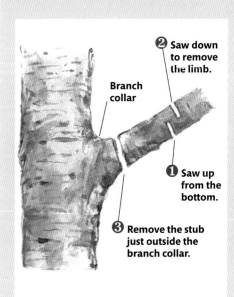

❷ Saw down to remove the limb.

Branch collar

❶ Saw up from the bottom.

❸ Remove the stub just outside the branch collar.

# Water for Your Plants

**The rainy season** in the Northwest is usually followed by a drought that can last from mid-July through October. This dry period makes watering a critical concern of gardeners. Though some plants will survive long dry periods once established, almost all plants will need regular watering the first few years after planting. And some will need summer watering their entire lives to look their best.

But there is more at stake than just the survival of plants. Conservation of water in summer is a growing concern in the region. Because outdoor landscapes use a large portion of urban water, efficient home watering systems can play an important role in conservation efforts.

So make water conservation part of your landscape planning from the beginning, including using plants that are native to the Northwest because these have become acclimated to the climate. The box below outlines effective water-saving practices for home landscapes. (See p. 189 for more on when and how much to water.) You can also consult your local water district for advice about watering gardens and lawns.

## Watering systems

One of the best ways to conserve water is to use an efficient delivery system. The simplest watering systems—watering cans and handheld hoses—are also the most limited and inefficient. They can be adequate for watering new transplants, containers, or widely separated individual plants. But sprinkling plants in an entire bed with a hose and nozzle for even an hour may provide less water than half an inch of rainfall. And wetting just the top few inches of soil this way encourages shallow root growth, making it necessary to water more frequently. To provide enough water to soak the soil to a depth of a foot or more, you need a system that can run untended for extended periods.

Hose-end sprinklers are easy to set up and leave to soak an area. But they're also inefficient: water is blown away by wind. It runs off sloped or paved areas. It is applied unevenly, or it falls too far away from individual plants to be of use to them. And because sprinklers soak leaves as well as soil, the damp foliage may breed fungal diseases.

**Low-volume irrigation.** For landscape plantings like those in this book, low-volume irrigation systems are the most efficient and offer the most flexibility and control. Frequently called "drip" irrigation systems, they deliver water at low pressure through a network of plastic pipes, hoses, and tubing and a variety of emitters and microsprinklers. Such systems are designed to apply water slowly and directly to the roots of targeted plants, so very little water is lost to runoff and evaporation or wasted on plants that don't need it. Because water is usually applied at soil level, the risk of foliar diseases is reduced. And because less soil is watered, weeds are also discouraged.

Simple low-volume systems can be attached to ordinary outdoor faucets or garden hoses and controlled manually, just like a sprinkler. You can set up such a system in less than an hour. Sophisticated systems include (1) their own attachment to your main water supply, (2) a

## Water-wise practices

**Choose plants carefully.** Many plants that do well in the Northwest's wet winters and dry summers are marked as "water-wise" plants at local nurseries and garden centers. Also, look for plants native to the region—they're adapted by nature for conditions here.

**Group plants with similar water needs.** Position plants that require the most water near the house, where they can be more easily tended and served by watering systems. Use drought-tolerant plants farther from the house.

**Plant in fall.** This way, new plants will have the cooler, wetter winter and spring seasons to become established before facing the summer drought.

**Mulch plantings.** A 2- to 3-in. layer of mulch reduces evaporation by keeping the soil cool and sheltering it from wind.

**Create water-retaining basins.** Use these to direct irrigation water to large plants. Make a low soil mound around the plant's perimeter, at its drip line. (Basins aren't necessary in drip-irrigated beds.)

**Limit lawn size.** Lawns demand lots of water. Reduce the size of your lawn by planting beds, borders, and less-thirsty ground covers.

**Water in the morning.** Lower morning temperatures and less wind mean less water will be lost to evaporation.

**Adjust watering to conditions.** Water less during cool weather in the spring and fall. During the rainy season, turn off automatic timers.

**Install, monitor, and maintain an irrigation system.** Even a simple drip system conserves water. Once it's installed, check and adjust the equipment regularly.

Connection to electronic controls

Control valve with backflow prevention device

Main water supply

Filter

### DRIP IRRIGATION SYSTEM

Pressure regulator

**Basic components of a drip irrigation system are shown here. Individual systems will vary. Several common types of emitters are shown; systems can incorporate others.**

network of valves and buried pipes that allow you to divide your property into zones, and (3) an electronic control device that can automatically water each zone at preset times for preset durations. Such systems often incorporate sprinkler systems for lawns.

A person with modest mechanical skills and basic tools can plan and install a low-volume irrigation system. Extensive multizoned systems (particularly those with their own attachment to the main water supply) are more difficult to design and install. If you tackle one, have a professional review your plans before you start. You can buy kits or individual system components from garden centers, nurseries, or specialty suppliers. (The main components of low-volume systems are outlined on this page.) Although most manufacturers provide helpful instructions, good criteria for choosing among different local suppliers are their knowledge of system design and installation and their ability to help you with both. A supplier may charge for this service, but good advice is worth the money.

**Low-volume-system components.** Any irrigation system connected to a domestic water supply needs a ***backflow prevention device*** (also called an anti-siphon device) at the point of connection to the water supply to protect drinking water from contamination. Check with local health or building officials for specific backflow requirements.

Install a ***filter*** to prevent minerals and flakes that slough off metal water pipes from clogging the emitters. You'll need to clean the filter regularly. Between the filter and emitters, all hoses and tubing should be plastic, not metal.

***Pressure regulators*** reduce the main's water pressure to levels required by the system's low-volume emitters.

***Supply lines*** deliver water from the source to the emitters. Some systems incorporate buried lines of rigid plastic pipe to carry water to plantings anywhere on the property. For aboveground use, you'll need flexible tubing designed specifically for low-volume irrigation.

***Emitters*** and ***soaker hoses*** deliver the water to the plants. A wide range of emitters are available for different kinds of plants and garden situations. Various drip fittings, bubblers, and microsprinklers can be plugged into the flexible plastic tubing. A single emitter or a group of emitters might serve individual or groups of plants. Soaker hoses and "ooze" tubes seep or drip water along their length. Consult with your supplier about which delivery systems best meet your plants' needs.

A ***timer*** or ***electronic controller*** helps ensure efficient water use. Unlike you, a controller won't forget and leave the water on too long. (It may also water during a rainstorm, however.) Used in conjunction with zoned plantings, these devices provide control and flexibility to deal with the specific water needs of groups of plants or even individual specimens. They also water your plants when you leave on vacation.

**Installation.** Permanent irrigation equipment should be installed early in the project. Lay underground piping that crosses paths, patios, or similar landscape features before installing any of these permanent features. It is best to lay pipes in planting areas, including lawns, after you have prepared the soil. That way, you won't damage the piping when digging. Install underground pipe in trenches; then temporarily cap the ends. Hook up the aboveground tubing and position emitters after planting.

½-in. supply line

Microsprinkler

¼-in. feedline

Stake

Individual emitter

Inline emitter

Punch-in emitter

¼-in. connector

# Making Paths and Walkways

**Every landscape** needs paths and walkways if for no other reason than to keep your feet dry as you move from one place to another. A path can also divide and define the spaces in the landscape and even be a key element in enhancing its beauty.

A walk has two main functional requirements: durability and safety. It should hold up through seasonal changes. It should also provide a well-drained surface that is easy to maintain.

A path's function helps determine its surface and its character. In general, heavily trafficked walkways leading to a door, garage, or shed need hard, smooth (but not slick) surfaces and should take you where you want to go fairly directly. A path to a backyard play area could be a strip of soft wood bark, easy on the knees of rambunctious children. A relaxed stroll in the garden might require only a hop-scotch collection of flat stones meandering from one prized plant to another.

Before laying out a walk or path, spend some time observing existing traffic patterns. If your path makes use of a route people already take (particularly children), they'll be more likely to stay on the path and off the lawn or flowers. Avoid areas that are slow to drain. When determining path width, consider whether the path must accommodate rototillers and wheelbarrows or two strollers walking abreast, or simply provide stepping-stone access for maintaining the plants.

## Dry-laid paths

You can make a path simply by laying bricks or spreading wood chips on top of bare earth. While quick and easy, this method has serious drawbacks. Laid on the surface, with no edging to contain them, loose materials are soon scattered, and solid materials are easily jostled out of place. If the earth base doesn't drain very well, the path will be a swamp after a rainstorm. Where winter temperatures dip below freezing and then warm up, the cycles of freezing and thawing expand and contract the soil, moving path and walkway materials laid on it. The effect of this "frost heaving" is minimal on loose materials such as wood chips or gravel, but it can shift brick and stone significantly out of line, making the path unsightly and potentially dangerous.

The method we recommend—laying surface material on an excavated base of sand or gravel, or both—minimizes these problems. Water moves through sand and gravel quickly, and such a base "cushions" the surface materials from any freeze-thaw movement of the underlying soil. Excavation can place the path surface at ground level, where the surrounding soil or an edging can contain loose materials and keep solid materials from shifting.

All styles, from a wood-bark path to a cut-stone entry walk, and all the materials discussed in this section can be laid on an excavated base of sand or gravel, alone, or in combination.

**Hard-surface walks**

Edging

2 in. builder's sand

Flagstone or precast pavers

Bricks

4 in. coarse gravel or crushed rock

**Loose-surface paths**

Edging

Water-permeable landscape fabric

Pea gravel, fine crushed rock, bark, or wood chips

4 in. coarse gravel or crushed rock

# Choosing a surface

Walkways and paths can be made of either hard or soft material. Your choice of material will depend on the walkway's function, your budget, and your personal preferences.

Soft materials, including bark, wood chips, pine needles, and loose gravel, are best for informal and low-traffic areas. Inexpensive and simple to install, they settle, scatter, or decompose and must be replenished or replaced every few years.

Hard materials, such as brick, flagstone, and concrete pavers are more expensive and time consuming to install, but they are permanent, requiring only occasional maintenance. (Compacted crushed stone can also make a hard-surface walk.) Durable and handsome, they're ideal for high-traffic, high-profile areas.

### Bark, wood chips, and pine needles

Perfect for a natural look or a quick temporary path, these loose materials can be laid directly on the soil or, if drainage is poor, on a gravel bed. Bagged materials from a nursery or garden center will be cleaner, more uniform, and considerably more expensive than bulk supplies bought by the cubic yard. Check with local tree services to find the best prices on bulk material.

### Gravel and crushed rock

Loose rounded gravel gives a bit underfoot, creating a soft but messy path. The angular facets of crushed stone eventually compact into a hard and tidier path that can, if the surrounding soil is firm enough, be laid without an edging. Gravel and stone type and color vary from area to area. Buy materials by the ton or cubic yard.

### Concrete pavers

Precast concrete pavers are versatile, readily available, and often the least expensive hard-surface material. They come in a range of colors and shapes, including interlocking patterns. Precast edgings are also available. Most home and garden centers carry a variety of precast pavers, which are sold by the piece.

**PRECAST PAVERS**

### Brick

Widely available in a range of sizes, colors, and textures, brick complements many design styles. When carefully laid on a well-prepared sand-and-gravel base, brick provides an even, safe, and long-lasting surface. If you buy used brick, pick the densest and hardest. Avoid brick with glazed faces; the glaze traps moisture and salts, which eventually damage the brick. If you live where it regularly freezes and thaws, buy bricks rated to withstand the weather conditions.

**RUNNING BOND**

**TWO BRICK
BASKET WEAVE**

**HERRINGBONE**

**DIAGONAL
HERRINGBONE**

### Flagstone

"Flagstone" is a generic term for stratified stone that can be split to form pavers. Limestone, sandstone, and bluestone are common paving materials. The surfaces of marble and slate are usually too smooth to make safe paving. Cut into squares or rectangles, flagstone can be laid as individual stepping-stones or in interesting patterns. Flagstones come in a range of colors, textures, and sizes. Flags for walks should be at least 2 in. thick. Purchased by weight, surface area, or pallet load, flagstones are usually the most expensive paving choice.

**CUT FLAGSTONE**

**CUT AND IRREGULAR
FLAGSTONE**

**IRREGULAR
FLAGSTONE**

### Drainage

Few things are worse than a path dotted with puddles or icy patches. To prevent these from forming, the soil around and beneath the path should drain well. The path's location and construction should ensure that rainwater does not collect on the surface. Before you locate a path, observe runoff and drainage on your property during and after heavy rains. Avoid routing a path through areas where water courses, collects, or is slow to drain.

While both loose and solid paving can sometimes be successfully laid directly on well-drained compacted soil, laying surface materials on a base of sand and gravel will help improve drainage and minimize frost heaving. For most situations, a 4-in. gravel bed topped with 2 in. of sand will work well. Very poorly drained soils may require more gravel, an additional layer of coarse rock beneath the gravel, or even drain tiles. If you suspect that your site has serious drainage problems, consult a landscape contractor.

Finally, keep water from pooling on a walk by making its surface higher in the center than at the edges. The center of a 4-ft.-wide walk should be at least ½ in. higher than its edges. If you're using a drag board to level the sand base, curve its lower edge to create this "crown." Otherwise crown the surface by eye.

## Edgings

All walk surfaces need to be contained in some fashion. Where soil is firm or tightly knit by turf, neatly cut walls of the excavation can serve as edging. An installed edging prevents damage to bricks or stones on the edges of paths. Walkway edgings are commonly made of 1- or 2-in.-thick lumber, thicker landscaping timbers, brick, or stone, as shown below. For a hidden edging, garden centers sell specially designed plastic edging strips that install on top of the gravel base and are covered by the adjacent soil.

### Wood edging

Wood should be rot-resistant redwood or cedar or some other wood pressure-treated for ground-contact use. If you're working in loose soils, fix a deep wooden edging to support stakes with double-headed nails. When the path is laid, pull the nails, and fill and tamp behind the edging. Then drive the stakes below grade. In firmer soils, or if the edging material is not wide enough, install it on top of the gravel base. Position the top of the edging at the height of the path. Dimension lumber 1 in. thick is pliable enough to bend around gradual curves.

**Treated dimensional lumber with support stakes**                **Landscape timbers with crossties laid on gravel base**

### Brick and stone edging

In firm soil, a row of bricks laid on edge and perpendicular to the length of the path adds stability. For a more substantial edging, stand bricks on end on the excavated soil surface; add the gravel base; and tamp the earth around the base of the bricks on the outside of the excavation. Stone edgings laid on end can be set in the same way. "End-up" brick or stone edgings are easy to install on curved walks.

**Bricks on edge, laid on gravel base**                **Bricks on end, laid on soil**

## Preparing the base

Having decided on location and materials, you can get down to business. The initial steps of layout and base preparation are much the same for all surface materials. Before you construct paths or walkways, check your irrigation plans. If underground water lines will cross any paths, be sure to lay the lines first.

### Layout

Lay out straight sections with stakes and string ❶. You can plot curves with stakes and "fair" the curve with a garden hose, or you can outline the curve with the hose alone, marking it with lime or sand.

### Excavation

The excavation depth depends on how much sand-and-gravel base your soil's drainage calls for, the thickness of the surface material, and its position above or below grade ❷. Mark the depth on a stake or stick and use this to check depth as you dig. Walking surfaces are most comfortable if they are reasonably level across their width. Check the bottom of the excavation with a level as you dig. If the walk cuts across a slope, you'll need to remove soil from the high side and use it to fill the low side to produce a level surface. If you've added soil or if the subsoil is loose, compact it by tamping.

### Edging installation

Some edgings can be installed immediately after excavation; others are placed on top of the gravel portion of the base ❸. (See the sidebar "Edgings" on the opposite page.) If the soil's drainage permits, you can now lay soft materials, loose gravel, or crushed stone on the excavated, tamped, and edged soil base. To control weeds and to keep bark, chips, or pine needles from mixing with the subsoil, you can spread water-permeable land-scape fabric over the excavated soil base.

### Laying the base

Now add gravel (if required); rake it level; and compact it ❹. Use gravel up to 1 in. in diameter or ¼- to ¾-in. crushed stone, which drains and compacts well. You can rent a hand tamper (a heavy metal plate on the end of a pole) or a machine compactor if you have a large area to compact.

If you're making a loose-gravel or crushed-stone walk, add the surface material on top of the base gravel. (See "Loose materials" on page 152.) For walks of brick, stone, or pavers, add a 2-in. layer of builder's sand, not the finer sand masons use for mixing mortar.

Rake the sand smooth with the back of a level-head rake. You can level the sand with a wooden drag board, also called a "screed" ❺. Nail together two 1x4s or notch a 1x6 to place the lower edge at the desired height of the sand, and run the board along the path edging. To settle the sand, dampen it thoroughly with a hose set on fine spray. Fill any low spots; rake or drag the surface level; and then dampen it again.

### PREPARING THE BASE

❶ Lay out the path with stakes, string, garden hose, and lime.

❷ Dig out path between layout string and lime lines.

❸ Install the edging.

❹ Rake out gravel base.

Lay out free-form curved sections with garden hose and mark with lime.

Mark straight sections with 1x2 stakes and string.

Drag board
Edging

❺ Level sand base with a drag board.

# Laying the surface

Whether you're laying loose or hard material, take time to plan your work. Provide access so delivery trucks can place materials close to the worksite.

## Loose materials

Install water-permeable landscape fabric over the gravel base to prevent gravel from mixing with the surface material. Spread bark or wood chips 2 to 4 in. deep. Spread loose pea gravel or crushed rock about 2 in. deep. For a harder, more uniform surface, add ½ in. of fine crushed rock on top of the gravel or coarser rock. You can let traffic compact crushed-rock surfaces or compact them by hand or with a machine.

## Bricks and precast pavers

Take time to figure out the pattern and spacing of the bricks or pavers by laying them out on the lawn or driveway, rather than disturbing your carefully prepared sand base. When you're satisfied, begin in a corner, laying the bricks or pavers gently on the sand so the base remains even ❶. Lay full bricks first; then cut bricks to fit as needed at the edges. To produce uniform joints, space bricks with a piece of wood cut to the joint width. You can also maintain alignment with a straightedge or with a string stretched across the path between nails or stakes. Move the string as the work proceeds.

As you complete a row or section, bed the bricks or pavers into the sand base with several firm raps of a rubber mallet or a hammer on a scrap 2x4. Check with a level or straightedge to make sure the surface is even ❷. (You'll have to do this by feel or eye across the width of a crowned path.) Lift low bricks or pavers carefully and fill beneath them with sand; then reset them. Don't stand on the walk until you've filled the joints.

When you've finished a section, sweep fine, dry mason's sand into the joints, working across the surface of the path in all directions ❸. Wet thoroughly with a fine spray and let dry; then sweep in more sand if necessary. If you want a "living" walk, sweep a loam-sand mixture into the joints and plant small, tough, ground-hugging plants, such as thyme, in them.

Rare is the brick walk that can be laid without cutting something to fit. To cut brick, mark the line of the cut with a dark pencil all around the brick. With the brick resting firmly on sand or soil, score the entire line by rapping a wide mason's chisel called a "brickset" with a heavy wooden mallet or a soft-headed steel hammer as shown on the facing page. Place the brickset in the scored line across one face and give it a sharp blow with the hammer to cut the brick.

If you have a lot of bricks to cut, or if you want greater accuracy, consider renting a masonry saw. Whether you work by hand or machine, always wear safety glasses.

**LOOSE MATERIALS**

Cover gravel base with water-permeable landscape fabric and add 2 to 4 in. of bark or wood chips.

**BRICKS AND PRECAST PAVERS**

To turn square corners, align the edging board with a carpenter's square.

❶ Begin laying in a corner.

❷ Check the surface with a level or straightedge. Fill under low bricks; tamp down high ones. Use a plank to distribute your weight if you must work on the path.

❸ Sweep fine, dry sand into the joints to fix the bricks or pavers in place.

# Stepping-stones

A stepping-stone walk set in turf creates a charming effect and is very simple to lay. You can use cut or irregular flagstones or fieldstone, which is irregular in thickness as well as in outline. Arrange the stones on the turf; then set them one by one. Cut into the turf around the stone with a sharp flat shovel or trowel, remove the stone; then dig out the sod with the shovel. Placing stones at or below grade will keep them away from mower blades. Fill low spots beneath the stone with earth or sand so the stone doesn't move when stepped on.

Cut around stepping-stone with shovel or trowel.

Remove sod and soil.

Set in place, filling with sand or soil to bed stone firmly.

## Cutting bricks

Wear safety glasses.

Scored line

Brickset chisel

## Cutting flagstones

Wear safety glasses.

Scored line

Wood batten

Brickset

## *Flagstones*

Install cut stones of uniform thickness as described for bricks and pavers. Working out patterns beforehand is particularly important—stones are too heavy to move around more than necessary. To produce a level surface with cut or irregular stones of varying thickness, you'll need to add or remove sand for each stone. Set the stone carefully on sand; then move it back and forth to work it into place ❶. Lay a level or straightedge over three or four stones to check the surface's evenness ❷. When a section is complete, fill the joints with sand or with sand and loam as described for bricks and pavers.

You can cut flagstone with a technique similar to that used for bricks. Score the line of the cut on the top surface with a brickset and hammer. Prop the stone on a piece of scrap wood, positioning the line of cut slightly beyond the edge of the wood. Securing the bottom edge of the stone with your foot, place the brickset on the scored line and strike sharply to make the cut.

FLAGSTONES

❶ Set flagstones in place carefully to avoid disturbing the sand base.

❷ Extend a straightedge over several stones to check the surface for evenness. Tap high spots to level.

# Laying a Patio

**You can make a simple patio** using the same techniques and materials we have discussed for paths. To ensure good drainage, an even surface, and durability, lay hard surfaces such as brick, flagstone, and pavers on a well-prepared base of gravel, sand, and compacted soil. (Crushed-rock and gravel surfaces likewise benefit from a sound base.) Make sure the surface drains away from any adjacent structure (house or garage); a drop-off of ¼ in. per foot is usually adequate. If the patio isn't near a structure, make it higher in the center to avoid puddles.

Establish the outline of the patio as described for paths; then excavate the area roughly to accommodate 4 in. of gravel, 2 in. of sand, and the thickness of the paving surface. (Check with a local nursery or landscape contractor to find out if local conditions require alterations in the type or amounts of base material.) Now grade the rough excavation to provide drainage using a simple 4-ft. grid of wooden stakes as shown in the drawings.

Drive the first row of stakes next to the house (or in the center of a freestanding patio), leveling them with a 4-ft. builder's level or a smaller level resting on a straight 2x4. The tops of these stakes should be at the height of the top of the sand base (finish grade of the patio less the thickness of the surface material) ❶. Working from this row of stakes, establish another row about 4 to 5 ft. from the first. Make the tops of these stakes 1 in. lower than those of the first row, using a level and spacer block, as shown below. Continue adding rows of stakes, each

## LAYING A SIMPLE PATIO

48 in.

Level — Straightedge

6 in.     **Slope = 1 in. in 48 in.**     1 in.

6 in.

**Attach a 1-in. block to straightedge for setting rows of stakes.**     Final grade

Level the row of stakes next to the house. Place subsequent rows 4 to 5 ft. apart, each 1 in. lower.

1x2 stake

❶ **Excavate roughly to depth. Then set a grid of stakes (4 to 5 ft. on center) to establish the grade at the height of the sand base.**

❷ **Using a tape measure or ruler, fine-tune the grade so the soil surface is 6 in. beneath the tops of all the stakes.**

1 in. lower than the previous row, until the entire area is staked. Then, with a measuring tape or a ruler and a shovel, fine-tune the grading by removing or adding soil until the excavated surface is 6 in. (the thickness of the gravel-sand base) below the tops of all the stakes ❷.

When installing the sand-and-gravel base, you'll want to maintain the drainage grade you've just established and produce an even surface for the paving material. If you have a good eye or a very small patio, you can do this by sight. Otherwise, you can use the stakes to install a series of 1x3 or 1x4 "leveling boards," as shown in the drawing below. (Before adding gravel, you may want to cover the soil with water-permeable landscape fabric to keep perennial weeds from growing; just cut slits to accommodate the stakes.)

Add a few inches of gravel ❸. Then set leveling boards along each row of stakes, with the boards' top edges even with the top of the stakes ❹. Drive additional stakes to sandwich the boards in place (don't use nails). Distribute the remaining inch or so of gravel and compact it by hand or machine, then add the 2 in. of sand. Dragging a straight 2x4 across two adjacent rows of leveling boards will produce a precise grade and an even surface ❺. Wet the sand and fill low spots that settle.

You can install the patio surface as previously described for paths, removing the leveling boards as the bricks or pavers reach them ❻. Disturbing the sand surface as little as possible, slide the boards out from between the stakes, and drive the stakes an inch or so beneath the level of the sand. Cover the stakes, and fill the gaps left by the boards with sand, tamping down carefully. Then continue laying the surface. Finally, sweep fine sand into the joints.

❸ **Add a few inches of gravel to the excavation.**

**Leveling board**

**Add another stake to sandwich the boards in place without nails.**

**Gravel subbase**

❻ **When you install the patio surface, remove leveling boards as you reach them.**

**Patio paving**

**Leveling board (removed)**

**Drive stakes below the surface, and fill gaps with sand.**

❹ **Set 1x3 leveling boards even with the top of the grade stakes. Then add sand.**

❺ **Drag a straight 2x4 across the leveling boards to grade and smooth the sand base.**

**For rectangular patios, equal diagonal measures will ensure square corners.**

**Work on plywood to avoid disturbing sand.**

# Installing a Pond

**It wasn't so long ago** that a garden pond like the one in this book required yards of concrete, an expert mason, and deep pockets. Today's strong, lightweight, and long-lasting synthetic liners and rigid fiberglass shells have put garden pools in reach of every homeowner. Installation does require some hard labor but little expertise: just dig a hole; spread the liner or seat the shell; install edging; and plant. We'll discuss installation of a pond with a liner in the main text; see below for installing a smaller, fiberglass pool.

### *Liner notes*

More and more nurseries and garden centers are carrying flexible pond liners; you can also buy them from mail-order suppliers specializing in water gardens. Synthetic rubber liners are longer lasting but more expensive than PVC liners. (Both are much cheaper than rigid fiberglass shells.) Buy only liners specifically made for garden ponds—don't use ordinary plastic sheeting. Many people feel that black liners look best; blue liners tend to make the pond look like a swimming pool.

### *Before you dig*

First, make sure you comply with local codes about water features. Then keep the following ideas in mind when locating your pond. Avoid trees whose shade keeps sun-loving water plants from thriving; whose roots make digging a chore; and whose flowers, leaves, and seeds clog the water, making it unsightly and inhospitable to plants or fish. Avoid low spots on your property; otherwise your pond will become a catch basin for runoff. Select a reasonably level spot. Use a carpenter's level on a straight board much like that shown on p. 162 to determine level, adding or removing soil as necessary.

## Small reflecting pool

A fiberglass shell or agricultural tank 2 ft. wide, 4 ft. long, and 2 to 3 ft. deep is ideal for the small pool on p. 85. Garden centers often stock pond shells in a variety of shapes.

Dig a hole about 6 in. wider on all sides than the shell. Hole depth should equal that of the shell plus 1 in. for a sand base. Compact the bottom of the hole and spread the sand; then lower the shell into place. Add temporary wedges or props if necessary to orient and level the shell. Slowly fill the shell with water, backfilling around it with sand or sifted soil so the backfill keeps pace with the rising water level. You can edge the pool with colored pavers as shown on p. 85, or overlap the edge of the shell with flagstones.

Paver on base of sand and gravel — Flagstone edging — Fiberglass pond shell or agricultural tank — Sand base, 1 in. thick — Sand/soil backfill

## A patio pond

The pond on pp. 82–83 incorporates a gently sloping river-rock "shore" at its shallow end. This helps create a more "natural" transition to the planting. The liner rests on a sand base (as described in the main text) and is covered with several inches of sand to cushion, and prevent damage from, the river rock.

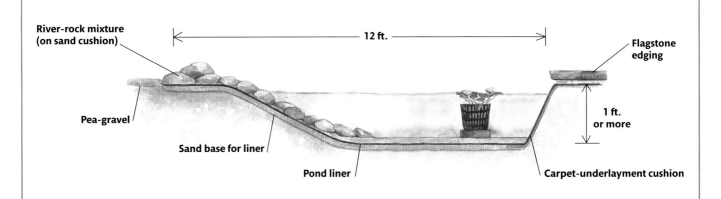

River-rock mixture (on sand cushion) — Pea-gravel — Sand base for liner — Pond liner — 12 ft. — Flagstone edging — 1 ft. or more — Carpet-underlayment cushion

Using graph paper, enlarge the outline of the pond provided on the site plan on p. 86, altering it as you wish. If you change the size of the pond, or are interested in growing a wider variety of water plants or adding fish, remember that a healthy pond must achieve a balance between the plants and fish and the volume, depth, and temperature of the water. Even if you're not altering the size of the pond, it's a good idea to consult with a knowledgeable person at a nursery or pet store specializing in water-garden plants and animals.

Calculate the liner width by adding twice the maximum depth of the pool plus an additional 2 ft. to the width. Use the same formula to calculate the length. So, for a 2 x 7 x 15-ft. pond, the liner width would be 4 ft. + 7 ft. + 2 ft. (or 13 ft.). The length would be 4 ft. + 15 ft. + 2 ft. (or 21 ft.).

### Water work

Unless you are a very tidy builder, the water you used to fit the liner will be too dirty to leave in the pond. (Spilled mortar can also make the water too alkaline for plants or fish.) Siphon or pump out the water; clean the liner; and refill the pond. If you're adding fish to the pond, you'll need to let the water stand for a week or so to allow any chlorine (which is deadly to fish) to dissipate. Check with local pet stores to find out if your water contains chemicals that require commercial conditioners to make the water safe for fish.

Installing the pond and plants is only the first step in water gardening. It takes patience, experimentation, and usually some consultation with experienced water gardeners to achieve a balance between plants, fish, and waterborne oxygen, nutrients, and waste that will sustain all happily while keeping algae, diseases, insects, and predators at acceptable levels.

## Growing pond plants

One water lily, a few upright-growing plants, and a bundle of submerged plants (which help keep the water clean) are enough for a medium-size pond. An increasing number of nurseries and garden centers stock water lilies and other water plants. For a larger selection, your nursery or garden center may be able to recommend a specialist supplier.

These plants are grown in containers filled with heavy garden soil (*not* potting soil, which contains ingredients that float). You can buy special containers designed for aquatic plants, or simply use plastic pails or dishpans. Line basketlike containers with burlap to keep the soil from leaking out the holes. A water lily needs at least 2 to 3 gal. of soil; the more, the better. Most other water plants, such as dwarf papyrus, need 1 to 2 gal. of soil.

After planting, add a layer of gravel on the surface to keep soil from clouding the water and to protect roots from marauding fish. Soak the plant and soil thoroughly. Then set the container in the pond, positioning it so the water over the soil is 6 to 18 in. deep for water lilies, 0 to 6 in. for most other plants.

For maximum bloom, push a tablet of special water lily fertilizer into the pots once or twice a month throughout the summer. Most water plants are easy to grow and carefree, although many are tropicals that die after a hard frost, so you'll have to replace them each spring.

**PLANTING WATER PLANTS**

**Set water plants in a container of heavy garden soil. Then cover the surface with gravel to keep soil from floating away.**

Gravel

1- to 3-gal. dishpan or special container

Heavy garden soil

## Excavation

If your soil isn't too compacted or rocky, a good-size pond can be excavated with a shovel or two in a weekend ❶. (Energetic teenagers are a marvelous pool-building resource.) If the site isn't level, you can grade it using a stake-and-level system adapted from the one described on pp. 162–163 for grading the patio.

Outline the pond's shape with garden lime, establishing the curves with a garden hose, or by staking out a large grid and plotting from the graph-paper plan. Many garden ponds have two levels. One end, often the widest, is 2 ft. deep to accommodate water lilies and other plants requiring deeper water, as well as fish. The other end is 12 to 16 in. deep for plants requiring shallower submersion. (You can also put plant pots on stacks of bricks to vary heights.) The walls will be less likely to crumble as you dig, and the liner will install more easily, if you slope the walls in about 3 to 4 in. for each foot of depth. Make them smooth, removing roots, rocks, and other sharp protrusions.

Excavate a shallow relief around the perimeter of the hole to contain the liner overlap and the width and thickness of the stone edging. To receive runoff after a heavy rain, create an overflow channel, as shown in the drawing on the opposite page. This can simply be a 1- to 2-in. depression a foot or so wide spanned by one of the edging stones. Lengths of PVC pipe placed side by side beneath the stone will keep the liner in place. Position the overflow channel to open onto a lower area of lawn or garden adjacent to the pond or to a rock-filled dry well.

**Section through pond**

17 ft.

2 ft.

12 to 16 in.

Slope in 6 to 8 in.

Slope bottom slightly to make draining the pond easier.

5 ft.

Slope in 3 to 4 in.

Slope in 3 to 4 in.

❷ Spread sand on horizontal surfaces; cushion walls with carpet underlayment.

INSTALLING A LINERED POND

❶ Dig hole with sloping sides to correct depth. Make sure that the perimeter of the hole is level.

Excavate shallow relief for edging flagstones.

### Fitting the liner

When the hole is complete, cushion the surfaces to protect the liner ❷. The drawing shows an inch-thick layer of sand on the bottom surfaces and carpet underlayment on the sloping walls. Fiberglass insulation also works well, as does heavy landscaping fabric.

Stretch the liner across the hole, letting it sag naturally to touch the walls and bottom but keeping it taut enough so it does not bunch up. Weight its edges with bricks or stones; then fill it with water ❸. The water's weight will push the liner against the walls, and the stones will prevent it from blowing around. As it fills, tuck and smooth out as many creases as you can. The weight of the water would make this difficult after the pond is full. If you stand in the pond to do so, take care not to damage the liner. Don't be alarmed if you can't smooth all the creases. Stop filling when the water is 2 in. below the rim of the pond, and cut the liner to fit into the overlap relief ❹. Hold it in place with a few long nails or large "staples" made from coat hangers while you install the edging.

### Edging the pond

Finding and fitting flagstones so there aren't wide gaps between them is the most time-consuming part of this task. Cantilevering the stones an inch or two over the water will hide the liner somewhat.

The stones can be laid directly on the liner, as shown below ❺. Add sand where necessary under the liner to level the surface so that the stones don't rock. Such treatment will withstand the occasional, careful traffic of pond maintenance. If you anticipate heavier traffic, you can bed the stones in 2 to 3 in. of mortar. It's prudent to consult with a landscape contractor about whether your intended use and soil require a footing for mortared stones.

**Elevation detail of pond overflow**

Flagstone edging, 12 in. or more wide

Cover pipe with flagstone.

Pond liner

To overflow area

Garden bed or lawn

PVC pipe, 1 or 2 in. dia., about 12 in. long

Carpet underlayment (walls)

1-in. layer of sand (horizontal surfaces)

❸ Spread liner and begin to fill with water. As water rises, tuck and smooth out as many creases as possible. Fill with water to within 2 in. of pond rim.

To overflow area

❺ Fit and lay flagstone edging. Add sand beneath the liner or stones where necessary to create a firm bed. Brush sand into joints when edging is complete.

Weigh down liner with stones.

❹ Trim liner to fit relief for flagstone edging. Fix liner in place with long nails or bent coat-hanger "staples."

# Building a Retaining Wall

**Contours and sloping terrain** can add considerable interest to a home landscape. But you can have too much of a good thing. Several designs in this book employ retaining walls to alter problem slopes. The wall shown on p. 60 eliminates a small but abrupt grade change, producing two almost-level surfaces and the opportunity to install attractive plantings and a patio on them. On p. 64 a retaining wall helps turn a steep slope into a showpiece.

Retaining walls can be handsome landscape features in their own right. Made of cut stone, fieldstone, brick, landscape timbers, or concrete, they can complement the materials and style of your house or nearby structures. However, making a stable, long-lasting retaining wall of these materials can require tools and skills many homeowners do not possess.

For these reasons we've instead chosen retaining-wall systems made of precast concrete for designs in this book.

Readily available in a range of sizes, surface finishes, and colors, these systems require few tools and no special skills to install. They have been engineered to resist the forces that soil, water, freezing, and thawing bring to bear on a retaining wall. Install these walls according to the manufacturer's specifications, and you can be confident that they will do their job for many years.

A number of systems are available in the Northwest through nurseries, garden centers, and local contracting suppliers. (Check the internet.) But they all share basic design principles. Like traditional dry-stone walls, these systems rely largely on weight and friction to contain the soil. In many systems, interlocking blocks or pegs help align the courses and increase the wall's strength. In all systems, blocks must rest on a solid, level base. A freely draining backfill of crushed stone is essential to avoid buildup of water pressure in the retained soil, which can buckle even a heavy wall. (In hilly terrain or where drainage is a concern, experts often recommend installing drainage pipe to remove excess water from behind retaining walls.)

The construction steps shown here are typical of those recommended by most system manufacturers for retaining walls up to 4 ft. tall; be sure to follow the manufacturer's instructions for the system you choose. For higher walls, walls on loose soil or heavy clay soils, and walls retaining very steep slopes, it is prudent to consult with a landscape architect or contractor. (Some cities and towns have regulations for retaining walls and landscape steps. Be sure to check with local authorities before beginning work.)

**Precast-system retaining wall**

Drawing represents typical construction; dimensions and specifications will vary depending on the system.

Cap block

Topsoil, 6 to 8 in. deep

Backfill of clean crushed stone

Undisturbed soil

"Batter" wall by offsetting each course.

Set first course partially or completely below grade.

Base, 24-in. trench filled with 4 in. of ⅜- to ¾-in. crushed stone

Original slope

New grade level

Excavate for wall; use to level surface behind wall.

30–45° from plumb

New grade

## Building a wall

Installing a wall system is just about as simple as stacking up children's building blocks. The most important part of the job is establishing a firm, level base. Start by laying out the wall with string and hose (for curves) and excavating a base trench.

As the boxed drawing shows, the position of the wall in relation to the base of the slope determines the height of the wall, how much soil you move, and the leveling effect on the slope. Unless the wall is very long, it is a good idea to excavate along the entire length and fine-tune the line of the wall before beginning the base trench. Remember to excavate back far enough to accommodate the stone backfill. Systems vary, but a foot of crushed-stone backfill behind the blocks is typical. (For the two-wall design, build the bottom wall first, then the top.)

Systems vary in the width and depth of trench and type of base material, but in all of them, the trench must be level across its width and along its length. We've shown a 4-in. layer of ⅜- to ¾-in. crushed stone (blocks can slip sideways on rounded aggregate or pea gravel, which also don't compact as well). Depending on the system and the circumstances, a portion or all of the first course lies below grade, so the soil helps hold the blocks in place.

Add crushed stone to the trench; level it with a rake; and compact it with a hand tamper or mechanical compactor. Lay the first course of blocks carefully ❶. Check frequently to make sure the blocks are level across their width and along their length. Stagger vertical joints as you stack subsequent courses.

Offset the faces of the blocks so the wall leans back into the retained soil. Some systems design this "batter" into their blocks; others allow you to choose from several possible setbacks.

As the wall rises, shovel backfill behind the blocks ❷. Clean crushed rock drains well; some systems suggest placing a barrier of landscaping fabric between the rock and the retained soil to keep soil from migrating into the fill and impeding drainage.

Thinner cap blocks finish the top of the wall ❸. Some wall systems recommend cementing these blocks in place with a weatherproof adhesive. The last 6 to 8 in. of the backfill should be topsoil, firmed into place and ready for planting.

**BUILDING A WALL**

❷ **As you add subsequent courses, backfill behind blocks with clean crushed rock.**

**Stagger joints.**

❸ **Cap blocks complete the wall. Use topsoil for final 6 to 8 in. of backfill.**

**Offset courses so wall leans into retained soil.**

**Rock base**

**Level**

❶ **After digging and leveling the trench, spread, level, and compact the base materials; then lay the blocks. Check frequently to see that they are level across their width and length.**

## Wall parallel with a slope: Stepped base

Construct walls running parallel to a slope in "steps," each with a level base.

Backfill so grade behind finishes level with top of wall.

Crushed-stone base

Finish grade in front of wall

## Wall parallel with a slope: Stepped cap

Sometimes the top of a wall needs to step up or down to accommodate grade changes in the slope behind.

Cap block

## A "return" corner

Where you want the slope to extend beyond the end of the wall, make a corner that cuts into the slope.

Step wall below grade to provide solid foundation.

Line of finish grade outside wall

### *Sloped sites*

If your slope runs parallel with the length of the wall, you can "step" the bottom of the wall and make its top surface level, as shown in the drawing, top left. Create a length of level trench along the lowest portion of the site. Then work up the slope, creating steps as necessary. Add fill soil to raise the grade behind the wall to the level of the cap blocks.

Alternatively, you can step the top of the wall, as shown in the drawing, middle left. Here, the base of the wall rests on level ground, but the top of the wall steps to match the slope's decreasing height. This saves money and labor on materials and backfill, while producing a different look.

Retaining walls, such as the one shown on p. 60, are frequently placed perpendicular to the run of a slope. If you want to alter just part of the slope or if the slope continues beyond your property, you'll need to terminate the wall. A corner that cuts back into the slope, bottom left, is an attractive and structurally sound solution to this problem.

### *Constructing curves and corners*

Wall-system blocks are designed so that curves, such as the one in the design on p. 64, are no more difficult to lay than straight sections. Corners may require that you cut a few blocks or use specially designed blocks, but they are otherwise uncomplicated. If your wall must fit a prescribed length between corners, consider working from the corners toward the middle (after laying a base course). Masons use this technique, which also helps to avoid exposing cut blocks at the corners.

You can cut blocks with a mason's chisel and mallet or rent a mason's saw. Chiseling works well where the block faces are rough textured, so the faces you cut blend right in. A saw is best for smooth-faced blocks and projects requiring lots of cutting.

# Steps

Steps in a low retaining wall are not difficult to build, but they require forethought and careful layout. Systems differ on construction details. The drawing below shows a typical design where the blocks and stone base rest on "steps" cut into firm subsoil. If your soil is less stable or is recent fill, you should excavate the entire area beneath the steps to the same depth as the wall base and build a foundation of blocks, as shown in the boxed drawing.

These steps are independent of the adjacent "return" walls, which are vertical, not battered (stepped back). In some systems, steps and return walls are interlocked. To match a path, you can face the treads with the same stone, brick, or pavers, or you can use the system's cap blocks or special treads.

**SOLID FOUNDATION: CROSS SECTION**

Cap block

Return wall

Slope path away from steps.

Slope treads ¼ in. per 12 in. toward front edge to promote runoff.

Stone base

In disturbed or problematic subsoil, make a solid foundation of blocks on a level gravel base.

**"Stepped" foundation**

Width and depth of treads will depend on size of system's block.

Return wall

Cap block

Surface steps with system-provided treads or stone, pavers, or brick, to match path. Set in mortar bed or weatherproof adhesive.

Increase width by adding full blocks.

Retaining wall

Path

Crushed-stone base

Wall block

In firm, undisturbed, or compacted subsoil, bed blocks on "steps" cut in the soil.

# Fences, Arbors, and Trellises

**Novices who have no trouble** tackling a simple flagstone path often get nervous when it comes time to erect a fence, an arbor, or even a trellis. While such projects can require more skill and resources than others in the landscape, the ones in this book have been designed with less-than-confident do-it-yourself builders in mind. The designs are simple, the materials are read-ily available, and the tools and skills will be familiar to anyone accustomed to ordinary home maintenance.

First, we'll introduce you to the tools and materials needed for the projects. Then we'll present the small number of basic operations you'll employ when building them. Finally, we'll provide drawings and comments on each of the projects.

## Tools and materials

Even the least-handy homeowner is likely to have most of the tools needed for these projects: claw hammer, crosscut handsaw, brace-and-bit or electric drill, adjustable wrench, combination square, measuring tape, carpenter's level, and sawhorses. You may even have Grandpa's old posthole digger. Many will have a handheld power circular saw, which makes faster (though noisier) work of cutting parts to length. A cordless drill/screwdriver is invaluable if you're substituting screws for nails. If you have more than a few holes to dig, consider renting a gas-powered posthole dig-ger. A 12-in.-diameter hole will serve for 4x4 posts; if possi-ble, get a larger-diameter digger for 6x6 posts.

### Materials

Of the materials offering strength, durability, and attractive-ness in outdoor settings, wood is the easiest to work and affords the quickest results. While almost all commercially available lumber is strong enough for landscape structures, most decay quickly when in prolonged contact with soil and water. Cedar, cypress, and redwood, however, contain natural preservatives and are excellent for landscape use. Alternatively, a range of softwoods (such as pine, fir, and hemlock) are pressure treated with preservatives and will last for many years. Parts of structures that do not come in contact with soil or are not continually wet can be made of ordinary construction-grade lumber, but unless they're regularly painted, they will not last as long as treated or nat-urally decay-resistant material.

In addition to dimension lumber, several of the designs incorporate lattice, which is thin wooden strips crisscrossed to form patterns of diamonds or squares. Premade lattice is widely available in sheets 4 ft. by 8 ft. and smaller. Lattice comes in decay-resistant woods as well as in treated and untreated softwoods. Local supplies vary, and you may find lattice made of thicker or narrower material.

### Fasteners

For millennia, even basic structures such as these would have been assembled with complicated joints. Today, with simple nailed, bolted, or screwed joints, a few hours prac-tice swinging a hammer or wielding a cordless electric screwdriver is all the training necessary.

All these structures can be assembled using nails. But screws are stronger and, if you have a cordless screwdriver, make assembly easier. Buy common or box nails that are galvanized, or screws treated with zinc dichromite, to pre-vent rust. Self-tapping screws ("deck" screws) require no pilot holes.

Galvanized metal connectors are available to reinforce the joints used in these projects. For novice builders, con-nectors are a great help in aligning parts and making assem-bly easier. (Correctly fastened with nails or screws, the joints are strong enough without connectors.)

### Finishes

Cedar, cypress, and redwood are handsome when left unfinished to weather, when treated with clear or colored stains, or when painted. Pressure-treated lumber is best painted or stained.

Outdoor stains are becoming increasingly popular. Clear or lightly tinted stains can preserve or enhance the rich red-dish browns of cedar, cypress, and redwood. Stains also come in a range of colors that can be used like paint. Because they penetrate the wood rather than forming a film, stains don't form an opaque surface, but stains won't peel or chip like paint and are therefore easier to touch up and refinish.

When choosing a finish, take account of what plants are growing on or near the structure. It's a lot of work to remove yards of vines from a trellis or squeeze between a large shrub and a fence to repaint; consider an unfinished decay-resis-tant wood or an initial stain that you allow to weather.

## Setting posts

Most of the projects are anchored by firmly set, vertical posts. In general, the taller the structure, the deeper the post should be set. Arbor posts should be at least 3 ft. deep. Corner and end posts of fences up to 6 ft. tall and posts supporting gates should also be 3 ft. deep. Intermediate fence posts can be set 2 ft. deep.

The length of the posts you buy depends, of course, on the depth at which they are set and their finished heights. When calculating lengths of arbor posts, remember that the tops of the posts must be level. The easiest method of achieving this is to cut the posts to length after installation. For example, buy 12-ft. posts for an arbor finishing at 8 ft. above grade and set 3 ft. in the ground. The convenience is worth the expense of the foot or so you cut off. The site and personal preference can determine whether you cut fence posts to length after installation or buy them cut to length and add or remove fill from the bottom of the hole to position them at the correct heights.

### Arbor posts

When laying out the arbor, take extra care when positioning arbor posts. The corners of the structure must be right angles, and the sides must be parallel with one another. Locating the corners with batter boards and string is fussy but accurate. Make the batter boards by nailing 1x2 stakes to scraps of 1x3 or 1x4, and positioning them about 1 ft. from the approximate location of each post as shown in the boxed drawing at right. Locate the exact post positions with string; adjust the string so the diagonal measurements are equal, which ensures that the corners of the structure will be at right angles.

At the intersections of the strings, locate the postholes by eye or with a plumb bob ❶. Remove the strings and dig the holes; then reattach the strings to position the posts exactly ❷. Plumb and brace the posts carefully. Check positions with the level and by measuring between adjacent posts and across diagonals. Diagonal braces between adjacent posts will stiffen them and help align their faces ❸. Then add concrete ❹ and let it cure for a day.

To establish the height of the posts, measure up from grade on one post, then use a level and straightedge to mark the heights of the other posts from the first one. Where joists will be bolted to the faces of the posts, you can install the joists and use their top edges as a handsaw guide for cutting the posts to length.

SETTING ARBOR POSTS

❶ Position the posts with batter boards, taut string, and a plumb bob.

Batter board

Taut string

Plumb bob

**BATTER BOARDS**
Set L-shaped batter boards at each corner and stretch string to position the posts exactly.

1x2 stakes and 1x3 boards

Taut string

Taut string

18 to 24 in.

For square or rectangular post layout, diagonal measurements should be equal.

❷ Remove the string to dig the holes; then reattach it and align the outer faces of the posts with the string while you plumb and brace them.

❸ Check distances between posts at top. Add diagonal bracing between posts to fix positions.

❹ Cement posts in place.

### Fence posts

Lay out and set the end or corner posts of a fence first, then add the intermediate posts. Dig the holes by hand or with a power digger ❶. To promote drainage, place several inches of gravel at the bottom of the hole for the post to rest on. Checking with a carpenter's level, plumb the post vertically and brace it with scrap lumber nailed to stakes ❷. Then add a few more inches of gravel around the post's base.

If your native soil compacts well, you can fix posts in place with tamped earth. Add the soil gradually, tamping it continu-ously with a heavy iron bar or 2x4. Check regularly with a level to see that the post doesn't get knocked out of plumb. This technique suits rustic or informal fences, where misalignments caused by shifting posts aren't noticeable or damaging.

For more formal fences, or where soils are loose or fence panels are buffeted by winds or snow, it's prudent to fix posts in concrete ❸. Mix enough concrete to set the two end posts; as a rule of thumb, figure one 80-lb. bag of premixed concrete per post. As you shovel it in, prod the concrete with a stick to settle it, particularly if you've added rubble to extend the mix. Build the con-

### SETTING A FENCE POST

❷ **Plumb the post, checking on adjacent faces with a level. Hold it in position with stakes and braces.**

❶ **Position the end or corner posts; then dig holes for them.**

❸ **Fill the hole with concrete and rubble.**

Post —

**Slope top surface for drainage.**

**3 ft. (typical)**

**Concrete and rubble (shown), or tamped earth**

**Coarse gravel**

**1 ft. (typical)**

crete slightly above grade and slope it away from the post to aid drainage.

Once the end posts are set, stretch a string between the posts. (The concrete should cure for 24 hours before you nail or screw rails and panels in place, but you can safely stretch string while the concrete is still wet.) Measure along the string to position the intermediate posts; drop a plumb bob from the string at each intermediate post position to gauge the center of the hole below ❹. Once all the holes have been dug, again stretch a string between the end posts, near the top. Set the intermediate posts as described previously; align one face with the string, and plumb adjacent faces with the carpenter's level ❺. Check positions of intermediate posts a final time with a measuring tape.

If the fence is placed along a slope, the top of the slats or panels can step down the slope or mirror it (as shown below). Either way, make sure that the posts are plumb, rather than leaning with the slope.

❹ **Stretch a string between the tops of the two end posts. Then locate positions of intermediate posts with a plumb bob.**

❺ **After digging the holes, stretch a string between the end posts to align intermediate posts. Use a level to plumb adjacent faces.**

## Fencing a slope

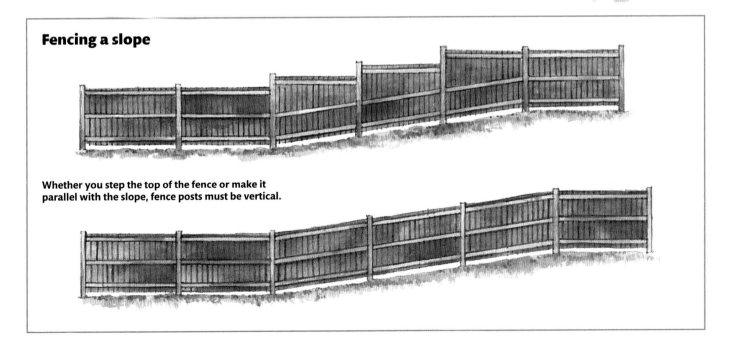

**Whether you step the top of the fence or make it parallel with the slope, fence posts must be vertical.**

## Joints

The components of the fences, arbors, and trellises used in this book are attached to the posts and to each other with the simple joints shown below. Because all the parts are made of dimensioned lumber, the only cuts you'll need to make are to length. For strong joints, cut ends as square as you can, so the mating pieces make contact across their entire surfaces. If you have no confidence in your sawing, many lumberyards will cut pieces to length for a modest fee.

Beginners often find it difficult to keep two pieces correctly positioned while trying to drive a nail into them, particularly when the nail must be driven at an angle, called "toenailing." If you have this problem, consider assembling the project with screws, which draw the pieces together, or with metal connectors, which can be nailed or screwed in place on one piece and then attached to the mating piece.

For one of the designs, you need to attach lattice panels to posts. The panels are made by sandwiching store-bought lattice

**Toenailed butt joints (use nails or screws)**

Post

Rail

Post

Rail

**Metal connectors for butt joints**

Joist hanger: nail through flanges to post and rail.

Angle clip

**Rafter-to-joist joints**

Rafter

Joist

Toenail

Rafter

Joist

Rafter tie

Joist

Rafter

between frames of dimension lumber (construction details are given on the following pages). While the assembled panels can be toenailed to the posts, novices may find that the job goes easier using one or more types of metal connector, as shown in the drawing at below right. Attach the angle clips or angle brackets to the post; then position the lattice panel and fix it to the connectors. For greatest strength and ease of assembly, attach connectors using self-tapping screws driven by a cordless or electric screwdriver or drill-driver.

In the following pages, we'll show construction details of the fences, arbors, and trellises presented in the Portfolio of Designs. (The page number indicates the design.) Where the basic joints discussed here can be used, we have shown the parts but left choice of fasteners up to you. Typical fastenings are indicated for other joints. We have kept the constructions shown here simple and straightforward. They are not the only possibilities, and we encourage experienced builders to adapt and alter constructions as well as designs to suit differing situations and personal preferences.

## Frame corner with metal connector

Nailing plate

Angled plate

## Attaching framed lattice panels to posts

Post

Post

Lattice panel

Lattice panel

Toenail frame to post with nails or screws.

Angle clip

Fix angle brackets to post, then to top and bottom edges of frame.

Fix angle clips to post, then to panel frame.

# Lattice-panel screen

## (pp. 16–17)

This screen serves as a decorative embellishment in the design on p. 16, but it can make an effective enclosure if you wish. The lattice is held in a frame made of 1x2s sandwiched between 1x3s and 1x4s. (The 1x4s add visual weight to the bottom of the screen.) Note how the parts overlap at the corners of the frame to form an interlocking joint.

Panels wider than 6 ft. are awkward to construct and to install. It is easiest to construct the panels on a large flat surface (a garage or basement floor). Lay out the 1x3s and 1x4 that form one face of the panel frame ❶. Then position and nail the 1x2s to them ❷. Add the lattice, then the other layer of 1x3s and 1x4 ❸. As you work, regularly check that the panel is square, its corners at right angles. (Use a framing square or measure across the diagonals to check that they are equal.) Lattice varies in thickness; if yours rattles in its groove, you can add ¾-in. quarter round as shown in the lower box to tighten the fit.

Depending on whether you have more confidence as a post setter or as a panel builder, you can build the panels first and then use them to space the posts, or you can set the posts first (see pp. 165–167) and build the panels to fit. Either way, attach the panels to the posts by toenailing (with nails or screws) or with metal connectors along the lengths of the upright members. Add the 1x4 cap after attaching the panels to the posts. Finials in a variety of styles are available at home and garden stores.

Finial · Lattice panel, to 6 ft. wide · 4x4 post · 1x4 cap · Lattice, 4-in. by 4-in. squares

40 in.

2-in. clearance

❶ Lay out one face of the panel on a flat surface, checking the corners with a framing square.

**PANEL CONSTRUCTION**

Framing square · 1x4 bottom frame rail · 1x3

❷ Nail the inner 1x2s in place, overlapping the joints at the corners.

1x2

1x3 · 1x4 bottom frame rail

❸ Place the lattice inside the 1x2 frame. Then nail the other face pieces in place, again overlapping the corner joints.

**CORNER DETAIL**

1x2 · 1x3 · 1x4

**SCREEN CONSTRUCTION DETAIL**

Finial · 4x4 post · 1x4 cap · 1x2 · 1x3 · ¾-in. quarter round (optional) · Lattice

# Homemade lattice trellis

## (pp. 54–57)

The trellis shown here supports climbing plants to make a vertical garden of a blank wall (or tall fence). Make two panels 48 in. wide for the design on p. 54–55. For the wide trellis on p. 56–57, we recommend making three 32-in.-wide modules (as shown here), which are simpler to make and handle than a single 8-ft.-wide trellis. Hung on L-hangers, these trellises are easy to remove when you need to paint the wall or fence behind. The design can readily be altered to suit other sizes and situations.

Start by cutting all the pieces to length. (Here we'll call the horizontal members "rails" and the vertical members "stiles.") Working on a large flat surface, nail or screw the two outer stiles to the top and bottom rails, checking the corners with a framing square. The 2x2 rails provide ample material to house the L-hangers.

Carefully attach the three intermediate stiles, then the 1x2 rails. Cut a piece of scrap 6 in. long to use as a spacer. Fix the L-shaped hangers to the wall or fence. Buy hangers long enough to hold the trellis several inches away from the surface, allowing air to circulate behind the foliage.

FRONT VIEW

32 in.

2x2 top rail

Make squares 6 in. by 6 in. (inside dimensions).

6 to 8 ft.

Unless otherwise noted, all parts are made of 1x2 stock.

Outer stile

Intermediate stile    Intermediate rail    2x2 bottom rail

CONSTRUCTION DETAILS

2x2 top rail

Hole for L-hanger

1x2 outer stile

1x2 intermediate stile

1x2 intermediate rail

Nail or screw each joint twice for rigidity.

Nail or screw through 1x2 stile into 2x2.

2x2 bottom rail

Hole for L-hanger

## TRELLIS HANGER DETAIL

2x2 top rail

L-hanger

Hang trellis on wall or fence for easy removal.

Stile

2x2 bottom rail

# Hideaway arbor

## (pp. 78–79)

This cozy enclosure shelters a bench and supports vines to shade the occupants. Once the posts are set in place, this project can be finished in a weekend.

Build the arbor before laying the pavers under it. After setting the posts (see pp. 165–167), attach the 2x10 joists with carriage bolts. (The sizes of posts and joists have been chosen for aesthetic effect; 4x4 posts and 2x6 or 2x8 joists will work, too.) Tack the joists in place with nails; then bore holes for

POST-TO-POST DETAIL

2x4 rafter

Hex nut

Washer

½x10 carriage bolt

2x10 joist

6x6 post

2x4 rafter, 7 ft. 6 in. long

Space rafters evenly.

6x6 post

Fix outer rafters to posts.

Bolt joists to post.

2x10 joist, 11 ft. 6 in. long

8 ft. o.c.

80 in. minimum from joist to ground

4 ft. o.c.

the bolts through post and both joists using a long electrician's auger bit. Fix the rafters by toenailing or using rust-protected metal rafter ties. Nail or screw the rafters at each end to the posts for added stability. For more privacy, you can add lattice between the posts at each end. (See p. 178 for a method of lattice panel construction.)

# Louvered fence

## (pp. 70–71)

Made of vertical slats set at an angle, this 6-ft.-tall fence allows air circulation to plants and people near the patio while providing a privacy screen. Be sure to check local codes about height and setback from property lines.

The slats are supported top and bottom by 2x4 rails; a 2x6 beneath the bottom rail stiffens the entire structure, keeps the slat assembly from sagging, and adds visual weight to the design. Set the posts (see pp. 165–167); then cut the rails to fit between them. Toenailed nails or screws or metal connectors are strong enough, but you can add a 2x4 nailer between the rails (as shown in the drawing at bottom right) to make positioning and assembly easier.

Position the 1x6 slats with a spacer block 1½ in. wide and angled 45° at its ends. Nailing or screwing down through the top rail is easy. Nailing up through the bottom rail is more difficult; instead, you could toenail through the edges or faces of the slats into the bottom rail. You may need to cut the final slat narrower to maintain the uniform spacing.

4 to 8 ft.

2x4 top rail

4x4 post

1x6 slat

2x4 bottom rail

2x6 base rail

6-in. clearance

6 ft.

2x4 top rail

4x4 post

1x6 slat

2x4 bottom rail

2x6 base rail

Alternative construction: fix 2x4 to post; nail or screw rails to its ends.

**SLAT ASSEMBLY**

4x4 post

Position first slat at 45°.

Position other slats with spacer block.

Toenail slats into position.

# Recycling-center screen

## (pp. 94–95)

Draped with vines, this is an attractive but unobtrusive screen between the recycling area and the rest of the backyard.

The screen is a snap to build. After setting the posts (see pp. 165–167), add the top and bottom rails. Cut the ends of those for the angled corners at 45° and toenail or screw them to the posts. Trim the ends of the "pickets" at a 45° angle, and fix them with a nail or screw into each rail. Position the pickets before fastening them to ensure even spacing. If you want a more solid-looking screen, offset the pickets so that those on one side fill the gaps left by those on the other. You can vary the size of the screen and the materials shown here. Keep in mind that the proportions are what make this simple design look good.

**PLAN VIEW**

4x4 post · 2x2 picket · 2x8 rail · 2 in. (approximate)

**FRONT ELEVATION**

4 to 8 ft. · 6 in. · 2 in. · 65 in. · 2 in. · 9 in. · Post cap (optional) · 2x8 top rail · 4x4 post · 2x2 picket · 2x8 bottom rail

**SIDE ELEVATION**

7 ft.

# Scene-setting fence

## (pp. 66–69)

This design provides privacy and an attractive backdrop for a perennial border. If the fence is used on a property line, be sure to check local codes for restrictions on placement and height.

This is a simple fence to construct. Assemble the panels on a flat surface, nailing or screwing the slats to the three 2x4 rails. You can lay out the arc at the top of each panel by "springing" a thin strip of wood, as shown on the facing page. Place the strip against a nail driven into a slat at the highest point of the arc in the center of the panel ❶. Enlist a couple of assistants to bend each end of the strip down to nails near each edge of the panel indicating the lowest points of the arc ❷. Pencil in the arc against the strip ❸. Then cut to the line. (A handheld electric sabersaw does the job quickly, but the curve is gentle enough to cut with a handsaw.)

**VIEW FROM BACK OF FENCE**

1x4 slat · 2x4 rail · 2x4 rail · 2x4 rail

Set the posts (see pp. 165–167) according to the widths of the finished panels. The 6x6 posts shown here add an eye-pleasing heft to the fence, an effect emphasized by setting the face of the panel 1 in. back from the faces of the posts. (Posts made of 4x4s will work just as well.) Metal connectors are the easiest means of attaching the completed panels to the posts. To allow yourself access to the rails when mounting the metal connectors, leave the last slats at each end off when you assemble the panels. We've shown a spherical finial attached to the top of each post; you can buy finials of various types at home centers.

## SPRINGING AN ARC

❶ **Position a thin strip of wood against nail driven into slat at top of arc.**

❸ **Scribe arc against bent strip.**

**Fence panel**

❷ **Pull ends of strip down to nails driven near low points of arc at panel edges.**

## FRONT ELEVATION

## SIDE ELEVATION

6 ft. o.c.

**Finial**

6 in.

6x6 post

1x4 slat

6 ft.

6 in.

**Assemble rails and slats; then fix panel to posts.**

**Finial**

**2x4 rail**

**6x6 post**

20 in.

**2x4 rail**

**1x4 slat**

20 in.

**2x4 rail**

12 in.

**Set slats back 1 in. behind face of post.**

# Entry arbor and fence

## (pp. 98–101)

This arbor makes an event of the passage from sidewalk to front door or from one part of your property to another. Two versions are shown in the Portfolio. One features a stand-alone arbor; the other adds a stylized picket fence. Construction details for both are shown here.

When the arbor stands on its own, a ladderlike trellis on each side gives the clematis something to climb. To provide a bit of visual interest, the spaces between the 1x2 rungs decrease from bottom to

**DETAIL OF ARBOR PEDIMENT**

3 in.
2x2 trellis "rafter"
2 in.
45°
2 in.
2x8 joist, 69½ in. long
4x4 post
1x2 ladder-trellis rung

**SIDE ELEVATION OF ARBOR WITH FENCE ASSEMBLY**

2x2 trellis "rafter"
2x8 top plate

3 in.
3½ in.
4 in.
4½ in.
5 in.
5½ in.
6 in.

Fence replaces bottom ladder-trellis rungs.

**SIDE ELEVATION OF FREESTANDING ARBOR**

3 in.
3½ in.
4 in.
4½ in.
5 in.
5½ in.
6 in.
6½ in.
7 in.
7½ in.
8 in.

**Fix 2x8 top plate to posts with ⅜ x 6 carriage bolts.**

**4x4 post**

**1x2 ladder-trellis rung**

**Starting at the top, increase the distance between each ladder-trellis rung by ½ in.**

**ELEVATION OF FENCE**

1x4 slat, 34 in. long
4x4 fence post
1x2 slat, 21½ in. long

2x4 top rail

2x2 midrail

2x4 bottom rail

9 in.
34 in.
11 in.

2-in. clearance
Space slats 1½ in. apart.

top. The drawings show how the fence is incorporated into the design. You can install ladder-trellis rungs above the fence as shown. If you want a more open arbor, replace the trellis rungs with heavy wires to support the vines.

Arbor and fence are both simple to make. The fence will go up quickest if you cut rails to length and nail or screw slats to them, and then attach these assembled sections to the posts.

**ARBOR AND FENCE**

2x2 trellis "rafter"

Note: Three trellis "rafters" were omitted here to show arbor construction.

2x8 top plate

4x4 fence post

8 ft.

2x8 joist

4x4 arbor post

Ladder trellis

Fence

4 ft. o.c.

6 ft.

Butt-join rails of long fence section to rails of short fence section fastened between posts.

# Preparing the Soil for Planting

**The better the soil,** the better the plants. Soil quality affects how fast plants grow, how big they get, how good they look, and how long they live. But on many residential lots, the soil is shallow and infertile. Unless you're lucky enough to have a better-than-average site where the soil has been cared for and amended over the years, perhaps for use as a vegetable garden or flower bed, you should plan to improve your soil before planting in it.

If you were planting just a few trees or shrubs, you could prepare individual planting holes for them and leave the surrounding soil undisturbed. However, for nearly all the plantings in this book, digging individual holes is impractical, and it's much better for the plants if you prepare the soil throughout the entire area that will be planted. (The major ex-ception is when you're planting under a tree, which is discussed on p. 180.)

For most of the situations shown in this book, you could prepare the soil with hand tools—a spade, digging fork, and rake. The job goes faster, though, if you use a rototiller, and a rototiller is better than hand tools for mixing amendments into the soil. Unless you grow vegetables, you probably won't use a rototiller often enough to justify buying one yourself, but you can easily borrow or rent a rototiller or hire someone with a tiller to come and prepare your site.

### Loosen the soil

After you've removed any sod or other vegetation from the designated area (see pp. 144–145), the first step is digging or tilling to loosen the soil ❶. Do this on a day when the soil is moist—not so wet that it sticks to your tools or so dry that it makes dust. Start at one end of the bed and work back and forth until you reach the other end. Try to dig down at least 8 in., or deeper if possible. If the ground is very compacted, you'll have to make repeated passes with a tiller to reach 8 in. deep. Toss aside any large rocks, roots, or debris that you encounter. When you're working near a house or other buildings, watch out for buried wires, cables, and pipes. Most town and city governments have a number you can call to request that someone help you locate buried utilities. Call before you dig.

After this initial digging, the ground will likely be very rough and lumpy. Whump the clods with the back of a digging fork or make another pass with the tiller. Continue until you've reduced all the clumps to the size of apples.

Once you've loosened the existing soil and dug it as deeply as possible, you may need to add topsoil to fill in low spots, refine the grade, or raise the planting area above the surrounding grade for better drainage or to make it easier to see a favorite plant. Unless you need just a small amount, order topsoil by the cubic yard. Consult the staff at your local nursery to find a reputable supplier of topsoil.

### Add organic matter

Common soil (and purchased topsoil, too) consists mainly of rock and mineral fragments of various sizes—which are mostly coarse and gritty in sandy soil, and dust-fine in clay soil. One of the best things you can do to improve any kind of soil for landscape and garden plants is to add some organic matter.

Organic materials used in gardening and landscaping are derived from plants and animals and include ground bark, peat moss, compost, and composted manures. Organic matter can be bought in bags or in bulk at nurseries and many municipal recycling centers. If possible, purchase only composted or aged ma-

## Common fertilizers and soil amendments

The following materials serve different purposes. Follow soil-test recommendations or the advice of an experienced gardener in choosing which amendments and fertilizers would be best for your soil. If so recommended, you can apply two or three of these at the same time, using the stated rate for each one.

| Material | Description | Amount for 100 sq. ft. |
|---|---|---|
| Compost | Amendment. Decomposed or aged plant parts and animal manures. | 8.3 cu. ft. |
| All-purpose fertilizer | Synthetic fertilizer containing various amounts of nitrogen, phosphorus, and potassium. | According to label |
| Organic fertilizer | Derived from a variety of organic materials. Provides nutrients in slow-release form. | According to label |
| Composted manure | Weak nitrogen fertilizers. Bagged steer manure is common. | Dependent on manure type and soil needs |

terial to amend your soil. Fresh manure can "burn" plant roots. Fresh bark and sawdust can "steal" nitrogen from the soil as they decay. If you buy uncomposted materials, ask at your nursery how best to use them as amendments (some require supplemental nitrogen).

How much organic matter should you use? Compost or aged material can be spread 2 to 3 in. thick across the entire area you're working on ❷. At this thickness, a cubic yard (about one heaping pickup-truck load) of bulk material will cover 100 to 150 sq. ft. If you're working on a large area and need several cubic yards of organic matter, have it delivered and dumped close to your project area. You can spread a lot of material in just a few hours if you don't have to cart it very far. Composted and aged manures, such as the bagged steer manure sold at nurseries, contain higher concentrations of nitrogen

and should be applied at much lower rates than other composts. They are more commonly used as slow-release fertilizers than as soil-improving amendments.

### Add fertilizers and mineral amendments

Organic matter improves the soil's texture and helps it retain water and nutrients, but these materials usually lack essential nutrients. To provide the nutrients that plants need, you typically need to use organic or synthetic fertilizers and powdered minerals. It's most helpful if you mix these materials into the soil before you do any planting, putting them down into the root zone as shown in the drawing ❸. But you can also sprinkle them on top of the soil in subsequent years to maintain a planting.

Getting a sample of soil tested is the most accurate way to determine how much of which nutrients is needed. (To

locate a soil-testing lab, look online or ask your Cooperative Extension Service.) Less precise, but often adequate, is seeking the advice of nursery staff. Test results or a good adviser will point out any significant deficiencies in your soil. Most soil just needs a moderate, balanced dose of nutrients.

The key is to avoid using too much of any fertilizer or mineral. Don't guess at this; measure and weigh carefully. Calculate your plot's area. Follow your soil-test results or instructions on a commercial product's package. If necessary, weigh out the appropriate amount, using a kitchen or bathroom scale. Apply the material evenly across the plot with a spreader or by hand.

## PREPARING THE SOIL FOR PLANTING

❶ Use a spade, digging fork, or tiller to dig at least 8 in. deep and break the soil into rough clods. Discard rocks, roots, and debris. Watch out for underground utilities.

❷ Spread a 2- to 3-in. layer of organic matter on top of the soil.

❸ Sprinkle measured amounts of fertilizer and mineral amendments evenly across the entire area, and mix thoroughly into the soil.

### Mix and smooth the soil

Finally, use a digging fork or tiller and go back and forth across the bed again until the added materials are mixed thoroughly into the soil and everything is broken into nut-size or smaller lumps ❹. Then use a rake to smooth the surface ❺.

At this point, the soil level may look too high compared with adjacent pavement or lawn, but don't worry. It will settle a few inches over the next several weeks and end up close to its original level.

### Working near trees

Plantings under the shade of an old tree can be cool lovely oases. But to establish the plants, you'll need to contend with the tree's roots. Contrary to popular belief, most tree roots are in the top few inches of the soil, and they usually extend beyond the perimeter of the tree's canopy. Always try to disturb as few roots as possible when planting beneath established trees. To do so, it's often best to dig individual planting holes. Avoid cutting large roots. To start ground covers and perennials, you can add up to 6 in. of soil under the canopy of many trees. Keep the new soil and mulch away from the trunk. Covering roots with too much soil can starve them of oxygen, damaging or killing them; soil or mulch next to the trunk can rot the bark.

Plantings beneath existing cedar, fir, and hemlock trees are normally problematic because the additional water needed to maintain the planting may damage or kill these trees. If you're uncertain about whether or how to plant beneath any established tree, or if your landscape plans call for significant grade changes beneath it, consult with a certified arborist.

❹ Use a tiller or digging fork to mix everything together, again working as deep as possible.

❺ Finish by smoothing the surface with a rake.

## Making neat edges

All but the most informal landscapes look best if you define and maintain neat edges between the lawn and any adjacent plantings. There are several ways to do this, varying in appearance, effectiveness, cost, and convenience. Attractive, easy-to-install edges include cut brick or stone and plastic strip. If you plan to install an edging, put it in after you prepare the soil but before you plant the bed.

### Cut edge

Lay a hose or rope on the ground to mark the line where you want to cut. Then cut along the line with a sharp spade or edging tool. Lift away any grass that was growing into the bed (or any plants that were running out into the lawn). Use a rake or hoe to smooth out a shallow trench on the bed side of the cut. Keep the trench empty; don't let it fill up with mulch.

**Pros and cons:** Free. Good for straight or curved edges, level or sloped sites. You have to recut the edge every four to eight weeks during the growing season, but you can cut 50 to 100 ft. in an hour or so. Don't cut the trench too deep; if a mower wheel slips into it, you may scalp the lawn. Crabgrass and other weeds may sprout in the exposed soil; if this happens, hoe or pull them out.

### Brick or stone mowing strip

Dig a trench about 8 in. wide and 4 in. deep around the edge of the bed. Fill it halfway with sand; then lay bricks on top, setting them level with the soil on the lawn side. You'll need three bricks per foot of edging. Sweep extra sand into any cracks between the bricks. In cold-winter areas, you'll probably need to reset a few frost-heaved bricks each spring. You can substitute cut stone blocks or concrete pavers for bricks.

**Pros and cons:** Good for straight or curved edges on level or gently sloped sites. Looks good in combination with brick walkways or brick houses. Fairly easy to install and maintain. Some kinds of grass and plants will grow under, between, or over the bricks.

## Plastic strip edging

Garden centers and home-improvement stores sell heavy-duty plastic edging in strips 5 or 6 in. tall and 20 or 50 ft. long. To install it, use a sharp tool to cut straight down through the sod around the edge of the bed. Hold the edging so the round lip sits right at soil level, and drive the stakes through the bottom of the edging and into the undisturbed soil under the lawn. Stakes, which are supplied with the edging, should be at least 8 in. long and set about 3 ft. apart.

**Pros and cons:** Good for straight or curved edges, but only on relatively level sites. Neat and carefree when well installed, but installation is a two- or three-person job. If the lip isn't set right on the ground, you're likely to hit it with the mower blade. Liable to shift or heave unless it's very securely staked. Hard to drive stakes in rocky soil. Some kinds of grass and ground covers can grow across the top of the edging.

**CUT EDGE**

Hose or rope

Sharp edging tool or flat shovel

Shallow trench slopes toward bed.

Lawn

Bed

**BRICK MOWING STRIP**

Fill cracks with more sand.

Lawn

Position top of bricks level with soil on lawn side.

Sand, 2 in. deep

Trench, 8 in. wide, 4 in. deep

Bed

**PLASTIC STRIP EDGING**

Drive stakes into firm soil under the lawn.

Position round lip at soil level.

Lawn

Bed

# Buying Plants

**Once you have chosen** and planned a landscape project, make a list of the plants you want and start thinking about where to get them. You'll need to locate the kinds of plants you're looking for, choose good-quality plants, and get enough of them to fill your design area.

### Where and how to shop

You may already have a favorite place to shop for plants. If not, look online for "Nurseries" and "Garden Centers." Take your shopping list, find a salesperson, and ask for help. The plants in this book are commonly available in the Northwest, but you may not find everything you want at one place. The salesperson may refer you to another nursery, offer to special-order plants, or recommend similar plants that you could use as substitutes.

If you're buying too many plants to carry in your car or truck, ask about delivery—it's usually available and sometimes free. Some nurseries offer to replace plants that fail within a limited guarantee period, so ask about that, too.

The staff at a good nursery or garden center will normally be able to answer most of the questions you have about which plants to buy and how to care for them. If you can, go shopping on a rainy weekday when business is slow so staff will have time to answer your questions.

Don't be lured by the low prices of plants for sale at supermarkets or stores that sell plants for only a few months unless you're sure you know exactly what you're looking for and what you're looking at. The staff at these stores rarely have the time or knowledge to offer you much help, and the plants are often disorganized, unlabeled, and stressed by poor care.

If you can't find a plant locally or have a retailer order it for you, you can always order online yourself from a nursery. Most mail-order nurseries produce good plants and pack them well, but if you haven't dealt with a business before, be smart and place a minimum order first. Judge the quality of the plants that arrive; then decide whether or not to order larger quantities from that firm.

### Timing

It's a good idea to plan ahead and start shopping for plants before you're ready to put them in the ground. That way, if you can't find everything on your list, you'll have time to keep shopping around, place special orders, or choose substitutes. Most nurseries will let you "flag" an order for later pickup or delivery, and they'll take care of the plants in the meantime. Or you can bring the plants home; just remember to check the soil in the containers every day and water if needed.

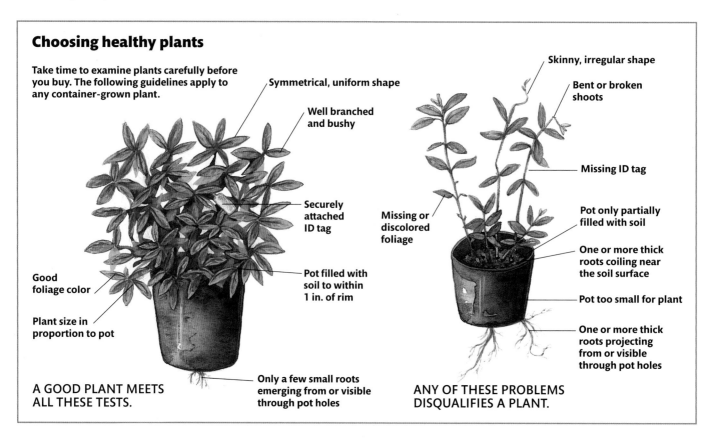

## Choosing healthy plants

Take time to examine plants carefully before you buy. The following guidelines apply to any container-grown plant.

Symmetrical, uniform shape

Well branched and bushy

Securely attached ID tag

Pot filled with soil to within 1 in. of rim

Good foliage color

Plant size in proportion to pot

Only a few small roots emerging from or visible through pot holes

**A GOOD PLANT MEETS ALL THESE TESTS.**

Skinny, irregular shape

Bent or broken shoots

Missing ID tag

Missing or discolored foliage

Pot only partially filled with soil

One or more thick roots coiling near the soil surface

Pot too small for plant

One or more thick roots projecting from or visible through pot holes

**ANY OF THESE PROBLEMS DISQUALIFIES A PLANT.**

## Choosing particular plants

# The Planting Process

If you need, for example, five azaleas and the nursery or garden center has a whole block of them, how do you choose which five to buy? Because the sales staff may be too busy to help you decide, you may need to choose by yourself.

Most plants today are grown in containers, so it's possible to lift them one at a time and examine them from all sides. Following the guidelines shown in the drawings on the opposite page, evaluate each plant's shape, size, health and vigor, and root system.

Trees and shrubs are sometimes sold "balled-and-burlapped," that is, with a ball of soil and roots wrapped tightly in burlap. For these plants, look for strong limbs with no broken shoots, an attractive profile, and healthy foliage. Then press your hands against the burlap-covered root-ball to make sure that it feels firm, solid, and damp, not loose or dry. (If the ball is buried within a bed of wood chips, carefully pull the chips aside; then push them back after inspecting the plant.)

To make the final choice when you're considering a group of plants, line them up side by side and select the ones that are most closely matched in height, bushiness, and foliage color. If your design includes a hedge or mass planting where uniformity is very important, it's a good idea to buy a few extra plants as potential replacements in case of damage or loss. It's easier to plan ahead than to find a match later. Plant the extras in a spare corner so you'll have them if you need them.

Sometimes a plant will be available in two or more sizes. Which is better? That depends on how patient you are. The main reason for buying bigger plants is to make a landscape look impressive right away. If you buy smaller plants and set them out at the same spacing, the planting will look sparse at first, but it will soon catch up. They'll both be larger, but you'll still be able to tell which one started bigger. For shrubs, the difference between one pot size and the next larger one usually represents one year's growth.

**Throughout the Northwest,** fall and early spring are the best times for planting. At those times of year, new plants have the upcoming wet season to become established before the onset of dry summer weather.

Although it's handy to plant a whole bed at once, you can divide the job, setting out some plants in fall and adding the rest in spring, or vice versa. If possible, do the actual planting on a cloudy day or evening when rain is forecast. Compared with preparing the soil, putting plants in the ground goes quite quickly. If you're well prepared, you can plant a whole bed in just an hour or two. On the following pages we'll give an overview of the process and discuss how to handle individual plants. If you're installing an irrigation system, remember that some of the components may need to be put in place after the soil is prepared but before planting.

### Try to stay off the soil

Throughout the planting process, do all you can by reaching in from outside the bed. Stepping on a newly prepared bed compacts the soil and makes it harder to dig planting holes. If you do need to step on the soil, use short boards or scraps of plywood as temporary stepping-stones. As soon as you can decide where to put them, lay permanent stepping-stones for access to plants that need regular maintenance.

### Check placement and spacing

The first step in planting is to mark the position of each plant. It's easy to arrange most of the plants themselves on the bed; use empty pots or stakes to represent plants that are too heavy to move easily. Follow the site plan for the design, checking the spacing with a yardstick as you place the plants.

Then step back and take a look. What do you think? Should any of the plants be adjusted a little—moved to the left or right, a little closer together or farther apart? Don't worry if the planting looks a little sparse. It *should* look that way at first. Plants almost always get bigger than you can imagine when you're first setting them out. And it's almost always better to wait for them to fill in rather than having to prune and thin a crowded planting in a few years. (You might fill between young plants with low-growing annuals, as suggested in the box on p. 184.)

### PLANTING POINTERS

**When working on top of prepared soil, kneel on a piece of plywood to distribute your weight.**

**Use empty pots or stakes to mark positions of plants not yet purchased or too heavy to move frequently.**

## Moving through the job

When you're satisfied with the arrangement, mark the position of each plant with a stake or stone, and set the plants aside so you won't knock them over or step on them as you proceed. Start planting in order of size. Do the biggest plants first, then move on to the medium-size and smaller plants. If all the plants are about the same size, start at the back of the bed and work toward the front, or start in the center and work to the edges.

## Position trees and shrubs to show their best side

Most trees and shrubs are slightly asymmetric. There's usually enough irregularity in their branching or shape that one side looks a little fuller or more attractive than the other sides do. After you've set a tree or shrub into its hole, step back and take a look. Then turn it partway, or try tilting or tipping it a little to one side or the other. Once you've decided which side and position looks best, start filling in the hole with soil. Stop and check again before you firm the soil into place.

## The fine points of spacing

When you're planting a group of the same kind of plants, such as perennials or ferns, it normally looks best if you space them informally, in slightly curved or zigzag rows, with the plants in one row offset from those of the next row. Don't arrange plants in a straight row unless you want to emphasize a line, such as the edge of a bed. After planting, step back and evaluate the effect. If you want to adjust the placement or position of any plant, now is the time to do so.

## Rake, water, and mulch

Use a garden rake to level out any high and low spots that remain after planting. Water enough to settle the soil into place around the roots. Mulch the entire planting area with 1 to 3 in. of composted bark, wood chips, or other organic matter. Mulch is indispensable for controlling weeds and regulating the moisture and temperature of the soil. If you're running out of time, you don't have to spread the mulch right away, but try to get it done within a week or so after planting.

## Using annuals as fillers

The plants in our designs have been spaced so they will not be crowded at maturity. Buying more plants and spacing them closer may fill things out faster, but in several years (for perennials; longer for shrubs) you'll need to remove plants or prune them frequently.

If you want something to fill the gaps between young plants for that first year or two, use some annuals. The best annual fillers are compact plants that grow only 6 to 10 in. tall. These plants will hide the soil or mulch and make a colorful carpet. Avoid taller annuals, because they can shade or smother your permanent plantings. And don't forget, filler plants will need water.

The following annuals are all compact, easy to grow, readily available, and inexpensive. Seeds of those marked with a symbol (✿) can be sown directly in the garden. For the others, buy six-packs or flats of plants. Thin seedlings according to seed packet or plant guidelines.

**Ageratum:** Fluffy blue, lavender, or white flowers. Choose dwarf types. Full sun (if watered) or partial shade.

**Annual chrysanthemum:** Bears white, pink, or yellow daisies all summer. Full sun.

**Dusty miller:** Silvery foliage, often lacy-textured. Full sun or partial shade.

**Dwarf calendula ✿:** Flowers in warm yellow and orange tones. Full sun.

**Garden verbena:** Bright red, pink, purple, or white flowers. Full sun.

**Geranium:** Red, pink, purple, or white flowers. Good for full sun.

**Impatiens:** Flowers in many colors. Slugs usually avoid them. Shade.

**Lobelia:** Dark blue, magenta, or white flowers. Best in full sun.

**Pansy and viola:** Multicolored flowers. Grow best in cool weather. Full sun.

**Sweet alyssum ✿:** Months of fragrant white or lilac flowers. Prefers cool weather. Full sun (if watered) or partial shade.

**Wax begonia:** Rose, pink, or white flowers. Good for shady sites but takes sun if watered regularly.

# Planting Basics

**Most of the plants** that you buy for a landscaping project today are grown and sold in individual plastic containers, but large shrubs and trees may be balled-and-burlapped; mail-order plants may come bare-root; and ground covers are sometimes sold in flats. In any case, the basic concern is the same: be careful what you do to a plant's roots. Spread them out; don't fold or coil them or cram them into a tight hole. Keep them covered; don't let the sun or air dry them out. And don't bury them too deep; set the top of the root-ball level with the surrounding soil.

*Planting container-grown plants*
The steps are the same for any plant, no matter what size container it's growing in. Dig a hole that's a little wider than the container but not quite as deep ❶. Check by setting the container into the hole—the top of the soil in the container should be slightly higher than the surrounding soil. Dig several holes at a time, at the positions that you've already marked out.

Remove the container ❷. With one hand, grip the plant at the base of its stems or leaves, like pulling a ponytail, while you tug on the pot with the other hand. If the pot doesn't slide off easily,

don't pull harder on the stems. Try whacking the pot against a hard surface; if it still doesn't slide off, use a strong knife to cut or pry it off.

Examine the plant's roots ❸. If there are any thick, coiled roots, unwind them and cut them off close to the root-ball, leaving short stubs. If the root-ball is a mass of fine, hairlike roots, use the knife to cut three or four slits from top to bottom, about 1 in. deep. Pry the slits apart and tease the cut roots to loosen them. This cutting or slitting may seem drastic, but it's actually good for the plant because it forces new roots to grow out into the surrounding soil. Work quickly. Once you've taken a plant out of its container, get it in the ground as soon as possible. If you want to prepare several plants at a time, cover them with an old sheet or tarp to keep the roots from drying out.

Set the root-ball into the hole ❹. Make sure that the plant is positioned right, with its best side facing out, and that the top of the root-ball is level with or slightly higher than the surface of the bed. Then add enough soil to fill in the hole, and pat it down firmly.

## PLANTING CONTAINER-GROWN PLANTS

❶ Dig a hole a little wider than the container but not as deep.

❷ Remove the plant from the container.

❸ Unwind any large, coiled roots and cut them off short. Cut vertical slits through masses of fine roots.

❹ Position the plant in the hole and fill in around it with soil.

## Planting a balled-and-burlapped shrub or tree

Nurseries often grow shrubs and trees in fields, and then dig them with a ball of root-filled soil and wrap a layer of burlap snugly around the ball to keep it intact. The problem is that even a small ball of soil is very heavy. A root-ball that is a foot wide is a two-person job. For larger root-balls, ask the nursery to deliver and plant it. Here's how to proceed with plants that are small enough that you can handle them.

Dig a hole three times the width of the root-ball but not quite as deep as the rootball is high. Firm the soil so the plant won't sink. Set the plant into the hole, and lay a stick across the top of the root-ball to make sure it's 1 to 2 in. higher than grade level, depending on the size of the caliper. Be sure to cut or untie any twine that wraps around the trunk. Fold the burlap down around the sides of the ball. Pull the burlap out altogether without damaging the roots. Fill soil all around the sides of the ball and pat it down firmly. Spread only an inch of soil over the top of the ball.

The top of the ball should be level with the surrounding soil. Cut twine that wraps around the trunk. Fold down the burlap.

## Planting bare-root plants

Mail-order nurseries sometimes dig perennials, roses, and other plants when the plants are dormant, cut back the tops, and wash all the soil off the roots to save space and weight when storing and shipping them. If you receive a plant in bare-root condition, unwrap it, trim away any roots that are broken or damaged, and soak the roots in a pail of water for several hours.

To plant, dig a hole large enough that you can spread the roots across the bottom without folding them. Start covering the roots with soil, then lay a stick across the top of the hole and hold the plant against it to check the planting depth, as shown in the drawing. Raise or lower the plant if needed in order to bury just the roots, not the buds. Add more soil, firming it down around the roots, and continue until the hole is full.

Dig a hole wide enough that you can spread out the roots. A stick helps position the plant at the correct depth as you fill the hole with soil.

## Planting ground covers from flats

Sometimes ground covers are sold in flats of 25 or more rooted cuttings. Start at one corner, reach underneath the soil, and lift out a portion of the flat's contents. Work quickly because the roots are exposed. Tease the cuttings apart, trying not to break off any roots, and plant them individually. Then lift out the next portion and continue planting.

Remove a clump of little plants, tease their roots apart, and plant them quickly.

## Planting bulbs

Plant spring-blooming bulbs in October and November. If the soil in the bed was well prepared, you can use a trowel to dig holes for planting individual bulbs; where you have room, you can dig a wider hole or trench for planting a group of bulbs all at once. The perennials, ground covers, shrubs, and trees you planted earlier in the fall or in the spring will still be small enough that you won't disturb their roots. As a rule of thumb, plant small (grape- or cherry-size) bulbs about 2 in. deep and 3 to 5 in. apart, and large (walnut- or egg-size) bulbs 4 to 6 in. deep and 6 to 10 in. apart.

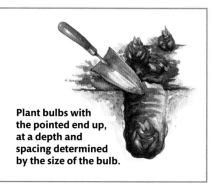

Plant bulbs with the pointed end up, at a depth and spacing determined by the size of the bulb.

## Planting on a hillside

Successful planting on a hillside depends on keeping the bare soil and young plants from blowing or washing away while they establish themselves. Rather than amending all the soil, prepare individual planting holes. Work from the top of the slope to the bottom. Push one or more wooden shingles into the slope just below a plant to help hold it in place. Mulch with heavier materials, such as wood chips, that won't wash or blow away. If the soil is loose, spread water-permeable landscape fabric over it to help hold it in place; slit the fabric and insert plants through the openings. Water with drip irrigation, which is less likely to erode soil than sprinklers are.

## Confining perennials

Yarrow, bee balm, artemisia, and various other perennials, grasses, spread by underground runners. To confine these plants to a limited area, install a barrier when you plant them. Cut the bottom off a 5-gal. or larger plastic pot, bury the pot so its rim is above the soil, and plant the perennial inside. You'll need to lift, divide, and replant part of the perennial every second or third year.

Position rim above soil surface.

Remove bottom of pot.

# Basic Landscape Care

**The landscape plantings** in this book will grow increasingly carefree from year to year as the plants mature, but of course you'll always need to do some regular maintenance. This ongoing care may require as much as a few hours a week during the season or as little as a few hours a year. You'll have to control weeds, use mulch, water as needed, and do spring and fall cleanups. Trees, shrubs, and vines may need staking or training at first and occasional pruning or shearing afterward. Perennials, ground covers, and grasses may need to be cut back, staked, deadheaded, or divided. Performing these tasks, which are explained on the following pages, is sometimes hard work, but for many gardeners it is enjoyable labor—a chance to get outside in the fresh air. Also, spending time each week with your plants helps you identify and address problems before they become serious.

## Mulches and fertilizers

Covering the soil in all planted areas with a layer of organic mulch does several jobs at once: it improves the appearance of your garden while you're waiting for the plants to grow, reduces the number of weeds that emerge, retards water loss from the soil during dry spells, moderates soil temperatures, and adds nutrients to the soil as it decomposes. Inorganic mulches such as landscape fabric and gravel also provide some of these benefits, but their conspicuous appearance and the difficulty of removing them if you ever want to change the landscape are serious drawbacks.

Many materials are used as mulches; the box on p. 188 presents the most common, with comments on their advantages and disadvantages. Consider appearance, availability, cost, and convenience when you're comparing different products. Most garden centers have a few kinds of bagged mulch materials, but for mulching large areas, it's easier and cheaper to have a nursery or other supplier deliver a truckload of bulk mulch. A landscape looks best if you see the same mulch throughout the entire planting area, rather than a patchwork of different mulches. You can achieve a uniform look by spreading a base layer of homemade compost, hay, or other inexpensive material and topping that with a neater-looking material such as bark chips or shredded bark.

It takes at least 2- to 3-in. layer of mulch to suppress weeds, but there's no need to spread it more than 4 in. deep. As you're spreading it, don't put any mulch against the stems of any plants, because that can lead to disease or insect problems. Put most of the mulch between plants, not right *around* them. Check the mulch during your spring and fall cleanups. Be sure it's pulled back away from the plant stems. Rake the surface of the mulch lightly to loosen it, and top it up with a fresh layer if the old material has decomposed.

### *Fertilizer*

Decomposing mulch frequently supplies enough nutrients to grow healthy plants, but using fertilizer helps if you want to boost the plants—to make them grow faster, get larger, or produce more flowers. Young plants or those growing in poor soils also benefit from occasional applications of fertilizer. There are dozens of fertilizer products on the market—liquid and granular, fast-acting and slow-release, organic and synthetic. All give good results if applied as directed. And observe the following precautions: don't overfertilize, don't fertilize when the soil is dry, and don't fertilize tender plants after late summer, because they need to slow down and finish the season's growth before cold weather comes.

# Mulch materials

### Bark products

Bark nuggets, chipped bark, shredded bark, ground bark, and composted bark are available in bags or in bulk. All are attractive, long lasting, medium-price mulches.

### Chipped tree trimmings

The chips available from utility companies and tree services are a mixture of wood, bark, twigs, and leaves. These chips cost less than pure bark products (you may be able to get a load for free), but they don't look as good and you have to replace them more often, because they decompose quickly.

### Sawdust and shavings

These are cheap or free at sawmills and woodshops. They make good path coverings, but they aren't ideal mulches, because they tend to pack down into a dense, water-resistant surface. Sawdust can also blow around.

### Hulls and shells

Ground coconut hulls, cocoa hulls, and nut shells can be picked up at food-processing plants and are sometimes sold at garden centers. They're all attractive, long-lasting mulches. Price varies from free to quite expensive, depending on where you get them.

### Tree leaves

A few big trees may supply all the mulch you need, year after year. You can just rake the leaves onto a bed in fall, but it's better to chop them up with the lawn mower, pile them in compost bins for the winter, and spread them where needed in late spring. Pine needles likewise make good mulch, especially for rhododendrons, azaleas, and other acid-loving shrubs. You can spread pine needles in fall, because they cling together and don't blow around.

### Grass clippings

A 1- to 2-in. layer of dried grass clippings makes an acceptable mulch that decomposes within a single growing season. Don't pile clippings too thick, though. If you do, the top surface dries and packs into a water-resistant crust, and the bottom layer turns into nasty slime.

### Hay and straw

Farmers sell hay that's unsuitable for fodder as "mulch" hay. Hay is cheap but likely to include weed seeds. Straw—the stems of grain crops such as wheat—is usually seed-free but more expensive. Both hay and straw are more suitable for mulching vegetable gardens than landscape plantings because they decompose quickly and must be renewed each year. They also tend to attract rodents.

### Gravel

A mulch of pea gravel or crushed rock, spread 1 to 2 in. thick, helps keep the soil cool and moist, and many plants grow very well with a gravel mulch. However, compared with organic materials such as bark or leaves, it's much more tiring to apply a gravel mulch in the first place; it's harder to remove leaves and litter that accumulate on the gravel or weeds that sprout up through it; it's annoying to dig through the gravel if you want to replace or add plants later; and it's tedious to remove the gravel itself, should you ever change your mind about having it there. Gravel mulches also reflect heat and can make a yard hotter than normal.

### Landscape fabrics

Various types of synthetic fabrics, usually sold in rolls 3 to 4 ft. wide and 20, 50, or 100 ft. long, can be spread over the ground as a weed barrier. Unlike plastic, these fabrics allow water and air to penetrate into the soil. A topping of gravel, bark chips, or other mulch can anchor the fabric and hide it from view. If you're planting small plants, you can spread the fabric and insert the plants through X-shaped slits cut in the fabric where needed. You can plant larger plants first, then cut and snug the fabric around them. Drip irrigation is best laid on top of the fabric, to make it easier to see clogs and leaks. It's also useful to lay fabric under paths, although it can be difficult to secure the fabric neatly and invisibly along the edges of adjacent planting beds. Removing fabric—if you change your mind—is a messy job. However, there are newer biodegradable fabrics that break down after a few years.

### Clear or black plastic

Don't even think about using any kind of plastic sheeting as a landscape mulch. The soil underneath a sheet of plastic gets bone-dry, while water accumulates on top. Any loose mulch you spread on plastic won't stay in an even layer. No matter how you try to secure them, the edges of plastic sheeting always pull loose, appear at the surface, degrade in the sun, and shred into tatters.

# Watering

Watering is a summertime necessity for most residential landscapes in the Northwest. To use water efficiently and effectively, it is helpful to know how to gauge when your plants need water, how much water they need, and how to ensure that you supply the desired amounts.

## Deciding whether water is needed

Many experienced gardeners can judge whether a plant needs water simply by looking at its leaves. But drooping or dull leaves can be caused by pests, disease, and overwatering as well as by water stress. A surer way to decide whether you need to water is to examine the soil. If the top 3 to 4 in. is dry, most annuals, perennials, and shallow-rooted shrubs such as rhododendrons will need to be watered. Most trees and larger shrubs need water if the top 6 to 8 in. is dry. You can dig in the soil to determine moisture content, but digging in an established planting can be harmful to roots.

There are several less-invasive methods of checking moisture. In the loose soil of a prepared bed, you can use a paint stirrer or similar piece of unfinished, light-colored wood as though it were a dipstick. Push it down through the mulch and 6 to 8 in. into the soil. Leave it there for an hour or so, and pull it out to see whether moisture has soaked in and discolored the wood or not. If so, the soil is moist enough for plants. If not, it's time to water.

Where ground is more compacted or where you want to gauge moisture at greater depths, you can push a ¼- to ½-in.-diameter iron bar into the soil. The bar will move easily through wet soil. When it encounters dry soil, the bar will become harder to push or it will feel different as you push.

Paying attention to rainfall also helps you gauge when plants may need water. In the Northwest, most landscape plants thrive if they get several inches of rain a month. Install a simple rain gauge on your property, and listen to weather reports. Mark significant rainfall amounts on a calendar for easy reference. During the drier summer months, you'll need to supply most if not all of your plants' water needs.

New plantings, even those of drought-tolerant plants, require frequent watering during the first year or two until the plants are established. In summer, new plantings may require water twice a week or more.

Early in the morning is the best time of day to water. The wind is calm, evaporation is low, and plant foliage will have plenty of time to dry off before nightfall, which helps reduce fungal growth.

## How much to water

Determining how much water to apply and how often to apply it is one of gardening's greatest challenges. Water too much and plants drown. Water too little and they dry out and die. The key to watering enough but not too much is to be a good observer. Examine your soil often, keep an eye on your plants, and make adjustments with the weather.

Established landscape plants vary in their water needs. When you do water, it is always best to water deeply, wetting a large portion of the plant's root zone. Shallow watering encourages shallow rooting, and shallow-rooted plants dry out fast and need watering more frequently. Furthermore, a water-stressed plant is also more susceptible to disease and insect damage.

If you decide your plants need a certain amount of water, you need to know how long to run your system to provide it. Different watering systems, from hose-end sprinklers to automated drip systems, deliver water at different rates. Manufacturers often provide rates for their products. You can determine a sprinkler's rate by setting tuna-fish cans in the area it covers and timing how long it takes to deposit an inch of water in one or more cans.

### CHECKING SOIL MOISTURE

**Stick a paint stirrer or similar piece of light-colored, unfinished wood down through the mulch and into the soil. Pull it up after an hour. If the bottom of the stick looks and feels damp, the soil is moist enough for plants.**

### MONITORING A SPRINKLER

**Set several tuna-fish cans throughout the area, and let the sprinkler run until about 1 in. of water has collected in each can.**

# Controlling weeds

Weeds are not much of a problem in established landscapes. Once the "good" plants have grown big enough to merge together, they tend to crowd or shade out all but the most persistent undesirable plants. But weeds can be troublesome in a new landscape unless you take steps to prevent and control them.

There are two main types of weeds: those that mostly sprout up as seedlings and those that keep coming back from perennial roots or runners. Try to identify and eliminate any perennial weeds before you start a landscaping project. (See p. 144.) Then you'll only have to deal with new seedlings later, which is a much easier job.

Annual and perennial weeds that commonly grow from seeds include annual bluegrass, bindweed, dandelions, oxalis, plantain, and spurge. Trees and shrubs such as big-leaf maple, alder, and cottonwood, produce weedy seedlings, too. For any of these weeds that grow from seeds, the strategy is twofold: try to keep the weed seeds from sprouting, and eliminate any seedlings as soon as you see them, while they are still small.

Almost any patch of soil includes weed seeds that are ready to sprout whenever that soil is disturbed. Preparing the soil for planting will probably cause an initial flush of weeds, but you'll never see that many weeds again if you leave the soil undisturbed in subsequent years. You don't have to hoe, rake, or cultivate around perennial plantings. Leave the soil alone, and fewer weeds will appear. Using mulch helps even more; by shading the soil, it prevents weed seeds from sprouting. And if weed seeds blow in and land on top of the mulch, they'll be less likely to germinate there than they would on bare soil.

In the Northwest, weed seedlings can emerge almost anytime except the drier months of August and September. Pull or cut them off while they're young and small, just a few inches tall. Don't let them mature and go to seed. Also, weeds that overwinter will be much stronger and harder to pull the following spring.

## Using herbicides

Two kinds of herbicides can be very useful and effective in maintaining home landscapes, but only if used correctly. You have to choose the right product for the job and follow the directions on the label regarding dosage and timing of application exactly.

**Preemergent herbicides.** Sold in granular or liquid form, these herbicides are designed to prevent weed seeds, particularly crabgrass and other annual weeds, from sprouting. Make the first application in early fall before the first rain. You'll probably need to make another application in spring before hot-weather season.

Make sure the herbicide you buy is registered for use around the kinds of ground covers, perennials, shrubs, or other plants

### WEEDS THAT SPROUT FROM SEEDS

**Simple root systems can be easily pulled while still small.**

Spurge                    Oxalis

### WEEDS THAT SPROUT BACK FROM PERENNIAL ROOTS OR RUNNERS

**Connected by underground runners, the shoots of these weeds need to be pulled repeatedly, smothered with a thick mulch, or killed with an herbicide.**

Creeping buttercup

Runner

**Use a disposable, sponge-type paintbrush to apply the herbicide selectively, painting only the weeds. Prepare the solution as directed for spray application. Use only enough to wet the leaves, so none drips off.**

### USING HERBICIDES ON PERENNIAL WEEDS

**Ready-to-use spot-weeder sprays are convenient, but you must aim carefully. Try using a sheet of cardboard as a backdrop to protect desirable plants from herbicide drift.**

# Caring for Woody Plants

you have. Granular forms are often used in smaller areas, liquid in larger areas. Apply them exactly as described on the product label. Wear heavy rubber gloves that are rated for use with farm chemicals, not household rubber gloves.

**Postemergent herbicides.** These chemicals are used to kill growing plants. Some kill only the aboveground parts of a plant; others are absorbed into the plant and kill it, roots and all. Postemergent herbicides are typically applied as sprays, which you can buy ready-to-use or prepare by mixing a concentrate with water. Look for those that break down quickly, and read the label carefully for registered applications, specific directions, and safety instructions.

Postemergent herbicides work best if applied when the weeds are growing vigorously. You usually have to apply enough to thoroughly wet the plant's leaves, and do it during a spell of dry weather. Applying an herbicide is an effective way to get rid of a perennial weed that you can't dig or pull up, but it's really better to do this before you plant a bed, as it's hard to spray herbicides in an established planting without getting some on your good plants. (Some postemergent herbicides are more selective, affecting only certain types of plants.) Aim carefully, shielding nearby plants as shown in the drawing, left, and don't spray on windy days. Brushing or sponging the herbicide on the leaves is slower than spraying, but you're sure to avoid damaging adjacent plants.

Using postemergent herbicides in an established planting may be the only way to get rid of a persistent perennial weed. For young weed seedlings, it's usually easier to pull them by hand.

**A well-chosen garden tree,** such as the ones recommended in this book, grows naturally into a pleasing shape, won't get too large for its site, is resistant to pests and diseases, and doesn't drop messy pods or other litter. Once established, these trees need very little care from year to year.

Regular watering is the most important concern in getting a tree off to a good start. Don't let it suffer from drought for the first few years. To reduce competition, don't plant ground covers or other plants within 2 ft. of the tree's trunk. Just spread a thin layer of mulch there.

Arborists now dismiss other care ideas that once were common practice. According to current thinking, you don't need to fertilize a tree when you plant it (in fact, unless they show obvious signs of deficiency or grow poorly, most landscape trees need little to no fertilizing). Keep pruning to a minimum at planting time; remove only dead or damaged twigs, not healthy shoots. Finally, research has shown that tree trunks grow stronger when they're not supported by stakes. However, most newly planted trees need some support, usually for no more than a year. It is very important that the supported trunk be allowed a certain amount of movement. Be sure to ask your nursery about proper staking for your tree.

## Pruning basics

Proper pruning keeps plants healthy and looking their best. There are two basic types of pruning cuts: heading and thinning. Heading cuts are made along the length of a branch or stem, between its tip and its base. These cuts induce vigorous growth in the dormant buds below the cut. Such growth is useful for filling in hedges and rejuvenating shrubs and perennials. But heading can drastically change the appearance of a plant, even destroying its natural shape. Heading can also produce weakly attached branches in trees and shrubs.

Thinning cuts remove stems and branches at their origin (the plant's crown or where the branch attaches to the trunk or a larger limb). Unlike heading, thinning does not produce vigorous growth. Instead, thinning opens the plant's interior to light and air, which improves its health, and redirects energy to newer branches and stems. And, by reducing congested growth, thinning often enhances the natural appearance of the plant. In most cases, thinning is the preferred pruning technique, especially for trees and shrubs.

**BUSHIER GROWTH**

For many plants, simple heading cuts can produce fuller, bushier growth. Cut off the ends of stems to induce growth from lower buds.

# Pruning roses

Roses are vigorous, fast-growing shrubs that need regular pruning to keep them shapely and attractive. Most of this pruning is done in late winter to early spring, just as the buds start to swell but before the new leaves start to unfold. Always use sharp pruning shears and cut back to a healthy bud, leaving no stub. Right after pruning is a good time to add fresh mulch around the plant.

Prune hybrid tea roses, such as 'Just Joey', to keep them neat, compact, and continuously producing long-stemmed flowers. Remove skinny or weak stems plus a few of the oldest stems (their bark is tan or gray instead of green) by cutting them off at their base. Prune off any shoots that got frozen or broken during the winter; remove old or weak shoots and crossing or crowded stems; and trim back any asymmetric or unbalanced shoots. Don't be afraid of cutting back too hard; it's better to leave just a few strong shoots than a lot of weak ones. If you cut old stems off 3 to 4 in. above ground level, new ones will grow to replace them. Cut damaged or asymmetric stems back partway and they will branch out. Cut just above an outward-facing bud to keep the center of the rose open.

Hybrid tea roses bloom on new growth, so if you prune in early spring, before new growth, you won't be cutting off flower buds. During the growing season, make a habit of removing the flowers as soon as they fade. This keeps the plant neat and makes it bloom longer and more abundantly. At least once a week, locate each faded flower, follow down its stem to the first or second five-leaflet leaf, and prune just above one of those leaves. (Follow the same steps to cut roses for a bouquet.)

Shrub roses, such as 'Flower Carpet' and *Rosa rugosa* 'Dwarf Pavement', as well as floribundas and other landscape roses also bloom on new growth. In winter, cut these bushy plants back by one-third to one-half. As for other roses, remove diseased or damaged canes when you see them. Try to cut stems at their base to avoid leaving stub ends, which are more susceptible to disease. In summer, remove spent flowers to keep plants tidy and promote additional bloom.

## PRUNING A HYBRID TEA ROSE

**In late winter or early spring, remove old, weak, or damaged shoots; stems that are crossing or crowded; and stems that stick out too far and look asymmetric. Don't be afraid to cut a lot away.**

## REMOVING FLOWERS

**Roses can look messy as they fade. Cut off by pruning the stem back to the first healthy five-leaflet leaf.**

**Cut blackened winter-damaged shoots back to healthy, green tissue.**

Old

Weak, crossing

BEFORE

AFTER

Five-leaflet leaf

# Shaping young trees

As a tree grows, you can affect its shape by pruning once a year, usually in winter. Take it easy, though. Don't prune just for the sake of pruning; that does more harm than good. If you don't have a good reason for making a cut, don't do it. Follow these guidelines:

▌**Use sharp pruning shears, loppers, or saws,** which make clean cuts without tearing the wood or bark.

▌**Cut branches back** to a healthy shoot, leaf, or bud, or cut back to the branch collar at the base of the branch, as shown at right. Don't leave any stubs; they're ugly and prone to decay.

▌**Remove any dead or damaged** branches and any twigs or limbs that are very spindly or weak.

▌**Where two limbs cross over or rub** against each other, save one limb—usually the thicker, stronger one—and prune off the other one.

▌**Prune or widen narrow crotches.** Places where a branch and trunk or two branches form a narrow V are weak spots, liable to split apart as the tree grows. Where the trunk of a young tree exhibits such a crotch or where either of two shoots could continue the growth of a branch, prune off the weaker of the two. Where you wish to keep the branch, insert a piece of wood as a spacer to widen the angle, as shown in the drawings below. Leave the spacer in place for a year or so.

## One trunk or several?

If you want a young tree to have a single trunk, identify the leader or central shoot and let it grow straight up, unpruned. The trunk will grow thicker faster if you leave the lower limbs in place for the first few years, but if they're

### WHERE TO CUT

When removing the end of a branch, cut back to a healthy leaf, bud, or side shoot. Don't leave a stub. Use sharp pruning shears to make a neat cut that slices the stem rather than tears it.

When removing an entire branch, cut just outside the slightly thickened area, called the branch collar, where the branch grows into the trunk.

in the way, you can remove them. At whatever height you choose—usually about 8 ft. off the ground if you want to walk or see under the tree—select the shoots that will become the main limbs of the tree. Be sure they are evenly spaced around the trunk, pointing outward at wide angles. Remove any lower or weaker shoots. As the tree matures, the only further pruning required will be an annual checkup to remove dead, damaged, or crossing shoots.

Several of the trees in this book, including vine maple, Japanese snowbell, and saucer magnolia are often grown with multiple trunks for a graceful, clumplike appearance. When buying a multiple-trunk tree, choose one with trunks that diverge at the base. Prune multiple-trunk trees as previously described for single-trunk trees. Remove some of the branches growing toward the center of the clump so that the center doesn't get too dense and tangled.

## AVOIDING NARROW CROTCHES

A tree's limbs should spread wide, like outstretched arms. If limbs angle too close to the trunk or to each other, there isn't room for them to grow properly and they may split apart after a few years, ruining the tree.

**SINGLE-TRUNK TREES: Correct narrow crotches on a young tree by removal or by widening the angle with a wooden spacer block. Choose well-spaced shoots to become the main limbs of a shade tree.**

**MULTIPLE-TRUNK TREES: Whether the stems of a multiple-trunk tree emerge from the ground or from a single trunk near the ground, widen angles if necessary to keep the trunks from touching.**

# Pruning shrubs

Shrubs are generally carefree plants, but they almost always look better if you do some pruning at least every other year. As a minimum, remove dead twigs from time to time, and if any branches are broken by storms or accidents, remove them as soon as convenient, cutting back to a healthy bud or branch or to the plant's crown. Also, unless the shrub produces attractive seedpods or berries, it's a good idea to trim off the flowers after they fade.

Beyond this routine pruning, some shrubs require more attention. (The entries in Plant Profiles, pp. 114-147) give more information on when and how to prune particular shrubs.) Basically, shrub pruning falls into three categories: selective pruning, severe pruning, and shearing. (See the drawings, below right.)

**Selective pruning** means using pruning shears to head back or thin individual shoots in order to refine the shape of the bush and maintain its vigor, as well as limit its size. This job takes time but produces a very graceful and natural-looking bush. Cut away weak or spindly twigs and any limbs that cross or rub against each other, and head all the longest shoots back to a healthy, outward-facing bud or to a pair of buds. You can do selective pruning on any shrub, deciduous or evergreen, at any time of year.

**Severe pruning** means using pruning shears or loppers to cut away most of a shrub's top growth, leaving just short stubs or a gnarly trunk. This kind of cutting back is usually done once a year in late winter or early spring. Although it seems drastic, severe pruning is appropriate in several situations.

It makes certain fast-growing shrubs, such as bigleaf hydrangea flower more profusely. It keeps others, such as spirea and 'Powis Castle' artemisia, compact and bushy.

One or two severe prunings done when a shrub is young can make it branch out at the base, producing a bushier specimen or a fuller hedge plant. Nurseries often do this pruning as part of producing a good plant, and if you buy a shrub that's already bushy, you don't need to cut it back yourself. Older shrubs that have gotten tall and straggly sometimes respond to a severe pruning by sprouting out with renewed vigor, sending up lots of new shoots that bear plenty of foliage and flowers. This strategy doesn't work for all shrubs, though—sometimes severe pruning kills a plant. Don't try it unless you know it will work (check with a knowledgeable person at a nursery) or are willing to take a chance.

**Shearing** means using hedge shears or an electric hedge trimmer to trim the surface of a shrub, hedge, or tree to a neat, uniform profile, producing a solid mass of greenery. Both deciduous and evergreen shrubs and trees can be sheared; those with small, closely spaced leaves and a naturally compact growth habit usually look best. A good time for shearing most shrubs is late spring, after the new shoots have elongated but before the wood has hardened, but you can shear at other times of year. You may have to shear some plants more than once a year.

If you're planning to shear a plant, start when it is young and establish the shape—cone, pyramid, flat-topped hedge, etc. Looking at the profile, always make the shrub wider at the bottom than on top; otherwise the lower limbs will be shaded and won't be as leafy. Shear off as little as needed to maintain the shape as the shrub grows. Once it gets as big as you want it, shear as much as you have to to keep it that size.

**SELECTIVE PRUNING.** Remove weak, spindly, bent, or broken shoots (red). Where two branches rub on each other, remove the weakest or the one that's pointing inward (orange). Cut back long shoots to a healthy, outward-facing bud (blue).

**SEVERE PRUNING.** In late winter or early spring, before new growth starts, cut all the stems back close to the ground.

**SHEARING.** Trim with hedge clippers to a neat profile.

### Making a hedge

To make a hedge that's dense enough that you can't see through it, choose shrubs that have many shoots at the base. If you can only find skinny shrubs, prune them severely the first spring after planting to stimulate bushier growth.

Hedge plants are set in the ground as described on pp. 185–186 but are spaced closer together than they would be if planted as individual specimens. This helps create the hedgelike look. We took that into account in creating the designs and plant lists for this book; just follow the spacings recommended in the designs. If you're impatient for the hedge to fill in, you can space the plants closer together, but don't put them farther apart.

A hedge can be sheared, pruned selectively, or left alone, depending on how you want it to look. Slow-growing small-leaved plants such as boxwood and box-leaf euonymus make rounded but natural-looking hedges with no pruning at all, or you can shear them into any profile you choose and make them perfectly neat and uniform. (Be sure to keep them narrower at the top.) Choose one style and stick with it. Once a hedge is established, you can neither start nor stop shearing it without an awkward transition that may last a few years before the hedge looks good again.

## Getting a vine off to a good start

Nurseries often sell crossvine, clematis, honeysuckle, and other vines as young plants with a single stem fastened to a stake. To plant the vine, remove the stake and cut off the stem right above the lowest pair of healthy leaves, usually about 4 to 6 in. above the soil ❶. This forces the vine to send out new shoots low to the ground. As soon as those new shoots have begun to develop (usually a month or so after planting), cut them back to their first pairs of leaves ❷. After this second pruning, the plant will become bushy at the base. Now, as new shoots form, use sticks or strings to direct them toward the base of the support they are to climb ❸.

Once they're started, twining vines such as the ones named above can scramble up a lattice trellis, although it helps if you tuck in any stray ends. The plants can't climb a smooth surface, however. To help them cover a fence with wide vertical slats or a porch post, you need to provide something the vine can wrap around. Screw a few eyebolts to the top and bottom of such a support and stretch wire, nylon cord, or polypropylene rope between them. (The wires or cords should be a few inches out from the fence, not flush against it.)

Some clinging vines, such as climbing hydrangea, can climb any surface by means of their adhesive rootlets and need no further assistance or care to get them well established.

After the first year, most vines need annual spring pruning to remove any dead, damaged, or straggly stems. If vines grow too long, you can cut them back anytime and they will branch out from below the cut. Don't prune a vine severely right before it blooms.

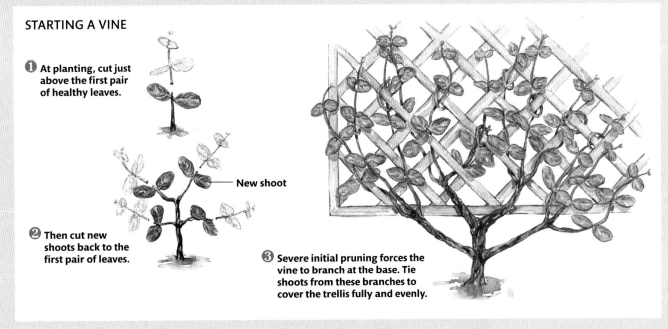

**STARTING A VINE**

❶ At planting, cut just above the first pair of healthy leaves.

New shoot

❷ Then cut new shoots back to the first pair of leaves.

❸ Severe initial pruning forces the vine to branch at the base. Tie shoots from these branches to cover the trellis fully and evenly.

# Caring for Perennials

**Perennials are simply plants** that send up new growth year after year. A large group, perennials include flowering plants such as daylilies and purple coneflower as well as grasses, ferns, and hardy bulbs. Although some perennials need special conditions and care, most of the ones in this book are adaptable and easygoing. Get them off to a good start by planting them in well-prepared soil, adding a layer of mulch, watering as often as needed throughout the first year, and keeping weeds away. After that, keeping perennials attractive and healthy typically requires just a few minutes per plant each year.

## Routine annual care

Some of the perennials that are used as ground covers, such as mondo grass and thyme, need virtually no care. On a suitable site, they'll thrive for decades even if you pay them almost no attention at all.

Most garden perennials, though, look and grow better if you clean away the old leaves and stems at least once a year. When to do this depends on the type of plant. Perennials such as daylily, penstemon, hosta, and Siberian iris have leaves and stalks that turn tan or brown after they're frosted in fall. Cut these down to the ground in late fall or early spring; either time is okay.

Perennials such as geranium, blue fescue grass, coralbells, and columbine are more or less evergreen, depending on the severity of the winter. For those plants, wait until after they've bloomed or until the fall; then cut back any leaves or stems that are discolored or shabby-looking. Don't leave cuttings lying on the soil, because they may contain disease spores. To avoid contaminating your compost, send diseased stems or leaves to the dump.

Right after you've cleared away the dead material is a good time to renew the mulch on the bed. Use a fork, rake, or cultivator to loosen the existing mulch, and add some fresh mulch if needed. Also, if you want to sprinkle some granular fertilizer on the bed, do that now, when it's easy to avoid getting any on the plants' leaves. Fertilizing perennials is optional, but it does make them grow bigger and bloom more than they would otherwise.

## Remove faded flowers

Removing flowers as they fade (called "deadheading") makes the garden look neater, prevents unwanted self-sown seedlings, and often stimulates a plant to continue blooming longer than it would if you left it alone, or to bloom a second time later in the season. (This is true for shrubs and annual plants as well as for perennial plants.)

Pick large flowers such as daisies, daylilies, irises, and lilies one at a time, snapping them off by hand. Use pruning shears on perennials such as hosta, epimedium, lavender, coralbells, and yarrow that produce tall stalks crowded with lots of small flowers, cutting the stalks back to the height of the foliage. Use hedge shears on bushy plants that are covered with lots of small flowers on short stalks, such as salvia, 'Moonbeam' coreopsis, basket-of-gold, and evergreen candytuft, cutting the stems back by about one-half their length.

Instead of removing them, you may want to let the flowers remain on purple coneflower, Siberian iris, 'Autumn Joy' sedum, and the various grasses. These plants all bear conspicuous seedpods or seed heads on stiff stalks that remain standing and look interesting throughout the fall and winter.

## Pruning and shearing perennials

Some perennials that bloom in summer or fall respond well to being pruned earlier in the growing season. Chrysanthemum, New England aster, Russian sage, and 'Autumn Joy' sedum all form tall clumps of stems topped with lots of little flowers. Unfortunately, tall stems are liable to flop over, and even if they don't, too-tall clumps can look leggy or top-heavy. To prevent floppiness, prune these plants when the stems are about 1 ft. tall. Remove the weakest stems from each clump by cutting them off at the ground; then cut all the remaining, strong stems back by about one-third. Pruning in this way keeps these plants shorter, stronger, and bushier, so you don't have to bother with installing stakes to keep them upright.

Some plants, such as 'Powis Castle' artemisia, are grown more for their foliage than for their flowers. You can use hedge shears to keep them neat, compact, and bushy, shearing off the tops of the stems once or twice in spring and summer.

**PRUNING A PERENNIAL**

Prune to create neater, bushier clumps of some summer- and fall-blooming perennials such as New England aster, chrysanthemums, and 'Autumn Joy' sedum. When the stalks are about 1 ft. tall, cut them all back by one-third. Remove the weakest stalks at ground level.

# Dividing perennials

Most perennials send up more stems each year, forming denser clumps or wider patches. Dividing is the process of cutting or breaking apart these clumps or patches. This is an easy way to make more plants to expand your garden, to control a plant that might otherwise spread out of bounds, or to renew an old specimen that doesn't look good or bloom well anymore.

Most perennials can be divided as often as every year or two if you're in a hurry to make more plants, or they can go for several years if you don't have any reason to disturb them. Fall is the best time to divide most perennials, but you can also do it in early spring.

There are two main approaches to dividing perennials, as shown in the drawings at right. You can leave the plant in the ground and use a sharp spade to cut it apart, like slicing a pie, and then lift out one chunk at a time. Or you can dig around and underneath the plant and lift it out all at once, shake off the extra soil, and lay the plant on the ground or a tarp where you can work with it.

Some plants, such as yarrow and some ferns, are easy to divide. They almost fall apart when you dig them up. Others, such as 'Autumn Joy' sedum, daylily, and most grasses, have very tough or tangled roots and you'll have to wrestle with them, chop them with a sharp butcher knife, pry them apart with a strong screwdriver or garden fork, or even cut through the roots with a hatchet or pruning saw. However you approach the job, before you insert any tool, take a close look at the plant right at ground level, and be careful to divide *between*, not *through*, the biggest and healthiest buds or shoots. Using a hose to wash loose mulch and soil away makes it easier to see what you're doing.

Don't make the divisions too small; they should be the size of a plant that you'd want to buy, not just little scraps. If you have more divisions than you need or want, choose just the best-looking ones to replant and discard or give away the others. Replant new divisions as soon as possible in freshly prepared soil. Water them right away, and water again whenever the soil dries out over the next few weeks or months, until the plants are growing again.

Divide hardy bulbs such as daffodils and crocuses every few years. Dig clumps after bloom but before the foliage turns yellow. Shake the soil off the roots, pull the bulbs apart, and replant them promptly, setting them as deep as they were buried before.

## DIVIDING PERENNIALS

**You can divide a clump or patch of perennials by cutting down into the patch with a sharp spade, like slicing a pie or a pan of brownies, then lifting out the separate chunks.**

**Or you can dig up the whole clump, shake the extra soil off the roots, then pull or pry it apart into separate plantlets.**

# Problem Solving

**Some plants** are much more suscep-tible than others to damage by severe weather, pests, or diseases. In this book, we've recommended plants that are gen-erally trouble-free, especially after they have had a few years to get established in your garden. But even these plants are subject to various mishaps and problems. The challenge is learning how to distin-guish which problems are really serious and which are just cosmetic and decid-ing how to solve—or, better yet, prevent—those problems that are serious.

## Pests, large and small

Deer and rabbits are liable to be a prob-lem if your property is surrounded by or adjacent to fields or woods. You may not see them, but you can't miss the dam-age they do—they bite the tops off or eat whole plants of daylilies and many other perennials. Deer also eat the leaves and stems of maples, azaleas, and many other trees and shrubs. Commercial or home-made repellents that you spray on the fo-liage may be helpful if the animals aren't too hungry and you use them often. (See the box below for thoughts on deer-proof plants.) But in the long run, the only solu-tion is to fence out deer and to trap and remove smaller animals.

Squirrels are cute but naughty. They normally don't eat much foliage, but they do eat some kinds of flowers and several kinds of bulbs. They also dig up new transplants, and they plant nuts in your flower beds and lawns. Meadow voles and field mice can kill trees and shrubs by stripping the bark off the trunk, usually near the ground. Gophers eat the roots of shrubs, trees, and perennials. Moles don't eat plants, but their digging makes a mess of a lawn or flower bed. Persistent trap-ping is the most effective way to control all of these little critters. (You can protect the roots of some plants from gophers by planting the plants in wire cages sold at many nurseries.)

Aphids, beetles, caterpillars, grubs, grasshoppers, spider mites, scale insects, slugs, snails, weevils, and countless other pests can cause minor or devastating damage in a home landscape. Most plants can afford to lose part of their foliage or sap without suffering much of a setback, so don't panic if you see a few holes chewed in a leaf. However, whenever you suspect that insects or related pests are at-tacking one of your plants, try to catch one of them in a glass jar and identify it so you can decide what to do.

## Identify then treat

Don't jump to conclusions and start spraying chemicals on a supposedly sick plant before you know what (if anything) is actually wrong with it. That's waste-ful and irresponsible, and you're likely to do the plant as much harm as good. Pinpointing the exact cause of a problem is even difficult for experi-enced gardeners, so save yourself frustration and seek out expert help from the beginning.

If it seems that there's something wrong with one of your plants—for exam-ple, if the leaves are discolored or have holes, spots, or marks on them—cut off a sample branch, wrap it in damp paper towels, and put it in a plastic bag (so it won't wilt). Take the sample to the nursery or garden center where you bought the plant, and ask for help. If the nursery can't help, contact the nearest office of your state's Cooperative Extension Service or a public garden in your area and ask if they have a staff member who can diagnose plant problems.

Meanwhile, look around your property and around the neighborhood, too, to see whether any other plants (of the same or different kinds) show similar symptoms. If a problem is widespread, you shouldn't have much trouble finding someone who can identify it and tell you what, if anything, to do. If only one plant is affected, it's often harder to diagnose the problem, and you may just have to wait and see what happens to it. Keep an eye on the plant, continue with watering and other regular maintenance, and see whether the problem gets worse or goes away. If nothing more has hap-pened after a few weeks, stop worrying. If the problem continues, intensify your search for expert advice.

Plant problems stem from a number of causes: insect and animal pests, diseases, and poor care, particularly in winter. Remember that plant problems are often caused by a combination of these; all the more reason to consult with experts about their diagnosis and treatment.

## Deer-proof plants?

Planting from lists of deer-proof plants often results in disappoint-ment. What's deer-proof in one area may not be in another. And if deer are really hungry, they'll eat almost anything. If you live in an area where deer are common, check with local nurseries for planting solutions or stroll through your neighborhood to see what's nibbled and what's not.

## DEER-CONTROL FENCING

Deer have been known to jump very tall fences. Experience shows that a wide midheight fence is one of the best ways to keep deer out. This fence is suitable for a larger property. It is about 6 ft. wide and 5 ft. high and consists of angled poles fixed to posts spaced about 10 ft. apart. Attach wires at 12-in. intervals to the poles. For advice on deer fences that work best in your area, consult your Cooperative Extension service.

There are several new kinds of insecticides that are quite effective but much safer to use than the older products. For example, insecticidal soap, a special kind of detergent, quickly kills aphids and other soft-bodied insects, but it's nontoxic to mammals and birds and breaks down quickly, leaving no harmful residue. Horticultural oil, a highly refined mineral oil, is a good control for scale insects, which frequently infest gardenias, camellias, and other broad-leaved evergreens. Most garden centers stock these and other relatively safe insecticides.

Before using any insecticide, study the fine print on the label to make sure that the product is registered to control your particular pest. Carefully follow the directions for how to apply the product, or it may not work.

### Diseases

Several types of fungal, bacterial, and viral diseases can attack garden plants, causing a wide range of symptoms such as disfigured or discolored leaves or petals, powdery or moldy-looking films or spots, mushy or rotten stems or roots, and overall wilting. As with insect problems, if you suspect that a plant is infected with a disease, gather a sample of the plant and show it to someone who can identify the problem before you do any spraying.

In general, plant diseases are hard to treat, so it's important to take steps to prevent problems. These steps include choosing plants adapted to your area, choosing disease-resistant plants, spacing plants far enough apart so that air can circulate between them, and removing dead stems and litter from the garden.

Perennials that would otherwise be healthy are prone to fungal infections during spells of humid weather, especially if the plants are crowded together or if they have flopped over and are lying on top of each other or on the ground. If your garden has turned into a jungle, look closely for moldy foliage, and if you find any, prune it off and discard (don't compost) it. It's better to cut the plants back severely than to let the disease spread. Plan to avoid repeated problems by dividing the perennials, replanting them farther apart, and pruning them early in the season so they don't grow so tall and floppy again. Crowded shrubs are also subject to fungal problems in the summer and should be pruned so that air can flow around them.

### Winter damage

Even though most of the Northwest enjoys cool, mild winters, occasional cold spells that damage normally hardy plants are not uncommon. After a cold spell, wait until at least midsummer to assess the severity of the damage. At that time, new growth will tell you just how far back a plant has been killed and you can prune out limbs that are brown and dead.

# Glossary

**Amendments.** Organic materials or minerals used to improve the soil. Peat moss, perlite, and compost are commonly used.

**Annual.** A plant that grows from seed, flowers, produces new seeds, and dies during a single growing season; a perennial plant treated like an annual in that it is grown for only a single season's display and then removed.

**Balled-and-burlapped.** Describes a tree or shrub dug out of the ground with a ball of soil intact around the roots; the ball is then wrapped in burlap and tied for transport.

**Bare-root.** Describes a plant dug out of the ground and then shaken or washed to remove the soil from the roots.

**Balled-and-burlapped**

**Bare-root**

**Compound leaf.** A leaf consisting of two or more leaflets branching from the same stalk.

**Container-grown.** Describes a plant raised in a pot that is removed before planting.

**Crown.** The part of a plant where the roots and stem meet, usually at soil level.

**Cultivar.** A cultivated variety of a plant, often bred or selected for some special trait such as double flowers, compact growth, cold hardiness, or disease and pest resistance.

**Deadheading.** Removing spent flowers during the growing season to improve a plant's appearance, prevent seed formation, and stimulate the development of new flowers.

**Deciduous.** Describes a tree, shrub, or vine that drops all its leaves in winter.

**Division.** Propagation of a plant by separating it into two or more pieces, each piece possessing at least one bud and some roots. Plants commonly divided include perennials, bulbs, grasses, and ferns.

**Division**

**Drainage.** Movement of water through soil. If water poured into a foot-deep hole drains completely in a few hours, the drainage is good.

**Drip line.** The circle of soil beneath a tree mirroring the circumference of the tree's canopy. This area benefits from direct rainfall and "drip" from leaves. Because many of the tree's feeder roots are found along the drip line and beyond, this area is the best for fertilizing and watering.

**Dry-laid.** Describes a masonry path or wall that is installed without mortar.

**Edging.** A barrier that serves as the border between lawn and a planting bed. Edgings may be shallow trenches or barriers of plastic, brick, or boards.

**Exposure.** The characterization of a site according to the sun, wind, and temperature acting upon it.

**Formal.** Describes a style of landscaping that features symmetrical layouts, with beds and walks related to adjacent buildings, and often with plants sheared to geometric or other shapes.

**Foundation planting.** Traditionally, a narrow border of evergreen shrubs planted around the foundation of a house. Contemporary foundation plantings often include deciduous shrubs, grasses, perennials, and other plants as well.

**Frost heaving.** A disturbance or uplifting of soil, pavement, or plants caused when moisture in the soil freezes and expands.

**Full shade.** Describes a site that receives no direct sun during the growing season.

**Full sun.** Describes a site that receives at least eight hours of direct sun each day during the growing season.

**Garden soil.** Soil specially prepared for planting to make it loose enough for roots and water to penetrate easily. Usually requires digging or tilling and the addition of some organic matter.

**Grade.** The angle and direction of the ground's slope in a given area.

**Ground cover.** A plant providing continuous cover for an area of soil. Commonly, a low, spreading foliage plant such as candytuft or creeping phlox.

**Habit.** The characteristic shape of a plant, such as upright, mounded, columnar, or vase-shaped.

**Hardiness.** A plant's ability to survive the winter temperatures in a given region without protection.

**Hardiness Zone.** A geographic region where the coldest temperature in an average winter falls within a certain range, such as between 0° and -10°F.

**Brick mowing strip**

**Hardscape.** Parts of a landscape constructed from materials other than plants, such as walks, walls, and trellises made of wood, stone, or other materials.

**Herbicide.** A chemical used to kill plants. Preemergent herbicides are used to kill weed seeds as they sprout, and thus to prevent weed growth. Postemergent herbicides kill plants that are already growing.

**Hybrid.** A plant with two parents that belong to different varieties, species, or genera.

**Interplant.** To use plants with different bloom times or growth habits in the same bed to increase the variety and appeal of the planting.

**Invasive.** Describes a plant that spreads quickly, usually by runners, and mixes with or dominates adjacent plantings.

**Landscape fabric.** A synthetic fabric, sometimes water-permeable, spread under paths or mulch to serve as a weed barrier.

**Lime, limestone.** Mineral compounds applied to soil to lower its pH, rendering it less acidic and thereby allowing plants to absorb nutrients better. Limestone also supplies calcium that plants need.

**Loam.** Soil rich in organic matter and with mineral particles in a range of sizes. Excellent for many garden plants.

**Microclimate.** A small-scale "system" of factors affecting plant growth on a particular site, including shade, temperature, rainfall, and so on.

**Mowing strip.** A row of bricks or paving stones set flush with the soil around the edge of a bed, and wide enough to support one wheel of the lawn mower.

**Mulch.** A layer of organic or other materials spread several inches thick around the base of plants and over open soil in a bed. Mulch conserves soil moisture, smothers weeds, and moderates soil temperatures. Where winters are cold, mulches help protect plants from freezing. Common mulches include compost, shredded leaves, straw, lawn clippings, gravel, newspaper, and landscape fabric.

**Native.** Describes a plant that is or once was found in the wild in a particular region and was not recently imported from another area.

**Nutrients.** Elements needed by plants. Found in the soil and supplied by fertilizers, nutrients include nitrogen, phosphorus, potassium, calcium, magnesium, sulfur, iron, and other elements, in various forms and compounds.

**Organic matter.** Partially or fully decomposed plant and animal matter. Includes leaves, trimmings, and manure.

**Peat moss.** Partially decomposed mosses and sedges. Dug from boggy areas, peat moss is often used as an organic amendment for garden soil.

**Perennial.** A plant with a life span of more than one year. Woody plants such as trees and shrubs are perennials, in addition to the "herbaceous perennials" more commonly cited, which have no woody tissue that persists from year to year.

**Pressure-treated lumber.** Softwood lumber treated with chemicals that protect it from decay.

**Propagate.** To produce new plants from seeds or by vegetative means such as dividing plant parts, taking root cuttings, and grafting stems onto other plants.

**Retaining wall.** A wall built to stabilize a slope and keep soil from sliding or eroding downhill.

**Rhizome.** A horizontal underground stem from which roots and shoots emerge. Some swell to store food. Branched rhizomes (those of iris, for instance) can be divided to produce new plants.

**Rootball.** The mass of soil and roots dug with a plant when it is removed from the ground; the soil and roots of a plant grown in a container.

**Rosette.** A low, flat cluster or crown of overlapping leaves.

**Selective pruning.** Using pruning shears to remove or cut back individual shoots in order to refine the shape of a shrub, maintain its vigor, or limit its size.

**Severe pruning.** Using pruning shears or loppers to cut away most of a shrub's top growth, leaving just short stubs or a gnarly trunk.

**Shearing.** Using hedge shears or an electric hedge trimmer to shape the surface of a shrub, hedge, or tree and produce a smooth, solid mass of greenery.

**Specimen plant.** A plant placed for individual display

**Spike.** An elongated flower cluster on which individual flowers are attached directly to the main stem or are on very short stalks attached to the main stem.

**Tender.** Describes a plant that is damaged by cold weather in a particular region.

**Underplanting.** Growing short plants, such as ground covers, under a taller plant, such as a shrub.

**Variegated.** Describes foliage with color patterns in stripes, specks, or blotches that occur naturally or result from breeding.

# Index

*NOTE: Page numbers in* **bold italic** *refer to illustrations.*

# Photo Credits

**Front Cover:** *top left* Rick Mastelli; *bottom* Jerry Pavia; *top right* Neil Soderstrom

**Back Cover:** *both* Jerry Pavia

**page 1:** Charles Mann

**page 7:** Charles Mann

**pages 14–15:** Jerry Pavia

**page 19:** *top* Saxon Holt; *middle* Richard Shiell; *bottom right* David McDonald

**page 24:** *top right* Saxon Holt; *top left* David McDonald; *middle right* Dan Keck; *bottom left* Charles Mann; *bottom right* Jerry Pavia

**page 31:** *top left & bottom right* Jerry Pavia; *middle left* Michael Thompson; *middle top right* Saxon Holt; *middle bottom right* Rick Mastelli; *bottom left* Charles Mann

**page 35:** *top left & bottom left* Richard Shiell; *top right* Michael Thompson; *middle left* Peter Pearsall U.S. Fish and Wildlife Service; *middle right & bottom right* Charles Mann

**page 39:** *top* Saxon Holt; *middle right & bottom center* Charles Mann; *bottom right* Jerry Pavia; *bottom left* Richard Shiell

**page 45:** *top left* Richard Shiell; *top right & top middle left* Galen Gates; *middle right* Wirestock Creators; *bottom right* Saxon Holt; *bottom left* Charles Mann

**page 49:** *top right & bottom right* Richard Shiell; *middle left* Charles Mann; *bottom left* LifeisticAC; *middle right & bottom middle* Jerry Pavia

**page 53:** *top* Neil Soderstrom; *middle left* David McDonald; *middle right* Michael Thompson; *bottom* Richard Shiell

**page 56:** *top & bottom left* Charles Mann; *middle left & bottom right* Jerry Pavia; *middle right* Rita Buchanan

**page 62:** *top & bottom right* Charles Mann; *middle left & middle right* Jerry Pavia; *center & bottom left* Saxon Holt

**page 69:** *top* Galen Gates; *middle right & bottom right* Jerry Pavia; *middle left* Richard Shiell

**page 73:** *top left, top right & middle right* Jerry Pavia; *middle top left* Richard Shiell; *bottom left* Charles Mann; *bottom right* Rita Buchanan

**page 77:** *top left, top right & middle top right* Jerry Pavia; *middle left* Rick Mastelli; *middle bottom right & bottom left* Charles Mann; *bottom right* Richard Shiell

**page 81:** *top* David McDonald; *middle left* Rita Buchanan; *middle center* Charles Mann; *middle right* Richard Shiell; *bottom both* Jerry Pavia

**page 84:** *top left* Charles Mann; *top right* Karen Bussolini; *middle right & middle bottom left* David McDonald; *top middle left* Michael Thompson; *bottom left* Tom Harrington/National Park Service; *bottom right* Jerry Pavia

**page 91:** *top left* Michael Thompson; *middle left* Jerry Pavia; *bottom left* Jill Lang/Dreamstime.com; *bottom right* Galen Gates

**page 97:** *top* Richard Shiell; *middle left & bottom left* Saxon Holt; *middle right* Michael Thompson; *bottom right* Jerry Pavia

**page 100:** *top left, bottom right & middle left* Richard Shiell; *top right* Dency Kane; *middle right* Michael Thompson; *bottom left* David McDonald

**page 105:** *top left & bottom left* Charles Mann; *middle left & bottom right* Neil Soderstrom; *middle right* Jerry Pavia

**page 111:** *top left* Charles Mann; *top right* Michael Thompson; *middle left* Galen Gates; *middle center* David McDonald; *middle right & bottom left* Richard Shiell; *bottom right* Jerry Pavia

**pages 112–113:** Jerry Pavia

**page 115:** Danita Delimont

**page 116:** Sunbunny Studio

**page 117:** *left* Richard Shiell; *top right* Charles Mann; *bottom right* Jerry Pavia

**page 118:** *bottom left* Photos Horticultural/Michael and Lois Warner; *bottom right* Richard Shiell

**page 119:** *top* David McDonald; *middle* Galen Gates; *bottom left* Charles Mann

**page 120:** *top* Galen Gates; *bottom* Jerry Pavia

**page 121:** *bottom left* Galen Gates; *bottom right* Charles Mann

**page 122:** *left* David McDonald; *right* Saxon Holt

**page 123:** *top* Rita Buchanan; *middle* David McDonald; *bottom* Richard Shiell

**page 124:** *top left* Bruce Dupree/Alabama Extension; *middle* Jerry Pavia; *bottom left* Richard Shiell; *bottom right* Karen Bussolini

**page 125:** *top left & middle right* Richard Shiell; *top middle right* Neil Soderstrom; *top right* Charles Mann; *bottom right* Saxon Holt

**page 126:** *top left & middle left* David McDonald; *top right* Galen Gates; *bottom* Saxon Holt

**page 127:** *top left* Charles Mann; *top right* Jerry Pavia; *middle left* Galen Gates; *middle right* Michael Thompson; *bottom right* Wayne Ray

**page 128:** *top & middle both* Jerry Pavia; *bottom* David McDonald

**page 129:** *top* Saxon Holt; *bottom* Richard Shiell

**page 130:** *top* Richard Shiell; *middle* Charles Mann; *bottom* Saxon Holt

**page 131:** *all* Charles Mann

**page 132:** *top left, middle top left, top right & bottom right* Jerry Pavia; *middle bottom left* Galen Gates; *bottom left* Saxon Holt

**page 133:** *top & middle* Jerry Pavia

**page 134:** *top & top middle* Jerry Pavia; *middle bottom & bottom* Richard Shiell

**page 135:** *top left* Jerry Pavia; *top middle* Dan Keck; *top right* Peter Pearsall U.S. Fish and Wildlife Service; *bottom right* Charles Mann

**page 136:** *top* Michael Thompson; *middle top* Richard Shiell; *middle bottom* David McDonald; *bottom* Wouter Hagens

**page 137:** *top* Richard Shiell; *middle* Jerry Pavia; *bottom* Saxon Holt

**page 138:** *top left* Jerry Pavia; *top right & middle* Michael Thompson; *bottom* Galen Gates

**page 139:** Richard Shiell

**page 140:** Saxon Holt

**page 141:** *top left* Charles Mann; *top middle* Richard Shiell; *top right* Lauren Springer Ogden; *bottom right* Saxon Holt

**page 142:** *left* Ruth Rogers Clausen; *right* Jerry Pavia

**page 143:** *top left* Karen Bussolini; *top middle* Charles Mann; *top right* Jerry Pavia; *bottom left* Courtesy of High Country Gardens; *bottom right* Richard Shiell

**page 144:** *top left* Richard Shiell; *bottom both* Rita Buchanan

**page 145:** *right both* Jerry Pavia; *bottom left* Tom Harrington/National Park Service

**pages 148–149:** Jerry Pavia

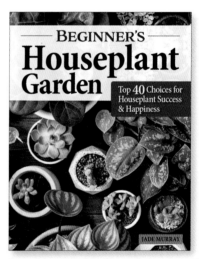